A Pilgrim's Progress:

ORESTES A. BROWNSON

A Pilgrim's Progress

ORESTES A. BROWNSON

A Pilgrim's
Progress:

ORESTES A. BROWNSON

By Arthur M. Schlesinger, Jr.

Originally entitled
ORESTES A. BROWNSON: A PILGRIM'S PROGRESS

LITTLE, BROWN AND COMPANY • BOSTON • TORONTO

A

Published simultaneously in Canada
by Little, Brown & Company (Canada) Limited

PRINTED IN THE UNITED STATES OF AMERICA

TO

MY MOTHER AND FATHER

ACKNOWLEDGMENTS

My principal obligation is to Professor Perry Miller for his generous advice and criticism. I am also indebted to other members of the Harvard faculty: Professors Howard Mumford Jones, Francis O. Matthiessen, Kenneth B. Murdock, André Morize and Arthur M. Schlesinger and Dr. Richard Leopold. The Reverend Robert Howard Lord of St. John's Seminary at Brighton kindly read the manuscript and improved it by his suggestions. The Reverend Thomas T. McAvoy, Archivist of Notre Dame University, afforded me many courtesies while I was examining the Brownson Papers. To Miss Marian Cannon I owe more than I can adequately express for her sympathetic encouragement and criticism at all stages of the work. Finally, my thanks are due Miss Elizabeth F. Hoxie for help in preparing the manuscript for publication and for making the index.

A. M. S., Jr.

INTRODUCTION

In the spring or summer of 1937, when I was casting about for a subject for a senior honors essay in history and literature at Harvard, my father suggested that I look at the article on Orestes A. Brownson in the *Dictionary of American Biography*. I did so and discovered that Brownson, a New England editor, a friend of Emerson's and Thoreau's, a Jacksonian Democrat, an early American convert to Roman Catholicism, had lived a diverse and fascinating life; that his writings, if voluminous, were readily available; and that he had thus far been pretty much overlooked in the new surge of interest in the flowering of New England. When I consulted with Professor Perry Miller, who was to be my tutor in my senior year, he thought Brownson a fine idea; and, as I brought the essay to him, section by section, in the winter of 1937-1938, he subjected it to the stringent and illuminating criticism which made him such an extraordinary teacher.

My father then encouraged me to turn the essay into a book. In the early summer of 1939 I went out to South Bend, Indiana, to go through the Brownson Papers at Notre Dame University; and I then completed a revision in time for publication by Little, Brown in 1939. It is perhaps of interest that the other senior honors essay at Harvard to be published in these years was written by a young concentrator in government, two years behind me, whom I then knew only by sight in the Yard — *Why England Slept* by John F. Kennedy, '40.

The study of Brownson helped fix my interest in the field which has ever since been my main professional preoccupation — intellectual history; and within this field it led particularly into the complex and tricky area where ideas and politics overlap and intersect. Thus Brownson's relationship to the political and intellectual conflicts of the age of Jackson gave a quite different impression of Jacksonian democracy from the uncouth backwoods revolt then conventionally depicted in the textbooks, as did the career of other New Englanders who turned up in the course of research, some well known but in other connections, like George Bancroft, others not known at all, at least to me, like Samuel Clesson Allen.

When I finished Brownson, I intended next to

write a life of Bancroft, a collateral ancestor of my mother's, with particular attention to the interplay of his careers as historian and politician; but an invitation to deliver the Lowell Lectures in 1941 diverted me into a larger consideration of the Jacksonian era. These lectures, somewhat pretentiously entitled "A Reinterpretation of Jacksonian Democracy," tried to understand why Eastern intellectuals like Brownson and Bancroft were so deeply engaged in Jacksonian emotions. They later became the basis for *The Age of Jackson*.

The age of Jackson was a time of the breaking-up of the religious and political creeds of the early republic, and Brownson was a product of the resultant intellectual mobility and confusion. His special talent was in expressing his view of the moment with exceptional clarity and power, and his writings thus open an astonishing variety of windows on his age. At the same time, one feels the pathos of modernity in this stormy pilgrim, this intellectually displaced person wandering passionately from one system to another until he came to relative rest in the historic certitudes of the Catholic Church. His life still touches contemporary nerves — from the antagonisms of capital and labor to the place of the Catholics in American society, from the nature of American culture to the death of God. For all the sad frustrations of his own life, Orestes Brownson remains, I believe, vigorously alive as a figure in American intellectual history.

ARTHUR M. SCHLESINGER, JR.

May 1966

CONTENTS

I. THE JOURNEY BEGINS, 1803–1832 . 3

II. FELLOW PILGRIMS, 1832–1836 . . 29

III. THE SLOUGH OF DESPOND, 1836–1840 . 61

IV. AT THE WICKET GATE, 1840–1842 . 112

V. THE PALACE BEAUTIFUL, 1842–1844 . 150

VI. THE DELECTABLE MOUNTAINS, 1844–
1860 185

VII. JOURNEY'S END, 1860–1876 . . 240

VIII. THE PILGRIM'S PROGRESS . . . 276

BIBLIOGRAPHY 299

INDEX 307

A Pilgrim's Progress:

ORESTES A. BROWNSON

A Pilgrim's Progress

ORESTES A. BROWNSON

CHAPTER I

THE JOURNEY BEGINS, 1803–1832

The measure of what is historically important is set by the generation that writes the history, not by the one that makes it. No historian can entirely escape judging by the standards of his day; in some sense he must always superimpose one set of values on another. Only a few figures in each age survive this process of sifting. They are men of many facets, reflecting light from whatever angle they are viewed. Others, not of the first importance, nor perhaps of the second, bulk large in the eyes of the people who knew them, but fade to vague names within a decade of their funerals, and in another may be wholly forgotten. Who in the America of 1860 remembered Herman Melville or knew of Stendhal or Karl Marx? But who did not know of N. P. Willis, of Eugene Sue, of Orestes Brownson?

1

At the end of the eighteenth century, Vermont, not ten years a state, was slowly yielding its green

hills to determined invaders from the south. Most of
the pioneers moved northward along the Connecticut
River, and many found its branch, the White River,
a convenient gateway to the promised land. At Stockbridge, one of the small towns that sprang up along
the rocky river valley, settled Sylvester Brownson,
native of Connecticut, with his New Hampshire wife,
Relief Metcalf. Brownson's forebears led back to
John Brownson of Waterbury, Connecticut, who had
migrated from England in time to distinguish himself in the Pequot War. As the family grew and
spread, the name lost a letter in the uncertainty of
colonial spelling. By 1800 the Bronsons, the most
important branch of the family, established their version as the preferred form. The Brownson line had
acquired little glory. Its most eminent son once remarked that he had never heard of any members of
note; [1] and the removal to Vermont was a confession
of its failure to get along in the settled part of the
country.

In 1803 Stockbridge had barely a hundred in-

[1] Genealogical information is to be found in Brownson's review of
Henry Bronson's *History of Waterbury, Conn.*, in *Brownson's
Quarterly Review* (hereafter cited as *BrQR*), Third New York
Series, I, 530–532 (October, 1860), and in Henry F. Brownson,
Brownson's Early Life, 3–4. Elizabeth Peabody believed Brownson
to be of French and Indian ancestry; but this theory, casually ad-
vanced in her *Reminiscences of Rev. Wm. Ellery Channing*,
353, finds no support elsewhere.

habitants. Sylvester Brownson, like the other settlers, found there a place to live, but hardly a living. The problem of forcing sustenance out of a thin unwilling soil was complicated by the presence of four young children who were of little help in growing the food they ate. On September 16, 1803, came two more, Orestes Augustus and Daphne Augusta. Sylvester died shortly after, and Relief, his wife, struggled for the next six years to keep the family together. She finally had to place the two youngest in the neighboring town of Royalton.

Young Orestes led a somber and solitary existence with the taciturn Vermont couple who took him in charge. The man was over sixty, his wife near fifty, and they sought only to make the child conscientious, truthful and God-fearing. Their life gave little outlet to the exuberance usually spent in boyhood rough-and-tumble. "Properly speaking, I had no childhood," Orestes wrote many years later.[2] The lonely boy turned hungrily to the small library which the severe Congregational morality of his foster parents had filled with volumes on theology. His early imaginings thus fed on dreams of heaven and hell. Religion is "connected with all I remember of my early visions, and entwined with all the endearing associations of childhood," he recalled when childhood was

[2] "The Convert," *Works*, V, 4.

still not far behind.[3] He later claimed that at the age
of nine he maintained the doctrine of free will against
the theology of Jonathan Edwards in stout argument with two elders; and, after he became a Catholic, he remembered early spiritual communication
with Jesus, Mary and the Angel Gabriel.[4] The power
of religion, re-enforced by the gray solitude of his
upbringing, nourished by the dark, leafy beauty of
Vermont hillsides and enriched by his eager imagination, worked itself deep into his emotions.[5] From
the first he was ambitious to become a minister.

Around him in Stockbridge and Royalton, religion was intense and primitive. The townspeople
hoped fervently to "get a change of heart," "be
born again"; but this was an inward matter, com-
pounded of ecstasy and fear and little connected
with rites or observances. Young Orestes was particularly impressed by the Methodists, whose preacher
conjured up hell-fire with a horrible urgency that
completely overbore the appeals of his competitors.
But just as the boy, then twelve, had solemnly decided to submit himself to Methodism, he was

[3] *The Philanthropist*, II, 114.
[4] "The Convert," *Works*, V, 5.
[5] Brownson frequently spoke with delight of Vermont, particularly after he moved to New York; see, for instance, "Beecher's
Norwood," *Catholic World*, X, 394–396 (December, 1869);
also *Works*, XIX, 533–544.

warned against it by an old woman who lived in a hut on the Royalton farm. Years later he recalled her as having told him to join only the church that had survived unchanged from the time of Christ and the apostles.

2

When Orestes was fourteen, his mother took the family from Vermont to Ballston Spa in upstate New York, about thirty miles from the Vermont border. Here he briefly attended a neighboring academy, probably until his earnings ran out and he had to return to work. This was all he had of formal education. His new job was in a printer's office, where he labored first as an apprentice and later as a journeyman. Though he toiled conscientiously at the presses, he was not engrossed by his work. From the theology of his childhood he had inherited problems which the pangs of loneliness and the emotional stirrings of adolescence were making sharp and fearful. Which was the way to salvation? Next to the thunder of this question, his daily life was vague and unimportant. He was badly buffeted by religious doubt and desire, and he knew not where to turn.

His aunt, a devoted disciple of Dr. Elhanan Winchester, a powerful Universalist preacher of the preceding century, early weakened the foundations of his orthodoxy by giving him a series of Universalist tracts, lent force by her fiery commentaries. Some books openly hostile to revealed religion only added to the boy's hopeless confusion. In anxious bewilderment, he began to grope for certainty in reason, but without finding warmth or satisfaction. Then on a beautiful Sunday in September 1822 he felt impelled to enter a Presbyterian church. At the close of the service, he stepped out into the tranquil sunlight in a mood of serenity that exposed barren reason in all its hatefulness. "Why does my heart rebel against the speculations of my mind?" he cried.[6] Logic must be a false guide. He would now yield to superior authority. The next month he joined the Presbyterian church at Ballston.

But baptism failed to bring peace. Ballston Presbyterianism was still the gloomy Calvinism of John Knox, and Brownson's earnest attempt to grasp its darker meanings succeeded so well that he found little of the comfort he had expected. The closely written diary he kept during these painful years grew heavy with anguished ponderings over sin and salvation. "Now ends another year," he wrote on the last day of 1822. "Yes, I have sinned every day, every hour, yea, and every breath has been drawn in in-

[6] "The Convert," *Works*, V, 10.

iquity: every thought and every imagination of my heart has been evil, only evil, and that continually." Notes of despair over the wickedness of man sounded recurrently. On Sundays they rose to a pitch of peculiar intensity. Only when he could forget human depravity and turn to the splendor of God did he seem genuinely cheerful.

He was behaving in the authentic tradition of Calvin. But he discovered no real satisfaction in beating his bosom and bewailing mankind. "[I] mourn the deadness of my own feelings," he noted unhappily early in 1823; and, a fortnight later, "How little do I feel religion, how cold, how dead in the service of the Lord!" Such entries became more frequent and more hopeless. "I see nothing in me that looks like religion; I am base; I am corrupt," he moaned. "Just returned from church . . . lost to every sense of religion. Feel an awful and desperately wicked heart." [7] He nervously implored God to grant him faith; but none came and his misery continued. In his deep loneliness and ardent desire for salvation, he had grasped too eagerly at a creed which could never become part of him. He felt strongly that he ought to believe man wholly evil; and for a time it seemed as if he did; but his grip of Calvinist doctrine was relaxing as the excitement of conversion disappeared,

[7] See diary, *passim*, Brownson Papers.

and soon he gagged at predestination and total depravity. His heart was once more rebelling against the speculations of his mind.

The details of his forswearing of Presbyterianism are not at all certain. In later years he told a lurid story of espionage, ostracism and perpetual constraint on the part of the preachers which took hell from the pulpit into the pews and made life in the church intolerable.[8] The Ballston pastor indignantly rebutted Brownson's charges and was content to explain Brownson's apostasy as a fall from grace.[9] But the facts of the matter are not really important. If Brownson's description did not reproduce them, it represented the cruel impression Presbyterianism made on him. The Calvinist dogmas did violence to his innermost impulses. He could not stomach the doctrines of predestination and eternal punishment. They embodied ideas of justice which the century was at the moment discarding, and attempts within the communion to soften them only made him doubt that they had divine authority. His deep unhappiness, whether ut-

----

[8] "The Convert," *Works*, V, 11–13. Elizabeth Peabody had an even wilder tale, according to which Brownson left the church because he refused to join in a secret plot to fasten Presbyterian control on the education of the country. This sounds like the work of a failing memory which badly garbled his Presbyterian adventure with his Owenite experience. Elizabeth Peabody, *op. cit.*, 353.

[9] *Princeton Review*, XXX, 390–392 (April, 1858).

tered in anguish over man's evil, as he expressed it at the time, or in protest at the repression of his personal liberty, as he explained it many years later, showed how repulsive Calvinism was to his most sacred feelings.

After a distressed two years Brownson gave up the battle. He had come to feel that Presbyterianism demanded faith on grounds that insulted reason; and he saw this feeling confirmed by Calvinist theology, which represented grace as superseding human nature rather than perfecting it, as well as by the behavior of his fellow communicants who dared not apply logic to their faith. If he had to choose between reason and faith — and he was compelled to make the choice — he would choose reason, which, after all, was man's distinctive faculty. His submission seemed to him now "the act of an intellectual desperado." [10] The next step was to reclaim his manhood.

3

In 1823, an earnest young man of twenty, he had begun to teach school in Stillwater, a village near Ballston Spa. Early in 1824, shortly after withdrawing from the Presbyterian communion, he left New York state for a teaching post in Detroit. There he

[10] "The Convert," *Works*, V, 18.

fell victim to the malarial breezes of Lake St. Clair. His life long hung in doubt and he was convalescent a considerable part of 1825. This illness gave him ample opportunity to meditate on the state of his soul. If Presbyterianism was too inhuman to know the road to salvation, which way should he turn next? His mother's sister, the devotee of Dr. Winchester, had bent his youthful thoughts toward Universalism. Indeed, it was the only form of rationalistic Christianity that he then knew of, as well as the chief refuge for apostate Calvinists. The ministers of the sect denied eternal damnation and asserted the salvation of all men, preaching that humanity sinned in Adam but was saved in Christ. Beyond this there was not much crystallization of doctrine, and Universalists were committed to little more than opposition to Calvinism. In the autumn Brownson applied to the Universalist General Convention for a letter of fellowship as a preacher.

In preparation for his new life, he painfully returned east, still pale and uncertain from long months in bed, and went to Vermont, where he continued his studies and gained practice in preaching. In the following June he was publicly ordained at Jaffrey, New Hampshire, a tall young man now, resolute in countenance and somewhat stern of expression. Three months later, coming back to New York, he preached for various periods at Ithaca, Geneva and finally Auburn. Meanwhile he would visit his family at Ballston Spa and occasionally hasten to Elbridge, where he saw Sally Healy, a dark, slender girl who had once been his pupil in the country school. In a few months they were married.

But Universalism proved no more satisfying to Brownson than Presbyterianism. At first it dulled the demands of his reason by placing God in a murky obscurity that made Him inaccessible to inquiry; but with God beyond the realm of definition or argument Brownson proceeded to test the Bible in the light of his logic. His mind already had that compelling analytical force which subjected every proposition to the severest strain and rejected those which snapped under the pressure. One by one, he found difficulties in the main tenets of Universalism. Since he could not defend universal salvation as a scriptural doctrine, he had to abandon the Bible as authoritative. This created new perplexities. If the Bible taught unsound doctrine, and at best only served to confirm the findings of reason, should not belief in its infallibility be everywhere attacked? Moreover, the Universalist notion that punishment was reformatory rather than vindictive seemed to end in blurring all distinction between good and evil; for, if the aim of punishment is to benefit him who suffers it, the innocent may as well receive it as the guilty. Virtue no longer has its reward, or sin its penalty: and all morality is undermined. He could not accept these conclusions, however powerfully they might issue from his premises, and in despair he decided that certain knowledge was limited to the world of the five senses.

At Auburn he had become the editor of the *Gospel Advocate and Impartial Investigator*, a semimonthly Universalist journal, and now he used its columns to chart the course of his growing doubt. His dangerous speculations alarmed the sober churchgoers of upper New York. One country boy returned home after listening to Brownson and found his parents in a rage at his wickedness in going, as they said, to hear the devil preach.[11] But more even than by his theological deviations, Brownson's position was endangered by his social heresies. As he shifted from Calvinism to liberal Christianity, he commenced to transpose his sense of sin to society, tracing evil to the organization of the world instead of to the souls of men. His mistrust of society sprang in part from his own feelings of loneliness and inferiority. "I am amiable and honest, I have intelligence and even some learning; I have wronged no one, and have helped the needy . . . ," he would write in pathetic solitude. "Yet nobody heeds me,

[11] Ludlow Williams to Brownson, March 5, 1860, Brownson Papers.

nobody loves me, nobody cares for me." "Call you this God's world? To me it seems more like the devil's world." "I am nobody, and if I venture to say anything, the only answer is, he is a poor devil, has not a red cent in his pocket — heed not his sayings." [12]

With the world gray and cheerless, and God reduced to the hazy and ineffective Heavenly Father of the Universalists, Brownson was forced back on his own efforts if life was to be improved. He began to grow concerned over politics. In the *Gospel Advocate* he vigorously opposed the attempts of the evangelical sects to stop the Sunday mails and otherwise exert political power. He became keenly interested in the affair of William Morgan, a stonemason of Batavia whose disappearance, supposedly at the hands of the Masons, was causing widespread excitement through the state. Believing that Morgan had been abducted and murdered, Brownson gave his political support for a time to his friend William H. Seward and the Anti-Masonic party.

By 1829 his position as a Universalist minister had become decidedly precarious. His growing indifference to church forms and growing concern with politics, made emphatic by his rugged outspokenness, caused considerable disquiet. Partly in response to criticism, he wrote "My Creed" for the *Gospel Ad-*

[12] H. F. Brownson, *Early Life,* 17–19.

vocate, a forthright and unrepentant declaration of independence from everything mystical and supernatural in religion. Men should be honest and benevolent, Brownson declared, and their main concern should be material comfort and intellectual development. "I BELIEVE, that if all mankind act on these principles they serve God all they can serve him." [13] But this confession of faith was too blunt and too flippant to quiet the murmurs. In October he published "A Gospel Creed," a theological embroiderment of his first creed which showed even more completely how his religion had become divested of piety and passion. It mentioned the after life only with apology, called Jesus "the greatest and best reformer ever vouchsafed us by heaven" [14] and, as a consequence of wrecking the great cosmic drama while retaining its characters, failed utterly to grapple with the master problems of evil and justice. But Brownson did not hold the "Gospel Creed" very important; he thought it necessary for everyone to believe his first declaration, but theology was, after all, a matter of opinion. In the end he only increased his disrepute among people who were already reaching the limits of tolerance. Meanwhile he was becoming more and more absorbed in social questions. Late in October 1829,

[13] *Ibid.,* 26. The entire creed is reprinted on pp. 25–29.
[14] *Ibid.,* 30. The entire creed is on pp. 30–34.

as he was passing through Utica, he stopped to hear a lecture on the evils of society by a notorious woman radical. He remained in excitement and fascination.

4

Frances Wright, a young Scotswoman, had first come to America in 1818. She came again in 1824 with Lafayette on his triumphal tour, and returned the next year to put into operation a scheme to solve the slavery problem that had gained the indorsement of Jefferson and Madison. The Negroes were to work out the price of their emancipation and at the same time receive industrial training which would prepare them for freedom. This was the famous Nashoba experiment. By 1828 it was evident that the plan was not working well. Concluding that slavery was only a symptom of a deeper complaint, Fanny Wright resolved to apply a more fundamental remedy. Her diagnosis revealed the basic ailment to be the failure of the American people to recognize the omnipotent rôle of environment in forming character. For this she blamed the clergy — who had an interest in sin, and therefore an interest in maintaining conditions out of which sin would arise.

Fanny decided to place the truth before America in a series of lectures. Unfortunately, however, her reputation had been stained by unlucky speculations about love. She had once suggested that in a more perfect society marriage would be based on moral obligation rather than on legal contract. This innocent hope was quickly interpreted as an argument for free love. Her appearance on the public lecture platform, in a day when few women strayed from the fireside, confirmed the general suspicion of her depravity. Her theme, moreover, was the evil of the clergy; and her plea was for a new system of education which would remake mankind: both were alike subversive and a bit ridiculous, and the newspapers took full advantage of each aspect. But Fanny Wright was an eloquent speaker — Brownson years later recalled her fine, rich, musical voice, her graceful manner, her tall commanding figure, her wit and sarcasm and deep, glowing enthusiasm [15] — and she held her audiences in spite of the strong popular disapproval.

Brownson stayed to talk with her after the lecture in Utica. When she came to Auburn they became closer friends. Fanny was then in her early thirties, a woman of uncommon charm and intelligence; and her ideas, already likely to interest Brownson, were irresistible when set forth by so pleasing a champion. He knew her for less than a year; yet she made an impression on him that resisted time and Catholicism,

[15] "The Convert," *Works*, V, 58.

and he always wrote of her with a touching mixture of regret and tenderness.

Brownson's growing concern with social questions had already led him to the writings of Robert Owen, the English manufacturer who had turned to constructing Utopias. Fanny Wright knew Owen, had borrowed liberally from his theories of education and was now associated with his son, Robert Dale Owen, in New York where they published the *Free Enquirer*, the *New Harmony Gazette* in new guise. She shared Brownson's fear of the evangelical sects and saw the advantage for her cause in acquiring this tall, intense man, so full of energy and vigor. In November he agreed to become a corresponding editor of the *Free Enquirer*. His rationalism, having weaned him from Presbyterianism, was now carrying him far beyond Universalism.

The Wright-Owen program had that inner consistency likely to attract a mind feeding more and more on logic, and less and less on experience. The premises granted, the conclusions were reasonable; and Brownson was so pleased, after the hodge-podge of Universalism, to find a body of ideas that survived systematization that he did not inquire immediately into their foundations. The program was built on the elder Owen's primary article of faith — that man was the passive creature of circumstance. Clearly,

then, the method of world reform would be to remold
the environment. Here entered the main plan —
"state guardianship," by which the state would undertake the education and training of all children from
the age of two. Owen and Fanny Wright hoped to institute this new educational system with the help of
the Workingmen's party.

It was this accidental alliance that gave the state-
guardianship proposal its significance. The depression
of 1828–1829 drove the city workers of New York
into the companionship bred by misery; and the
Workingmen's party staggered blindly forth, not
knowing what direction to take and catching at any-
one offering to serve as guide. Almost immediately
it came on two diverging paths to Utopia. Thomas
Skidmore, a machinist and disciple of Tom Paine,
advocated agrarianism — the equal division of property among all — while Owen, Fanny Wright and
George H. Evans urged the state-guardianship
scheme. Brownson, who became editor of the Genesee
Republican and Herald of Reform (published at Le-
roy, New York), strongly supported the Owenite
faction.[16] But the workingmen really wanted little
more than higher wages and the ten-hour day. When

[16] Brownson's contributions to the *Free Enquirer* had little to
do with the workingmen's movement and amounted on the whole
to a defense of his own course. Richard Leopold, "Robert Dale
Owen" (MS.), 163.

they became used enough to their political existence to examine the proposals at which they had snatched, they quickly repudiated agrarianism. A year or so later they rejected Owen's plan, as much because of the bad odor of atheism and radicalism his sponsorship gave it as because of its intrinsic defects. They had no genuine interest in far-reaching measures.

Brownson's open partnership with the forces of Satan was too much for his Universalist brethren, who became increasingly bitter toward him and forced him to leave the *Gospel Advocate*. He felt he should be congratulated for speaking out honestly rather than condemned for not concealing his doubts, and was enraged. But he overestimated the courage of his fellows, who denounced him less because his ideas were false than because they thought it bad policy to ventilate them. Brownson always believed that many other Universalists shared his uncertainty, if not his rashness. He now plunged enthusiastically into work for the new party. But with time the program suffered more and more from the queries of his experience. Finally he could stand it no longer and withdrew from its activities. Owen attributed Brownson's change of heart to the necessity of supporting a family.[17] There were more cogent reasons, however; for Brownson

[17] R. D. Owen to N. P. Trist, February 23, 1831, Trist Papers, VII, Leopold, *op. cit.*, 166.

was not inclined to let personal comfort stand between him and his vision of truth. But he was never a party man. He stood for no convictions but his own, and hated taking responsibility for the opinions of others. He never wholly accepted the Owen-Wright theory of education, and never believed that man was a helpless victim of his environment. He decided, moreover, that the workingmen were too weak to gain political power. "Money commands the supplies, and can hold out longer than they who have nothing but their manhood." [18] Labor's salvation, he concluded, must be looked for in other fields than politics. In the autumn of 1830 he voted for the Democratic candidate for governor. He had already ended his connection with the *Free Enquirer*, and shortly after the election he disposed of the Genesee *Republican*. This ended his experiment with political radicalism.

Brownson came away with a concrete understanding of the power of capital. He concluded that a party dedicated to the cause of labor would lead, not to victory, but to systematic oppression by mobilized business interests. The one hope seemed to lie in securing the co-operation of all classes, and this could be achieved only by moral suasion. Reform must come from within men before it could come from without.

[18] "The Convert," *Works*, V, 64.

Owen's error lay in presupposing the results of his measures as a condition of their introduction.

He did not draw this lesson clearly at the time, because of inward troubles of his own. In after years, however, it remained with him as a heritage of his days with Robert Dale Owen and that graceful, charming and unfortunate woman whom he never quite forgot, Fanny Wright.

5

During the year 1830, while Brownson was losing his faith in the Workingmen's party, he was fighting hard to preserve a deeper faith — his belief in God. His fatal passion for unraveling the logical implications of ideas had already shown the inadequacy of Universalism. This created an inner torment of doubt, intensified by the strain — unbearable for a man of Brownson's transparent honesty — of having to profess doctrines as a preacher that he could not believe as a man. His creed of 1829 had rejected heaven for earth, eternity for time and God for humanity. He acknowledged a Supreme Being, but it had all the strength and immediacy of a mathematical formula, and not half the importance. His belief had changed from a living religion to a perfunctory sentiment. But he was incorrigible in tracing notions to their logical extremes, and he soon proceeded from the unresolved moralism known as liberal Christianity to actual agnosticism.

"My doubts were first awakened by reading Paley's natural theology," [19] he wrote shortly after. When Paley's classic proofs of the existence of God failed to convince him, his faith in logic left no option but skepticism. Hume and Dr. Thomas Brown, moreover, had analyzed causality into a simple relation of antecedence and consequence which excluded the idea of creative power and thus of God.[20] Lured on by these tight little syllogisms, Brownson strayed far away from the reality of his feelings into a new realm that he found intellectually secure but emotionally terrifying. Here he lingered in an agony of doubt, sternly renouncing God and shivering in the bleak, dark universe his logic had left him. His wife grieved bitterly at her husband's disbelief. Finally, after a few months, Brownson himself realized how idle it was to hold out against the Lord. Why take logical conclusions for fact, particularly when the logic ignored

[19] *The Philanthropist*, II, 113.

[20] "Letter to the Editor," *BrQR*, Last Series, II, 541 (October, 1874), *Works*, XX, 429. Dr. Thomas Brown was a Scotch metaphysician whose powerful restatement of Hume's criticism of causality had great influence on Brownson. Brown showed in particular that "power" can mean nothing more than invariable sequence. He denied the skeptical implications of his doctrine, but Brownson apparently found the denials unconvincing.

the deepest promptings of his being? He now turned to the God he could not deny. Agnosticism vanished, like Owenism, when confronted by the things his heart told him were true. "I have . . . a witness within," he wrote, "and having this witness, I can find its testimony corroborated by the whole of external nature. I forgot the spirit, looked only at the flesh, and this witness was unheeded. It was therefore I doubted." [21]

Charles Elwood, or the Infidel Converted,[22] the fictional account Brownson wrote of his adventure in skepticism, shows abundantly how intellectual the experience was, its anguish coming from his struggle to believe in things he found essentially incredible, not from the terrifying vacancy of actual doubt. In the novel he tried to justify the religious impulse and

[21] *The Philanthropist,* II, 115.

[22] *Charles Elwood* was first written in 1834 under the title *Letters to an Unbeliever in Answer to Some Objections to Religion.* Later Brownson modified some of the arguments and recast the book in novel form. This version was published in 1840, but was soon withdrawn in America because of Brownson's discontent with it, though it was several times reprinted in England. The manuscript of *Letters to an Unbeliever* is in the Brownson collection. *Charles Elwood* as a novel is heavy and dull; but as a study in belief it is singularly persuasive and has the flavor that comes from immersion in actual experience. Edgar Allan Poe remarked of it, "In logical accuracy, in comprehensiveness of thought, and in the evident frankness and desire for truth in which it is composed, we know of few theological treatises which can be compared with it." "A Chapter on Autography," *Graham's Magazine,* November 1841–January 1842, Poe, *Works,* IX, 201.

show that logic was an incomplete guide for life. As
Dr. Francis Wayland remarked in the *Christian Review*, it should have been called *Charles Elwood, or
Christianity Converted;* for the only conversion was
in the hero's discovery at the end that he had all along
been a Christian and not an unbeliever.[23] Wayland's
quip justly characterized the episode. Brownson destroyed his uncertainty, not by a burning mystic experience, but by a restatement of Christianity; he
achieved, not a new faith, but a new name.

He had already resolved to resume preaching as an
independent minister when, during his convalescence
from infidelity, a friend read him William Ellery
Channing's sermon on "Likeness to God." This eloquent affirmation of the divinity of man, which
Brownson later called "the most remarkable [ser-
mon] since the Sermon on the Mount," [24] formulated
excitingly the Christianity Brownson had just described to himself, and precipitated his restored religious sentiment in the shape of something he could
label Unitarianism. "You, sir, have been my spiritual
father," he told Channing ten years later.[25] The ex-

[23] "Charles Elwood Reviewed," *Boston Quarterly Review* (hereafter cited as *BoQR*), April, 1842, *Works*, IV, 326.
[24] "New Views of Christianity, Society and the Church,"
Works, IV, 46.
[25] "The Mediatorial Life of Jesus," *Works*, IV, 140.

cursion into doubt, like the excursion into politics, ended with a deep conviction that religious principles were necessary.

On the first Sunday of February, 1831, Brownson returned to the pulpit in Ithaca. "I belong to no party, I disclaim all sectarian names," he told his congregation,

. . . Should I assume the name of any party, it should be Unitarian, as that denomination approximates nearer, in my estimation, to the spirit of Christianity than any other. Unitarian discourses are mostly practical; their lessons inculcate charity, a refined moral feeling and universal benevolence . . . but I discover no necessity of assuming any name that can become the rallying point of a sect . . . I am an independent preacher, accountable to my God, to truth, to my country, to the people of my charge, but to no other tribunal.[26]

With uncertainty banished once more, Brownson felt that he had something to say; and he indulged his temperamental need for self-expression by editing and publishing a fortnightly journal called *The Philanthropist*. Meanwhile his first child, a son, was born; and he had to struggle to keep his family clothed and fed through the biting winter. An itinerant printer years later remembered hearing Brownson's earnest

[26] *The Philanthropist*, II, 86.

preaching on a frosty Sunday afternoon to a very small congregation.[27]

His ministry in Ithaca was characteristic of the disciples of Channing. Religion, he told the few who came to hear him, was a way of life, not a creed; its end was moral behavior, not spiritual salvation; its object was to be one with God in goodness and thus be one with men. "My aim is to do right," said Brownson impatiently to a Presbyterian minister who asked him if he were not a sinner. "I am not conscious of being a sinner." [28] He stood in his pulpit, still a social reformer, not a priest.

[27] John Duffey to Brownson, January 27, 1857, Brownson Papers.
[28] *The Philanthropist*, II, 202.

CHAPTER II

FELLOW PILGRIMS, 1832–1836

Dr. Channing's writings had drawn Brownson's attention for the first time to the Unitarians as a sect. He liked their habit of letting each preacher stand on his own private convictions; and the cultivation and intelligence of the few members he met charmed him. With the death of the *Philanthropist* in the summer of 1832, his last interest in Ithaca vanished. He thereupon offered himself to a Unitarian congregation in Walpole, New Hampshire, and was accepted as its minister.

The removal to New England opened new intellectual vistas. The atmosphere was for the moment contemplative rather than active, and Brownson's mental world enlarged immensely before his eyes. He plunged into philosophy and theology, learned French and a little German and gained excited entry to a whole new literature. He delivered four sermons a week and many Lyceum lectures; and he made frequent visits to Boston, a hundred miles by stage, where he met the leading Unitarians.

As an author, Brownson was irrepressible. He speedily began to contribute articles on the French philosophers and on the alliance between Christianity and social progress to such Unitarian journals as the *Christian Register* and the *Unitarian,* and soon to the most dignified of them all, the *Christian Examiner.* This brought him more conspicuously to Boston's attention. As Harriet Martineau found two years later, "Prudence is now reigning supreme over the elderly classes of Boston generally, and too many of the young"; [1] but some younger men, disciples of the great Channing, did not rest content with ministers who tailored their words to the prejudices of their congregations. George Ripley, then acting editor of the *Register,* was in particular attracted by the Walpole preacher with his "pithy, lucid and direct" style and saw in him an intellect whose vigor and devotion might be most valuable in reviving the Unitarian cause.[2]

Brownson early met Channing and told him that he owed his rescue from infidelity to the "Likeness to God." Channing, with Boston reserve, responded that he could not regard a stranger, "not brought up among us, and who has made important changes of

[1] Harriet Martineau, *Society in America,* II, 198.
[2] Ripley to Brownson, January 15, 1833, H. F. Brownson, *Early Life,* 104.

religion," as an old friend, but that he highly approved of Brownson's treatment of Christianity as a principle of reform.[3] Early in 1834 Brownson named his third son after the good Doctor. In Ripley Brownson found a more congenial soul. They shared an aptitude for philosophy, an enthusiasm for foreign thinkers, and great hopes for the future. Ripley borrowed Constant from Brownson and loaned him Jouffroy; and in March 1834 he tried to induce Brownson to come to Boston and preach to the indifferent and skeptical who kept away from the ordinary churches.[4]

The Unitarians of Canton, Massachusetts, however, had just asked Brownson to be their minister, and Ripley's plan lapsed for the time. In May Brownson was installed. Ripley preached the sermon; and Adin Ballou also took part in the exercises.[5] Brownson remained for two years in Canton, where he became a very useful member of the community. He organized a Lyceum, and he started a small library. One summer (1835) he was called upon to examine a Harvard sophomore who wanted to teach the town school. "The two sat up talking till midnight," as Ellery Channing described it later, "and Mr. Brownson informed the school committee that Mr. Thoreau

[3] Channing to Brownson, January 11, 1834, *ibid.*, 106–108.
[4] Ripley to Brownson, undated, 1834, March 26, 1834, *ibid.*, 110–111, 104–106.
[5] Adin Ballou, *Autobiography*, 254.

was examined, and would do, and would board with him." [6] Thoreau and Brownson spent a stimulating summer, reading German together and walking the shady banks of the cool Neponset River. These six weeks gave young Thoreau his first continuous association with a mature and provocative intelligence. "They were an era in my life," he wrote Brownson, "the morning of a new *Lebenstag*. They are to me as a dream that is dreamt, but which returns from time to time in all its original freshness." [7]

Brownson had meanwhile gained wide attention for his writings on French philosophy. The first book he read at Walpole was Benjamin Constant's huge work in five octavo volumes, *De la Réligion Considérée dans sa Source, ses Formes et ses Développements*. Constant expressed, with formidable appeal to history and psychology, the conclusion Brownson had drawn from his flirtation with atheism: that the whole of life does not yield itself to logical expression, and the most important sentiments exist beyond the reach of the intellect. The religious principle, then, was not impugned by the absence of syllogistic demonstration. Its mere existence was enough to prove its reality. Upon this analysis Constant built a theory of

---

[6] William Ellery Channing, *Thoreau, the Poet-Naturalist*, 32.
[7] Thoreau to Brownson, December 30, 1837, H. F. Brownson, *op. cit.*, 204–206.

progress by which man rose through the ages on the steppingstones of his dead institutions, each discarded as the idea it represented came to need purer embodiment. From Constant Brownson proceeded to Saint-Simon, whose *Nouveau Christianisme* announced so eloquently the faith that was to inspire the new age. Brownson caught fire from the strange brilliance of the French nobleman. He read with excitement the interpretation of Christianity as the gospel of social reform, for he had himself already decided that reform could come only through religion; and he hailed joyously Saint-Simon's fervent conviction that the "organic" epoch, the era of reconstruction, was at hand. Saint-Simon became to the young minister "in our day the truest interpreter of the thought of Jesus." [8] Brownson listened to him with the devotion of a true disciple and cherished his dream of a Christian Utopia.

The lesson of Constant and Saint-Simon was plain, and Brownson might well have proclaimed it if he had never heard of them. Man's vital need in 1834 was a new and purified embodiment of the religious sentiment. The Reformation signalized the failure of Catholicism; and Protestantism, as Brownson wrote in the *Christian Examiner*, was no church, but a chaos

[8] "Leroux on Humanity," *BoQR*, V (July, 1842), *Works*, IV, 101.

of sects, attesting the sickness of the time but containing nothing positive enough to serve as a cure. A universal church was needed, a church which would replace the confused and anachronistic and tyrannical sects of the day. Brownson's battle cry in conversation, in the Unitarian reviews, and in his sermons, became the *Church of the Future.*

2

Though Brownson's application to Constant and Saint-Simon, and soon to Jouffroy and Cousin, developed his philosophical tastes, he remained chiefly concerned with reform. His philosophy served to make his sympathy for the workingmen intellectually respectable, and it gave their cause significance by placing it in the cosmos. He could then proceed without apology to his main job.

He had been, on the whole, a political agnostic until he joined with Fanny Wright in the New York Workingmen's party. In 1824 he had supported Calhoun and then Crawford; in 1828 he voted — foolishly, as he said later — for Adams.[9] In the few years after 1830 he paid little attention to actual political struggles, since he was convinced that all politicians

[9] "Popular Government," *Democratic Review,* XII (May, 1843), *Works,* XV, 285.

were equally cynical; but he still cared deeply about the welfare of labor. From his retirement at Walpole he could take only a theoretical interest in the workingmen. In Canton, however, he lived in the midst of a population that was largely working-class. Though his concern with abstractions still continued, he was drawn more and more to the social problem as it confronted him.

Experience with the Workingmen's party had left Brownson with the conviction that social reform must depend on moral reform. As early as 1831, in a Fourth of July address at Ovid, New York, he cried, " 'Tis the slavery of the mind which paves the way to that of the body, and the slavery of individuals which induces that of nations": the fault, dear citizens, is not in our rulers but in ourselves that we are underlings. "There can be no bad government when the people, as individuals, are wise, virtuous and independent." [10] Three years later, in an essay on "Christianity and Reform" in the *Unitarian*, he re-echoed his faith in the significance of personal morality. "There is no such thing as reforming the mass without reforming the individuals who compose it." Why has reform been ordinarily the ally of infidelity? Because those who profit by the existing abuses always fight

[10] *An Address on the Fifty-Fifth Anniversary of American Independence Delivered at Ovid, Seneca County, New York*, 8, 11.

change, and the clergy are usually in the privileged class: see the French Revolution. The spirit of Jesus, the spirit of radical reform, is forgotten when the church grows corrupt.[11] Brownson's analysis was going below the surface; he was beginning to sense the social background of individual selfishness.

On the Fourth of July 1834 at Dedham he made his chief utterance on social conditions before his removal to Boston. Here he attacked the surviving forms of inequality, the laws which bore most heavily on offenses committed by the poor, and particularly the injustice in barring wage-earners from a decent education, thus making them meat for demagogues. Education, Brownson argued, would raise the workers above artificial distinctions and enable them to destroy inequalities in the law. The Dedham address was published, and Brownson sent copies to many of his fellow ministers. Some, like the timorous James Walker, then editor of the *Christian Examiner* and later president of Harvard, thought Brownson too inflammatory: "I am extremely anxious that on this subject you will proceed, independently indeed, but yet cautiously and circumspectly."[12]

The most penetrating observations on the speech, however, occurred in a remarkable letter to Brownson

[11] H. F. Brownson, *op. cit.*, 96–100.
[12] Walker to Brownson, August 2, 1834, *ibid.*, 120–121.

from the Workingmen's candidate for governor, Samuel C. Allen of Northfield.[13] The Gospel, Allen believed, was "good news to the poor, *as a class*"; what frustrated the mission of Jesus was that its preachers "have attached themselves to the privileged classes, and have lent themselves to uphold an order of things wholly irreconcilable with its principles." "What have governments been," demanded Allen, "and what are they now, but the combination of the rich and powerful to increase their riches, and extend their power?" "Individual character is very much formed by social institutions, and among them that of property in all its aspects is of chief influence." Property "asserts the right to get whatever it can get of labor or its fruits with the consent of the owner" without regard to justice. This notion, "false in theory, and subversive alike of morals and happiness," has stamped its character on the administrative policy of nations, through the efforts of the property holders, joining to gain by

[13] Allen to Brownson, August 18, 1834, *ibid.*, 113–118. Samuel Clesson Allen [Jr.] was born in Northfield in 1793, the son of Samuel Clesson Allen, member of Congress and later professor of political economy at Amherst. The younger Allen was nominated for governor in 1833 and 1834 by the Workingmen's party; from 1837 to 1843 he served in the state legislature as a Democrat. He later moved to East Boston where he became postmaster and died in 1860. See Herbert C. Parsons, *A Puritan Outpost* (New York, 1937), 494 and *passim*; Commons *et al.*, *History of Labour in the United States*, I, 315 ff.; A. B. Darling, *Political Changes in Massachusetts*, *passim*.

fraud or force the powers of government. "What have the laboring class to expect from their justice or charity? What from a government in their control? Its legislation and jurisprudence, the ministrations of religion and justice, when held and directed by theory will afford no relief to the laborers *as a class*." "All wealth is the product of labor and belongs of right to him who produces it, and yet how small a part of the products of its labor falls to the laboring class!" The workers must unite: "The rod of the oppressor must be broken, he will not throw it away." "I may say," Allen concluded, "and in this perhaps I differ from you, that I do not think any extensive or permanent reform can be effected without change in the economical relations of society." In a postscript Allen criticized Brownson's indifference to party strife. The struggle over the Bank expressed fundamental issues, he declared, and the people must rally around Jackson.

This extraordinary document, with its mature social theory, illuminates the defects in the moralistic attitude toward social reform, which substantially was Channing's and that of most of the Boston intellectuals as well as Brownson's. Like all people who see things strongly, the moral reformers saw things simply. They ignored the relationship between ethical conduct and the social setting. It is not, of course, an accident that a century ago reformers tended to appeal to man's soul while today they appeal to his environment. The conviction that reform is a personal problem was almost justified by an age in which the environment was so simple that its influence could be easily overlooked. The Industrial Revolution had not yet made the economic system so impersonal that a morality which had evolved out of man-to-man relationships was obsolete. Brownson lived in a world that was relatively uncomplicated. It was a world which persuaded Jackson that the operations of government were simple enough to be understood by any intelligent citizen; its deepest feelings were voiced by Emerson, who made self-reliance the holiest way of life. Brownson was but generalizing from that segment of experience that seemed most vital to him. He was nearly right; in America of the 1830's individual reform might almost have been enough. Almost, but not quite. After all, Brownson, in the very essay in which he reduced reform to a private concern, showed a lively realization that change would be opposed by the privileged classes — look at France! But his intellectual recognition of this truth vanished when he turned from France to America and spoke from the depths of his own past: then he felt he could restrict reform to an appeal to individual souls.

Brownson looked on society and saw an organism; Allen looked and saw the class struggle. This is less an incompatibility of views than a difference of emphasis. Neither is an objective description of society; both are descriptions of states of mind toward society, and they are as objectively contradictory as the convexity and concavity of a lens. The difference lies in the attitudes they imply and the emotions they arouse. One presupposes progress by harmony; the other progress by discord. One believes moral change to be necessary for social change; the other finds moral change impossible without social change. It is at this point that the difference becomes crucial and finds its way into action. One believes in the efficacy of political agencies; the other — but it has never been clear just how the moral reformers hoped to make men virtuous, and there is their fatal weakness.

Brownson's disdain for Andrew Jackson was typical of his position. Obviously the man was arrogant, illiterate, self-interested — his motives were not chaste enough for a reformer's consideration. Allen, less concerned with absolutes and more aware of the things men live by, saw that Jackson was fighting the people's battle. Political opportunism, perhaps, but a thousand times more effective than the Channing program of regenerating individual souls. Brownson looked on education — the cultivation of the soul — as the instrument of social reform. Here, most glaringly, appears the tragic flaw in the moralistic approach. If virtue depends on proper schooling, and proper schooling is impossible until the country becomes sufficiently virtuous to establish it, how is a corrupt nation to be started on the road to paradise? Brownson had no means, except religious conversion, of improving education. His social thought still had too much the hothouse flavor. It needed a little exposure to the frosts and storms, the buffetings of circumstance, that confused the actual situation.

3

Early in 1836 Brownson moved to Mount Bellingham in Chelsea, and in May began to hold independent services in Boston. He was a striking figure in the pulpit, two inches over six feet, slim and active, with black hair brushed straight back from his forehead and deep-set eyes of mixed gray and hazel that seemed black when he grew excited. But his excitement never turned into frenzy, nor his indignation into bombast; he was becoming an able orator who impressed foreigners and staid Bostonians alike with his dignity and eloquence.

Away from the pulpit his manners still carried with them the robust honesty of the country. He made little attempt to defer to Boston, and his heartiness somewhat dismayed New England gentility. Many who knew Brownson but slightly were suspicious of this tall lean man, whom they saw striding violently down narrow Boston streets to Benjamin Greene, the publisher, his coattails swinging out behind, or waiting for the Chelsea ferry, with half a dozen books under his arm and a quid of tobacco in his mouth. After performing marriage ceremonies he took the first kiss from the bride, and once when he exchanged pulpits with Dr. Channing, he found himself hungry after a lunch with Channing and bought another at a hotel before the afternoon sermon.[14] In conversation with his friends he tended to shout and to pound on the table. Most of the Unitarian intellectuals were interested in developing their agreements; but Brownson looked on argument as argument, and, confident of his mastery of logic, never hesitated to halt the expansive soliloquies of the Transcendentalists at all doubtful points. No one was safe from this rustic bluntness. Even Emerson was commanded to make himself clear, and once was driven to exclaim in confusion, "I feel myself to be in the midst of a truth I do not comprehend, but which comprehends me."[15]

[14] H. F. Brownson, *Latter Life*, 245, and *Early Life*, 160.
[15] F. B. Sanborn, ed., *The Genius and Character of Emerson*, 163.

Such conduct gained Brownson a reputation for contentiousness that has survived when most other things about him have been forgotten. On another occasion he picked an argument with the ingenuous Charles Lane, the English friend of Bronson Alcott, who later joined the Alcotts at Fruitlands. Overpowered by the other's vehemence, Lane took paper and pencil from his pocket and tried to still the flood by asking Brownson to name the three profoundest men in America. Lane was a simple soul, and, when Brownson specified himself as the third, he accepted it with wonderful solemnity and repeated the story to Emerson. "Brownson never will stop and listen," Emerson commented, "neither in conversation, but what is more, not in solitude." [16] But good George Ripley, more patient than the others, and perhaps less dedicated to fostering his own personality, bore with the gaunt Vermonter and encouraged his booming discussions. Ripley alone pierced through Brownson's proud and confident bearing to the lonely man beneath. The others found him lacking in sympathy, cold and dogmatic, but Ripley warmed to him and became his friend.

At home Brownson was a stern husband who looked to his wife for obedience before affection. As his daughter remarked years later, he was never intended

[16] R. W. Emerson, *Journals*, VI, 297.

for home life.[17] Not even family affection broke into his abiding loneliness. He studied a great deal, sometimes till long after midnight, always in his swallow-tail coat, waiting eagerly for the strong, black coffee Sally brought him morning and evening. He might read from his own library of three hundred and twenty volumes, or he might borrow books from Ripley or Dr. Channing or another of his Unitarian friends: his lamp burned constantly, and his family saw little of him. Then on certain evenings Brownson would send for his eldest son to play a game of chess. They would draw up cane-bottom chairs and sit down, sometimes for hours. Brownson loved the game and suffered intensely when he lost; he would play endlessly, if the mood was on him — "There was no respite," his son cried half a century later.[18]

Brownson may indeed have brought rudeness to Boston, but he also brought strength, and strength was badly needed. Most of the clergy were timid, afraid to touch the burning questions of the day. The people, bored with the monotonous services which stuffed them with convention and snubbed their urgent needs, were leaving the churches. Some went to Abner Kneeland, an unfrocked Universalist preacher,

[17] Sarah Brownson to H. F. Brownson, October 1, 187?, Brownson Papers.
[18] O. A. Brownson, Jr., to H. F. Brownson, February 22, 1887, Brownson Papers.

who started a Society of Free Enquirers and began to expound pantheism in the *Boston Investigator*. His success alarmed the conservative, and the protest at his indictment for blasphemy in 1834 alarmed them further. A small deaf Englishwoman, who spent the winter of 1835–1836 in Boston, was alike shocked by the cowardice of most of the respectable ministers and delighted by the fervor of the young men who wanted to grapple with truth. One day she took her ear trumpet to hear a new preacher at the Lyceum Hall on Hanover Street. She came away, deeply stirred. "The people are requiring a better clergy," Harriet Martineau later wrote in her chapter on religion in America. "Even in Boston, as far behind the country as that city is, a notable change has already taken place. A strong man, full of enlarged sympathies, has not only discerned the wants of the time, but set himself to do what one man may to supply them." [19] In her appendix she reprinted part of a discourse by Orestes Brownson on "The Wants of the Times."

Brownson was, to the most nearsighted, a strong man. He inevitably found his friends among the few men of Boston who were bold enough to think independently and eloquent enough to speak out their thoughts excitingly. In the fall of 1836 he met with

[19] Harriet Martineau, *op. cit.*, II, 357–358.

half a dozen of them — Ralph Waldo Emerson, George Ripley, F. H. Hedge, Convers Francis, James Freeman Clarke, Bronson Alcott — at Ripley's home where they formed a loose society known as the Transcendentalist Club. Hedge later said that "Brownson met with us once or twice, but became unbearable, and was not afterward invited." [20] Brownson no doubt proved unbearable to some; for the lesser Transcendentalists luxuriated in a windy and diffuse thought of a kind calculated to drive the logical Brownson to fury. As Hecker remarked, "No one loves to break a lance with him, because he cuts such ungentlemanly gashes." [21] But his connection with the Club was much longer than Hedge, who undoubtedly disliked him, cared to remember. It met at his home in Chelsea, and he was known generally as one of its leading members.[22]

The question of whether he was ever a Transcendentalist is purely verbal. In later years he confessed and denied it as it suited his polemic purposes. He certainly shared many of the Transcendentalist tastes and enthusiasms. He was a member of the Club; he thrilled to the symphonies of Beethoven; he took part in the conversations at Elizabeth Peabody's book-

[20] Quoted by Lindsay Swift, *Brook Farm*, 7.
[21] Walter Elliott, *The Life of Father Isaac Hecker*, 181.
[22] George W. Cooke, *Ralph Waldo Emerson*, 57.

store; he compared Carlyle favorably to Michel-angelo, Van Dyck, Titian, Rembrandt, Wordsworth and Shelley within a page.[23] His sentiments were frequently Emersonian, if expressed without Emerson's bell-like ring. "The age tends too much to association;" he would declare, "people are beginning to act only in crowds, and the individual is fast being lost in the mass."[24] "Truth is the property of no one sect, righteousness is the exclusive boast of no one denomination. All have some truth, all have some errors. To join any one, you must support its falsehoods as well as its truths, or they will cast you out of the synagogue."[25] "The world is not to be regenerated by the exertions of reformers who have but one idea, and who fancy that one idea embraces the universe."[26]

Outsiders generally regarded him as one of the elect. The *Western Messenger*, journal of liberal Unitarianism on the frontier, paid as much attention

[23] "Carlyle's French Revolution," *BoQR*, I, 410–411 (Oct., 1838). This essay may not, however, have been written by Brownson. Theodore Parker noted W. H. Channing as the author in his copy of the magazine; Clarence L. F. Gohdes, *The Periodicals of American Transcendentalism*, 49. Judging by the style alone, I should incline to ascribe the article to Channing; but H. F. Brownson used his father's own papers when he edited the *Works* and would hardly have included this essay in the *Works* if he had not been certain of its authorship.

[24] *Address on Intemperance* (February 26, 1833), 13.

[25] Sermon at Ithaca, New York, February, 1831, *Early Life*, 52.

[26] "Ultraism," *BoQR*, I, 380 (July, 1838).

to Brownson as to Emerson or Channing;[27] and
Blackwood's Magazine called him the Coryphaeus
of the sect.[28] The Transcendentalists approved highly
of Brownson's *Boston Quarterly Review* — Alcott
thought it in 1839 "the best journal now current on
this side of the Atlantic," Ripley called it "the best
indication of the culture of philosophy in this country,"
and Parker preferred it to the *Dial*[29] — but, when
Brownson tried to persuade them to make the *Boston
Quarterly Review* their organ instead of founding a
new magazine, they scurried to cover. Alcott talked
it over with Emerson and Margaret Fuller, and the
three determined to go ahead with their own plans.[30]
This crisis indicates Brownson's position: enough of a
Transcendentalist to have his proposal considered, but
too much a Brownsonian for it to be accepted. His
mind demanded too great a show of rigorous think-

[27] Gohdes, *op. cit.*, 34.

[28] "Transcendentalism," *BrQR*, 1845–1846, *Works*, VI, 25.

[29] Quotations from Alcott's journal, March 27, 1839, T. W.
Higginson, *Margaret Fuller Ossoli*, 143; George Ripley, "Brownson's Writings," *Dial*, I, 31 (July, 1840). Parker to Convers
Francis, December 18, 1840: "Apropos of 'The Dial': to my
mind it bears about the same relation to 'The Boston Quarterly'
that Antimachus does to Hercules, Alcott to Brownson, or a band
of men and maidens daintily arrayed in finery, 'walking in a
vain show,' with kid mitts on their 'dannies,' to a body of stout
men in blue frocks, with great arms and hard hands, and legs like
the Pillars of Hercules." O. B. Frothingham, *Theodore Parker*,
139.

[30] Higginson, *op. cit.*, 148.

ing ever to partake of the naïvetés and extravagances of die-hard Transcendentalism.[31]

Such as it was, his Transcendentalism was Cousinian in form rather than Emersonian or Orphic. Brownson suffered from a passion for exact definition. When Emerson was restated according to Brownson's ideas of meaningfulness, he sounded remarkably like the French philosopher. The Oversoul through Brownson's eyes became Cousin's impersonal reason; the divinity in man was translated into the instinctive human impulse toward religion; and self-reliance was simply Emerson's phrasing of Cousin's doctrine of spontaneity. Emerson actually had things to say that went far deeper than Transcendentalism; but his friends necessarily read him with their own pale torches and found in him only what their much feebler lights permitted them to see. Like the others, Brownson disregarded Emerson's warning that words

[31] Brownson made the most judicious of his many pronouncements on whether or not he was a Transcendentalist in the *BoQR*, III, 322–323 (July, 1840): "So far as Transcendentalism is understood to be the recognition in man of the capacity of knowing truth intuitively, or of attaining to a scientific knowledge of an order of existence transcending the reach of the senses, and of which we can have no sensible experience, we are Transcendentalists. But when it is understood to mean, that feeling is to be placed above reason, dreaming above reflection, and instinctive intimation above scientific exposition, in a word, when it means the substitution of a lawless fancy for an enlightened understanding . . . we must disown it, and deny that we are Transcendentalists."

referred to things. They all looked in his glowing essays for phrases they knew as intellectually fashionable, not for the realities of experience that Emerson meant these phrases to signify. Every generation has its own sacred words, which guarantee ideas an entrance to all enlightened minds; but, though the profoundest thinker of the day may use the same words and very probably may have given them their magic, he is likely to be saying quite different things from the people who shine by reflected light. Brownson, a lesser man, extracted from Emerson a version of Transcendentalism that he might have developed without ever going to Concord.

4

Ever since Ripley suggested in 1833 that he come to Boston as an independent preacher, Brownson had been eager to give his *Church of the Future* outward and visible form. Two years later, while still at Canton, he was appointed chairman of a Unitarian committee on the diffusion of Christian truth. The other members, Ezra Stiles Gannett and Joseph Allen of Northborough, recommended cautiously that the Unitarian clergy be more fervent in its preaching and that it distribute suitable religious tracts more widely; but Brownson seized the opportunity to sketch the

Church of the Future. Religion must keep up with the times; Brownson thought it idle to reprove the times for no longer being religious. He proposed to the committee that it search for a new principle of Christian organization, some new plan of union which the whole world would welcome. Gannett and Allen looked fishily at their chairman's excessive enthusiasm and skeptically advised him to go to Boston and try the experiment himself.[32] These Unitarians were too used to nay-saying to salute the everlasting Yea. The church had a chill in its bones that eventually caused its Emersons, its Ripleys, its Parkers and its Brownsons to seek warmth elsewhere.

For a moment Brownson thought he saw in Channing the Paul of the new Church. Though they became steady friends, and Brownson found much in the older man to admire, he soon recognized that eloquence did not mean profundity, or philanthropy, vigor. Channing's part was to intervene after others, less polished but more original, had laid the question open.[33] Brownson sought the new Messiah, but could not find him among his acquaintances. As for himself, he could be no more than a John the Baptist crying in the wilderness.

[32] Gannett to Brownson, April 9, 1835, Allen to Brownson, April 25, 1835, H. F. Brownson, *Early Life*, 126–129, 131–134.

[33] Brownson's brilliant characterization of Channing is to be found in "The Convert," *Works*, V, 77–79.

Since the aspirations nearest his heart did not thrive in the cold sobriety of Unitarianism, Brownson determined to restrict his confidences to George Ripley. The two were fascinated by the French philosophers who had given Brownson's scheme its intellectual justification; and neither was disturbed by the prospect of making lonely experiments for the sake of truth in a dark and disheartening world. Ripley's faith later created Brook Farm. In 1835, still in the Unitarian ministry, he warmly encouraged Brownson in his plan of world salvation. "In the formation of my mind, in systematizing my ideas, and in general development and culture, I owe more to him than to any other man among Protestants," Brownson later said of Ripley. "We have since taken divergent courses, but I loved him as I have loved no other man." [34] Chiefly through Ripley, Brownson was enabled to move to Boston. Channing and others also urged him to come, thinking that Brownson's own experience with agnosticism would prepare him peculiarly for preaching to the laboring class and winning back to Jesus the disciples of the imprisoned Kneeland.[35] Brownson, accepting the invitation, intended to go beyond Channing's expectation. He would pro-

---

[34] "From motives of delicacy" Brownson did not name the person of whom he was speaking; but there can be little doubt that he was referring to Ripley. *Ibid.*, 81.

[35] *Ibid.*, 82; Elizabeth Peabody, *op. cit.*, 354.

claim the *Church of the Future* in the hope that the new Messiah would appear.

During May and June of 1836 Brownson held religious meetings in the Lyceum Hall in Boston. On the last Sunday of May he preached the discourse on "The Wants of the Times" which so excited Harriet Martineau. The old churches, Brownson began, are failures; they have lost their hold on the people, and what they now offer finds no response in their hearts. Their preaching ignores the vital aspirations of the day — the demand for free inquiry, the tendency to democracy and the craving for reform. "All over the Christian world," Brownson declaimed, his face working convulsively, "a contest is going on, not as in former times between monarchs and nobles, but between the people and their masters, between the many and the few, the privileged and the underprivileged." Religion alone can assure the victory of the people, for religious love alone can elicit the sacrifice necessary for basic reform. And, if religion is to live, it *must* ally itself with the people. This is simply to apply the Christianity of Jesus. If I repeated the words of Jesus in the marketplaces of this city, he cried, "You would call me a 'radical,' an 'agrarian,' a 'trades-unionist,' a 'leveller.' " Jesus is "the prophet of the workingmen." [36] My object is to

[36] Martineau, *op. cit.*, II, 402–415. The quotations are from 405 and 412.

fulfill the Gospel; to help found the kingdom of peace on earth; to establish the new church, the *Church of the Future,* the Society for Christian Union and Progress.

Brownson pushed ahead the organization of his new society in the next month. Its three articles, he loudly proclaimed, were intellectual liberty, social progress and a more spiritual morality than animated the ministers who took care not to offend State Street. To free-thinkers he sought to prove that Christianity was compatible with free inquiry; to the reformers he presented it as the religion of progress and equality; and to those convinced of the corruption of existing churches he affirmed the true Christian morality. "A multitude flocks around him," wrote Miss Martineau, "the earnest spirits of the city and the day. . . . The rising-up of this new church in Boston is an eloquent sign of the times." [37]

The philosophical justification of the Society for Christian Union and Progress soon appeared in Brownson's first book, *New Views of Christianity, Society and the Church.* He drew chiefly on French authors, on Saint-Simon and especially Cousin, in this work, and he was also indebted to Heine, Schleiermacher and to Dr. Follen's treatise on *Religion and the Church.* Cousin, whose mark on Brownson was be-

[37] *Ibid.,* II, 358.

coming clearer, had first come to his attention in 1833. Brownson shared the popular belief that all systems had their truth and were wrong only when they became exclusive; and Cousin's eclectic principle suggested a way of philosophizing from this conviction. In *New Views* he applied Cousin's method to religion. The *Church of the Future* must contain the partial truths of all the churches of the past in a shining new synthesis. Brownson founded his historical analysis on a dialectical theory borrowed chiefly from Heinrich Heine and Saint-Simon. Civilization, said *De L'Allemagne*, was a struggle between exclusive spiritualism and exclusive materialism. Heine had named the protagonists Hebraism and Hellenism; but Brownson, after examination, declared them to be Catholicism and Protestantism. He wrote, indeed, partly to answer the contention of the Saint-Simonists, and especially of Heine, that Christianity could not be the social ideal of the future. Christianity had assumed these two embodiments, argued Brownson; but each was inadequate because each reflected the truth in fragments. One fitted man to die, the other fitted him to live; one nourished only his soul, the other only his flesh. But Jesus, the God-Man, symbolized the essential unity of spirit and matter. The *Church of the Future* must combine the affirmations of Catholicism and Protestantism into one glorious whole: the body sanctified, the spirit humanized, the two flowing together in the ineffable harmony of a Beethoven symphony. *New Views* announced the idea. Let humanity become convinced of its truth and eager for its fulfillment, and the great man — who figured in so many hopes of the day — will appear and realize it for the world.

It is idle to argue with such a book. Carlyle remarked to Theodore Parker that the new views were as old as Voltaire, and laughed about Brownson; [38] but he might have traced them back to Julian the Apostate without denying their value. Every generation has had to rediscover them to save the churches of the world from crumbling from infectious decay. The work would persuade few who did not already concede its conclusions; but to these it demonstrated that their belief represented the climax of human destiny. The learned and skeptical could quibble with every line, for it was packed with ignorant remarks and inaccurate observations. But *New Views* was not history. Brownson dealt with propositions, not with facts; the historical chapters consisted of various abstractions, of which the most prominent were "materialism" and "spiritualism," acting out their logical implications against a backdrop of history. His style

[38] Frank B. Sanborn and William T. Harris, *A. Bronson Alcott*, II, 369, quoted from a letter of Theodore Parker.

was breathless, elliptic, compressed. He affirmed and deduced, but paused not to explain. His confidence in logic, as usual, misled him, and he frequently argued himself out of touch with what history agrees to be the facts. Brownson's abstractions, however, expressed sharply felt sentiments of his own. He was reading these sentiments into history, but that was his right: the important thing to Brownson, and to his audience, was not the history but the sentiments.

New Views was a bold and striking utterance of the profound discontent that had been fermenting in Boston and was beginning to rise to the surface. The cold respectability of Unitarianism had too long suppressed the anxiety for inward experience, the deep thirst for spiritual consolation. Young men were starved by the emotional thinness of the religion offered by most of their ministers. They could no longer accept the doctrine of John Locke, who blankly denied that the soul could of its own yearning perceive God. They needed something new and alive, and *New Views* was one evidence that the need was becoming articulate. Brownson's searching criticism of Protestantism formulated the feelings that had tormented Emerson and Ripley into resigning their pulpits. "With Protestants, religion has existed, but as a reminiscence, a tradition. . . . Men labor six days for this world and at most but

one for the world to come. . . . Right yields to
expediency, and duty is measured by utility." The
world must learn the new faith: "All things are holy,
and all doctrines are sacred. All the productions of
the ever-teeming brain of man . . . are but so many
manifestations of humanity, and humanity is a mani-
festation of the Divinity." [39] The future religion of
man is one that he can never outgrow: the religion
of progress.

The spirit within, confined too long by Unitarian
austerity, was bursting forth on all sides. There was
an air of excitement and anticipation in Boston.
Others, besides Brownson, were looking for the
"providential" man who would end the confusion
and perplexity. "There is a great feeding on the mul-
berry leaves," exulted Ripley, "and it will be hard
if silken robes are not woven for the shining ones." [40]
Young men were beginning to enter the lists against
established ministers, instead of whispering dissatis-
faction in their studies: Emerson published *Nature*;
Convers Francis, *Christianity as a Purely Internal
Principle*; Ripley, *Discourses on the Philosophy of
Religion*; Alcott, *Conversations with Children on
the Gospels*; and W. H. Furness, *Remarks on the
Four Gospels*. William Lloyd Garrison, unable to

[39] *Works*, IV, 22, 23–24, 54.
[40] Ripley to Bancroft, September 20, 1837, Bancroft Papers.

draft the clergy in his crusade against slavery, was leading another attack on the churches. Men suddenly knew that faith should be living. These half-dozen books of 1836 attested the vitality of the soul; and the high priest of conservatism, Andrews Norton, sat, as his enemies said, in a room with the shutters closed and meditated on the latest forms of infidelity.[41]

To Brownson's disappointment, *New Views* made very little stir. The liberals acknowledged its existence — Emerson discussed a question out of it with Charles Shackford — and Bronson Alcott, observing that it was about as thick as *Nature*, declared its author to be one of the best men in the liberal church.[42] But they did not thrill to Brownson's clarion call. He decided sadly that he had made

[41] *BoQR*, III, 269 (July, 1840).

[42] R. W. Emerson, *op. cit.*, IV, 166; "Alcott's 'Conversation' on the Transcendental Club and *The Dial*," ed. Clarence Gohdes, *American Literature*, III, 16. This conversation was based on Alcott's journal. Quoted from Alcott's diary: "Emerson and Hedge promise more than others amongst us; with Furness, Brownson and Ripley, they furnish the best talent in the liberal church." Sanborn and Harris, *op. cit.*, I, 269. *Cf.* George Ripley, "I do not count it clearly impossible for new life to be breathed into the languid veins of our liberal Christianity; and with such men as Brownson, and the brave, young writers in the Western Messenger, I almost hope to see the time, when religion, philosophy and politics will be united in a holy Trinity, for the redemption and blessedness of our social institutions." Ripley to Bancroft, September 20, 1837, Bancroft Papers.

the announcement too soon. His friends appreciated
his statement of the problem, for it was largely their
own; but they were not prepared for the breath-
taking grandeur of his solution. Boston was awaken-
ing to the idea, but it was not ready for the institution.

CHAPTER III

THE SLOUGH OF DESPOND, 1836–1840

Brownson's new church found its God in man and looked for its heaven on earth. It conceived salvation in terms of ethics, not religion. Its hope was to transform worldly society into the Kingdom of God. Indeed, underneath his religious terminology, Brownson was fighting to help the working class. He believed wholeheartedly that Saint-Simon had stated with inspired accuracy the aim of Christianity in his noble formula: "Religion should direct society toward the great end of the most rapid possible amelioration of the lot of the poorest class." [1] His church was flooded with humanitarianism; he was struggling to make social reform honorable by wedding it to religion.

Most of the young men rebelling against the cold immobility of John Locke and Andrews Norton were also rebelling against the cold immobility of Massachusetts Federalism. George Ripley, as Brownson told George Bancroft, had philosophized him-

[1] *Nouveau Christianisme* (1832), 20.

self into democracy; Dr. Channing had democratic instincts; and even Mr. Emerson in *Nature* "has a presentiment of social progress which is really cheering." [2] Ripley seconded his friend's enthusiasm, writing, "Almost to a man those who shew any marks of genius or intellectual enterprise are philosophical democrats." [3] But the others tended to be democrats in their libraries and Whigs at the voting-booths. Brownson alone put his distrust of State Street into energetic performance.

His tenderness for the workingmen aroused considerable suspicion among the conservative; but his colleagues in the Boston churches, conceiving the Society for Christian Union and Progress as a missionary venture to the infidel, were more approving. Brownson frequently exchanged pulpits with them, even preaching once in the stronghold of Congregational orthodoxy, the Park Street Church itself. Channing, with his innocent faith that, once the workers were united by religious principles, they would easily secure their rightful place in the world, looked on the Society and Brownson with particular approval. "I comprehend how, to such a man, the present social state should be full of deformity," he wrote to Elizabeth Peabody. "I pre-

[2] Brownson to Bancroft, September 24, 1836, Bancroft Papers.
[3] Ripley to Bancroft, September 20, 1837, Bancroft Papers.

fer his morbidly sensitive vision on these points
to the stone-blindness of multitudes who condemn
him." [4]

At first, the Society justified Channing's confidence and deduced its program from his social philosophy. Yet, very early after moving to Chelsea,
Brownson began to outgrow Channing's guileless
reliance on inner reform. This trust was all very
well for a simple, undeveloped economic life; but
Brownson saw that in a community as complex as
Boston a revival of neighborly friendliness could
achieve little. Most men of the day lacked the
head or the heart thus to generalize from their experience.

Even for Brownson, his shrewd observations
worked but slowly into his thinking. His article
on "Education of the People" in the *Christian Examiner* of June 1836 contained glimmerings of a
recognition that morality might be influenced by
social conditions. "In some states of society there
must be a social growth before there can be — in
relation to a part of the community — an individual
growth," he wrote; [5] but he went on to urge educa-

[4] Channing to Miss Peabody, September 1, 1837, Peabody,
Reminiscences of Rev. Wm. Ellery Channing, 395. William
Henry Channing gives a slightly different verson of this letter
in his *Memoir of William Ellery Channing*, III, 54.

[5] *Christian Examiner*, 3rd series, II, 160 (June, 1836).

tion as the means of rescuing the underprivileged. He had not yet begun to see the problem of persuading the privileged classes to aid — or allow — the elevation of the workers when their own privileges were likely to be the price.

In July Brownson, who had been for some time without a magazine of his own, became the editor of the *Boston Reformer*, a weekly journal of the new humanitarianism. He gave it a fine motto, "We know no party but mankind"; but this he tended to interpret as "We know no party but Brownson," and he rode the *Reformer* as a hobby horse, from which he tilted at whatever was for the moment vexing him. Its columns were filled with reports of his sermons, brief articles by himself and paragraphs from other journals praising or (more generally) denouncing him. But, beneath these Brownsonian trappings of flippancy, pugnacity and arrogance, the *Reformer* had a markedly moral tone. Its editor planned to save both religion and reform by uniting them: "The people are going ahead and ahead they will go; with the clergy, if the clergy choose; without them, if the clergy choose to stay behind." [6] Consequently he opposed the Workingmen's party, approved the ten-hour day but excluded collective bargaining, and gave Martin Van Buren only the

[6] *Boston Reformer*, July 21, 1836.

mildest endorsement in the election of 1836. In the fashion of his day, he prescribed psychotherapy as a cure for what he later determined to be cancer.

Like Channing, he thought manual-labor schools to be the best direct way of helping the workers. These schools not only would make labor highly respectable by placing it on the same level with study and literature, but would refine the working-men, cultivate their souls and make them more able to converse in the parlors of the liberal ministers. They would thereby achieve immediate social equality. Any trifling changes they desired in the law would follow as a matter of course. On Channing's encouragement, Brownson even took steps toward preparing a specific plan by enlisting the readers of the *Reformer* in a search for relevant information.[7]

But, while Channing and Brownson were fiddling away, Rome began to burn. Speculators had piled up fuel all over America, largely in the shape of worthless stock or depreciated bank notes. Jackson's Specie Circular of July provided the spark. Already the flames were eating into the economic structure. Financial gamblers had spun out credit far beyond its capacity to be redeemed; and the young economy was not expanding fast enough to take

[7] Channing to Brownson, July 19, 1836, H. F. Brownson, *Early Life*, 190–193.

up the slack. Then the Barings failed in Great Britain, throwing their American securities on the market. Bankruptcies followed, domino-fashion, all through the United States. In May 1837 the banks of New York City suspended; and in that year over six hundred failed. Private bank notes were hopelessly discredited. Everywhere factories were closed, wages cut, men thrown out of work. The depression hit America with added impact because of the concentration in cities of laborers who could not fall back on their own corn or their own cattle. Such suffering was new in the national experience.

Brownson found his audience largely among the working class; and he realized early their helplessness in the contortions of a floundering economy. As the Panic of 1837 deepened into a way of life, he gradually began to see that the complicated financial system had somehow burst the bonds of a personal morality. His pious theories were crumbling when confronted by the desperate facts of misery and starvation. As he told Channing, there was more hatred of the rich than he had ever expected.[8] In the face of this bitterness, which no appeals to the soul could placate or answer, he had to recast his plans of reform. It was treacherous to ask hungry people to put their trust in religion

[8] William Henry Channing, *op. cit.*, III, 53.

and manual-labor schools. Prayer would not supply them with another meal; and, while State Street
might, it did not choose to. He recalled the Saint-
Simonian warning that there was a difference between the *proprietaire* and the *ouvrier* and decided
that the benefit of State Street was not necessarily the
benefit of Chelsea mechanics. He read the *Paroles
d'un Croyant* of Lamennais and was fired by its fine
faith in the people's struggle against oppression. The
religious solution had come to seem a hoax. If the
people wanted liberty, praying was not enough:
they must fight for it.

"Babylon is falling," he chose as the text of a
sermon in May 1837, "and the merchants of the
earth shall weep and mourn over her; for no man
buyeth their merchandize any more." The fall of
Babylon, his hearers quickly discovered, was the
fall of "the SPIRIT OF GAIN," the collapse of this
"system of universal fraud and injustice," of which
the depression was so clear a portent. "Society for
long ages has been in perpetual strife," he told his
startled congregation. "The struggle can be ended
only by giving to all, not equal wealth, but equal
chances to wealth." There is no other way out. "The
two causes are hostile in their very nature, and can
never co-exist but in a state of war. One party or
the other must be exterminated before the war will

end." "The contest is now between the privileged and the underprivileged," he repeated with solemn emphasis, "and a terrible one it is. The slave snaps his fetters, the peasant feels an unwonted strength nerve his arm, the *people* rise in stern and awful majesty, and demand in strange tones their ever despised and hitherto denied rights. They rise and swear in a deep and startling oath that *justice shall reign*." [9] There could be no doubt with which side Orestes Brownson was allying himself.

He now acted vigorously in the cause of justice. On the Fourth of July he spoke to a thousand people at a Democratic mass meeting on Bunker Hill. Later in the month, in the *Reformer* (the editorship of which he resumed after six months' rest), he contemptuously attacked the orthodox doctrine that the interests of the rich and those of the poor were the same.[10] The argument he used took sharpest form four years later in his parable of the wolf and the lamb:

The lamb is necessary to the wolf; for without the lamb the wolf might want a dinner; and the wolf is necessary to the lamb, for without the wolf the lamb might fail to be eaten. "Therefore," says the benevolent wolf to the lamb,

[9] *Babylon Is Falling*, 3, 4, 10, 20, 21.
[10] Brownson reprinted this article in the *BoQR*, IV, 146–149 (April, 1841).

"do not be hostile to us, nor excite your brother lambs against us; for you see we wolves and you lambs are mutually necessary to each other. We are as dependent on you for something to eat, as you are on us to be eaten." "But I don't want to be eaten," exclaims the lamb in great trepidation. "Not want to be eaten!" replies the wolf. "Now that's odd. You and I are very far from thinking alike, and I must needs consider you very unreasonable, and radical in your mode of thinking." [11]

The depression was showing Brownson that reform, to be effective, must be quick and practical: at best, half the people would starve to death before individual regeneration could hope to remedy matters that had gone beyond individual control; and at worst the do-nothing policy gave complete control of government to the business classes. The important thing, he decided, was to feed people, not to pray for them: the need of the moment was action. What was the cause of the distress? Plainly, the banks which refused to pay their just debts. And why were they not compelled to? Because of "the moral obtuseness of the community which could tolerate, nay, defend, in those moneyed corporations conduct which would have been severely censured and even punished in the case of private individuals." He feared that a system of special

[11] "Conversations with a Radical," *BoQR*, IV, 35–36 (January, 1841).

legislation had been fixed on the country, "which, if not arrested, would bring us under the absolute control of associated wealth." [12]

George Bancroft, like Samuel C. Allen a few years before, had already offered Brownson a key to the situation. In 1836, as a leading Democrat, he wrote Brownson an insinuating letter to get his support for Van Buren and ended, with a flourish: "It is now for the yeomanry and the mechanics to march at the head of civilization. The merchants and the lawyers, that is, the monied interest broke up feudalism. The day for the multitude has now dawned." [13] On Brownson's return to the *Reformer*, Bancroft sent him a detailed analysis of the political scene in terms of economic interest. "To the national administration I give unfaltering support . . . because its overthrow would instal slavery, corporations, and mercantile privilege in the chair of state," he concluded. "I am too familiar with your writings not to know that our principles accord in many essential points; I would fain hope we might view practical subjects alike also." [14]

Bancroft's hope was rapidly justified. Circum-

[12] "Popular Government," *Democratic Review*, XII (May, 1843), *Works*, XV, 285.

[13] Bancroft to Brownson, September 21, 1836, H. F. Brownson, *Early Life*, 179–181.

[14] Bancroft to Brownson, July 9, 1837, *ibid.*, 184–188.

stances compelled Brownson to recognize the justice of Bancroft's analysis. A year with Fanny
Wright had convinced him that a labor party could
achieve nothing, and he turned to inner reform;
but deeper experience with actual conditions destroyed his belief in the Channing method. The
Democratic party was the party of the people, not
simply of the workingmen. If he wanted action, the
Democrats alone were likely to provide the right
kind. He thereupon determined to give them his
support. Channing, of course, was shocked when
Elizabeth Peabody told him of Brownson's latest
vagary. "I grieve to hear what you say of Mr.
Brownson," he wrote her. "I did hope that the
study of great truths, universal principles, would
give calmness and stability to his mind, and so they
would, were it not for an unhappy organization." [15]
But Brownson had discovered that, however consoling great truths or universal principles, calmness
or stability of mind, might be, they did not fill
people's stomachs.

[15] Channing to Miss Peabody, September 1, 1837, Peabody,
op. cit., 395. Channing's social views were moralistic almost to
sentimentality. He once told a group of English miners, "Your
true strength lies in growing intelligence, uprightness, self-respect,
trust in God, and trust in one another. These cannot fail to secure
to you your just share of social privileges." Channing to the
Mechanic Institute of Slaithwaite, England, March 1, 1841,
W. H. Channing, *op. cit.*, III, 57.

His alliance with Bancroft was soon signalized. Van Buren had rewarded Bancroft's services in 1836 by appointing him Collector of the Port of Boston. Early in 1838 Bancroft offered Brownson the stewardship of the United States Marine Hospital at Chelsea. The duties involved mainly visits of inspection and superintendence: they would take little time, and Brownson's family badly needed the additional income. Brownson, who cherished his own independence rather more than he did his family's comfort, at first declined, but, on being assured that the job would in no way affect his freedom in political discussion, he accepted.[16] He had already turned to augmenting his income and promoting the cause of reform by lecturing. That year he went to New York City where the Loco-Focos, the party of people's rights, were finding new encouragement in Van Buren's policy. A boy of German stock named Isaac Hecker was deeply moved by this "handsome man, tall, stately and of grave manners" who urged on so eloquently the fight against monopoly and privilege.[17]

Yet, with all his activity, Brownson felt that he was not expressing himself effectively enough. The

[16] H. F. Brownson, *Early Life*, 211–213.

[17] Isaac T. Hecker, "Dr. Brownson and the Workingman's Party Fifty Years Ago," *Catholic World*, XLV, 204 (May, 1887).

reception of *New Views* had shown that the world, even that Boston, had to be more extensively prepared for the *Church of the Future,* while in the Whig party, solidified by the Panic of 1837, Brownson saw a genuine threat to popular liberties. He needed a more powerful weapon to carry on his two battles, and in the fall he resolved to found a new magazine.

2

Late in December, when the first year of the depression was reaching its grim close, the *Boston Quarterly Review* appeared in Boston bookshops. Brownson again! exclaimed the conservatives sadly; why wasn't he content to give his articles to the respectable *Christian Examiner,* or to print them in his own sheet, the *Reformer?* Other journals were indeed open to Brownson, but the laws of hospitality required him to act as a guest. He lacked the perfect freedom he hoped to find in a quarterly of his own. There, moreover, he could write more fully and soberly than in a weekly like the *Reformer.* He now felt more than ever the urgency of setting forth his principles to the public. The great Movement, commenced by Jesus of Nazareth, was in peril; and

with this Movement, whether it be effecting a reform in
the Church, giving us a purer and more rational theology; in
philosophy seeking something profounder and more inspirit-
ing than the heartless Sensualism of the last century; or
whether in society demanding the elevation of labor with
the Loco foco, or the freedom of the slave with the Abolition-
ist, I own I sympathize, and I thank God that I am able to
sympathize.[18]

The *Boston Quarterly* won the immediate respect
of the young men, tired of the austere monotony
of the *Christian Examiner* and the *North American
Review*. "It is high time," Thoreau wrote Brownson, "that we knew where to look for the expression of *American* thoughts. It is vexatious not to
know beforehand whether we shall find our account
in the perusal of an article. But the doubt speedily
vanishes when we can depend upon having the
genuine conclusions of a single reflecting man."[19]
Thoreau was more accurate than he probably anticipated in calling the *Quarterly* the work of a single
man. Brownson invited others to take part, but less
for his own sake, as his son remarked, than for
the subscribers'.[20] Among the contributors were Ban-

[18] "Introductory Remarks," *BoQR*, I, 6 (January, 1838).

[19] Thoreau to Brownson, December 30, 1837, H. F. Brownson,
Early Life, 206.

[20] H. F. Brownson, *Middle Life*, 137. One reader respectfully
asked Brownson, "Feeling a strong sympathy with the spirit of
your magazine, I am induced to the presumption of inquiring if

croft, Ripley, Alcott, Margaret Fuller, Theodore
Parker, Alexander H. Everett, Elizabeth Peabody,
Sarah H. Whitman, W. H. Channing, John S.
Dwight and Albert Brisbane. However, Brownson's
volubility had few limits and, except during his
ill health at the end of 1839, he managed to fill
most of the pages himself. Ripley, indeed, thought
that the *Boston Quarterly* stood alone in the
history of periodical works. "It was undertaken by
a single individual, without the coöperation of
friends, with no external patronage, supported by
no sectarian interests, and called for by no motive
but the inward promptings of the author's own
soul." [21]

Brownson's "inward promptings" were for the
moment unmistakable, and he gave them clear expression in the first issue. As the shadows of the
depression lengthened, the deformities of society
were thrown into sharp relief, and his social thought
acquired a new keenness. The excesses of the reformers on every side warned him of the need for
caution, however; and he took care to formulate a
sound theory of action in order to save the country from remedies which might prove worse than

all articles are rejected there except from its able editor, however
carefully or wisely written." Jane E. Locke to Brownson, February 4, 1850, Brownson Papers.
    [21] "Brownson's Writings," *Dial*, I, 30 (July, 1840).

the disease. In his essay on "Democracy" he laid down what he believed to be a solid basis for government. In substance, "Democracy" was an elaboration of the theory he had already advanced in the *Reformer*. "We make justice paramount to the popular will," he had written in 1836, "and acknowledge allegiance to the popular will only so far as it is in harmony with our convictions of the Just." [22] He developed this criticism of majority rule in the *Quarterly* article, pointing out the evil results for society — demagoguery, corruption, conformity, social tyranny — as well as the danger to morality in defining the Right by public opinion. "By bounding the state by justice, we declare it limited; we deny its absolute sovereignty; and, therefore, save the individual from absolute slavery." [23] The belief that justice was essential to the state was not new. It had come to America with the *Mayflower;* but few Americans in 1838 thought systematically about government, and Brownson's statement of principles was a novelty.

If majority rule was the danger, what were the bulwarks of minority rights? It soon became evident that Brownson looked to the state-rights doctrine as the guardian of liberty. The people could not

[22] H. F. Brownson, *Early Life*, 182.
[23] "Democracy," *BoQR*, I, 44 (January, 1838).

control the government, he thought, unless the states retained their integrity; for centralization would open the way to control by a small group. The American democracy had started from the distribution of powers. The assurance of liberty must lie in keeping local authorities independent. In the details of his state-rights argument Brownson followed Calhoun.[24]

The people's sovereignty, then, was limited only by justice as embodied in state rights. Having settled the theory, Brownson proceeded to contemplate the scene before him. "The old feudal nobility is extinct," he wrote, "and the *Bourgeoisie*, or middle class, is now on the throne." It is generally accounted the most virtuous class. Perhaps so; "it demands a laboring class to be *exploited*, but it loves order, peace and quiet. These, however, it knows are incompatible with the existence in the community of an ignorant, vicious and starving populace; it, therefore, will attend to the wants of the lower classes up to a certain point." Do not deprecate this monarchy of the middle classes: it is merely playing its part in history. "It has a mission to execute, and when it shall have executed its mission it will then give way to the monarchy, not of a class, not of an

[24] This argument is developed in "Slavery — Abolitionism," *BoQR*, I, 238-260 (April, 1838).

order, but of Humanity." [25] The task for reform is not to destroy the past but to perfect it, to cling to institutions until the onward pressure of opinion forces their abandonment. Truth is omnipotent, and it is on the march.

Brownson did not favor revolution, but he proposed to assist truth on its way. The social problem, as it narrowed down from his theory to the America of 1838, became the problem of securing the triumph of the people's party. Inner reform he recanted in a brilliant paragraph that destroyed the bases of the Channing theory:

This position is not tenable. If it were, it would be fatal to all progress, and be most heartily pleasing to all tyrants. The plain English of it is, perfect the individual before you undertake to perfect society; make your men perfect, before you seek to make your institutions perfect. This is plausible, but we dislike it, because it makes perfection of institutions the end, and that of individuals merely the means. Perfect all your men, and no doubt, you could then perfect easily and safely your institutions. But when all your men are perfect, what need of perfecting your institutions? And wherein are those institutions, under which all individuals may attain to the full perfection admitted by human nature, imperfect? [26]

[25] "Democracy," *BoQR*, I, 62–63 (January, 1838).

[26] *BoQR*, I, 127 (January, 1838). Internal reform in the sense advocated by Channing should not be confused with superficially similar remarks by Emerson. Channing regarded internal reform as a practical method of improving society, an alternative to

In similar fashion he turned his fierce gaze on other mirages likely to lure moral energy from its true path. The abolitionists were early victims of his relentless logic. In April 1838 he lashed out at them for agitating the slavery question at a time when all thoughts should be turned to the urgent financial problems. For a brief moment in 1836, when a mob prevented his speaking at the Boston Anti-Slavery Society, Brownson had looked on the abolitionists with some kindliness; [27] but now their activities had taken on a different color and seemed to carry a threat to basic rights. Slavery, he conceded, was an evil; but the abolitionists, in their fury at the slaveholders, had become simple-minded in their criticism and dangerous in their program. "Reformers should war against systems, not against men. . . . Slavery is not an individual but a social institution, and society, not the individual conscience alone, is responsible for it." [28] It was idle, Brownson thought, to consign the Southerners to hell: they were not, after all, the only men in America to profit by unjust social institutions. But,

---

Fourierism or Owenism. Emerson rarely thought of problems in these terms; his remarks simmer down to psychological observations about the necessity of inward desire (*not* of inward perfection) as the preamble to reform.

[27] *Boston Reformer*, August 4, 1836.

[28] "Slavery — Abolitionism," *BoQR*, I, 240 (April, 1838).

far more than the myopic social vision, he feared abolitionism as a menace to liberty. Seeing in minority rights the one safeguard against the rule of consolidated capital, Brownson was forced to hold the state-rights doctrine sacred. The friends of the people, he declared, must fight all movements tending to strengthen the national government, or claiming for citizens of one state jurisdiction over the internal affairs of another. Perhaps the abolitionists were lawless in a good end, but who could guarantee that their methods might not be converted to the service of despotism? In another number of the *Quarterly* he ended the discussion by sardonically advising the abolitionists to exercise their philanthropy in the wretched slums of the North.[29]

The eccentric reformers suffered too for deflecting attention from national politics. Aren't they carrying the joke a little too far? Brownson asked with the scorn of a man engaged in improving conditions practically,

the land is overspread with them, and matters have come to such a pass, that a peaceable man can hardly venture to eat or drink, to go to bed or to get up, to correct his children or kiss his wife, without obtaining the permission and the direction of some moral . . . society.[30]

[29] "Abolition Proceedings," *BoQR*, I, 500 (October, 1838).
[30] "Ultraism," *BoQR*, I, 379 (July, 1838).

Brownson also developed his talent for nosing out anything savoring of Whiggism. He pointed mournfully to the happy future for corporations in the "vested rights" doctrine, and opposed the establishment of a state board of education as the entering wedge of centralization.[31] Even when, in the fashion of the day, he criticized America's literary dependence on England, his complaints turned into savage attacks on conservatism. The Whigs, Brownson argued, nourished this dependence, lest their power be undermined if national literature should become American and democratic instead of English and conservative. Class lines were ruling literary criticism: it was lawful to praise Irving; but Cooper was under the ban of all the quarterlies — save Brownson's; Bryant could hardly hazard another volume of poems; Channing was condemned as a Loco-Foco with his eye on Congress; and Bancroft was endured because only a democrat could write the history of the United States.[32] As the class lines drew tighter, Brownson decided that the want of a great social crisis explained the tepidity and imitativeness of American literature. "The whole matter of wealth and labor . . . must come up, be dis-

[31] "The American Democrat," *BoQR*, I, 376 (July, 1838); "Education of the People," *BoQR*, II, 393–434 (October, 1839).
[32] "Grund's Americans," *BoQR*, I, 163–165 (April, 1838).

cussed and disposed of," he told the students at Brown in the fall of 1839. "In the struggle of these two elements, true American literature will be born." [33]

These random war cries, however, were but echoes of the profound alarm with which he watched America stumble through the depression. His brilliant historical analysis made the class struggle the dynamic force in the evolution of society. The middle class, he thought, had served its turn for humanity by destroying feudalism. Its interests had now diverged from those of the masses, and it was intent only on maintaining its power. But "all classes, each in turn, have possessed the government; and the time has come for all predominance of class to end; for Man, the People to rule." [34] The scarcity that followed the Panic of 1837 left nerves raw and tempers quick: Brownson was convinced that the class war was entering on an acute phase. In England, he predicted, the struggle would end in violence; but the equalitarian heritage of the Revolution, however much it had been traduced by

[33] "American Literature," an oration delivered before the United Brothers Society of Brown University, September 3, 1839, *BoQR*, III, 75–76 (January, 1840).

[34] "Tendency of Modern Civilization," *BoQR*, I, 237 (April, 1838).

Hamilton and the party of Money, promised a more harmonious solution in the United States.[35]

A prime cause of the depression had been the grotesque overexpansion of credit by promoters and speculators working through a loose and defective banking system. The tribunes of the people — Jackson, Benton, Van Buren — had fought to end this wild manipulation of credit, but without success. All Benton's efforts to persuade a Congress, partly in the hire and largely under the influence of the United States Bank, to end speculation in the public lands by requiring payment in specie won him only the nickname of "Old Bullion"; and the main advances toward a more sober financial system were made by executive order. After the bubble burst, Van Buren summoned a special session of Congress and recommended immediate deflation, proposing that all taxes be paid in hard money, and that the government take charge of its own funds, depositing them in "sub-treasuries" instead of in private banks where they served only to support pyramids of credit. Calhoun backed the president; but Webster and Clay attacked Van Buren as callous to the interests of the business and financial classes and hopefully

[35] *BoQR*, I, 123 (January, 1838); "Tendency of Modern Civilization," *supra*, 236–237.

urged the rechartering of the United States Bank. Though Van Buren's policy was seconded by the workingmen, as the establishment of a safe banking system by the Loco-Focos in New York soon showed, Congress defeated the Sub-Treasury plan in 1837 and again in 1838.

The people's first move toward victory, Brownson declared, should be to put the monetary system out of the reach of the capitalists, thus restoring the country to economic health and insuring it against future financial dyspepsia. He saw clearly enough that the people could never command the government until it was divorced from the special interests of business. In his reading of American history, he found three policies which had stolen the government from the people, each tending to concentrate control in the counting-houses. Internal improvements, the protective tariff and the alliance of government and banking had given the money changers free entry to the temple. Jackson abruptly slammed all three doors by the Maysville veto, the tariff of 1832 and the veto of the United States Bank bill. But Wall Street and State Street were rallying desperately, and the fight was becoming critical. If the Biddles retrieved their credit monopoly, American liberties would be more seriously imperiled than in the earlier period of the Bank's domination, because of the growing class antagonism. But the passage of Van Buren's Sub-Treasury plan would drive the bankers out of the capitol and restore the government to its constitutional purity.

The mounting pressure forced Brownson soon to discard all pretense of political nonpartisanship and become an avowed Democrat. The Whigs as the party of entrenched greed easily slipped into his pattern of the class struggle: "in the last analysis the dominant idea of the Whigs is not MAN, but PROPERTY; and the contest between them and the democracy was rightly declared by Mr. Benton to be a contest between MAN and MONEY." [36] But Boston intellectuals, unhappily for Brownson, were Whigs by instinct and Democrats only by effort. Webster's massive brow had mesmerized most of them into a reverence that was not shattered until he performed perhaps his most disinterested act and supported the Compromise of 1850. Even Emerson, the wisest of them all, believed that though the Democrats might have the best cause, the Whigs had the best men.[37] Democracy, in short, was disreputable. Boston preferred a government run by gentlemen like Rufus Choate to one run by ruffians like Jackson and knaves like Van Buren. Brownson's appeal for the Sub-

[36] "Democracy and Reform," *BoQR*, II, 508 (October, 1839).
[37] "Politics," *Works* (Standard Library Edition), III, 201.

Treasury plan would be ineffectual until he justified the existence of the Democratic party.

There followed during the next two years a series of articles in the *Quarterly* discussing the philosophies behind the parties. Leaving the defense of the details of Van Buren's policy to the accomplished pen of Alexander H. Everett, Brownson devoted himself to demonstrating that the Democratic party was fulfilling the mission of Jesus. He renewed his plea that the churches preach democracy lest they withdraw themselves altogether from the hearts of the people and die of inanition.[38] As for political parties, he discovered them to be essential in the advance of humanity, since God gave man the will-to-progress without giving him the power to achieve it as an individual;[39] and Whiggism he barred from serious consideration because it clearly inherited the atheistic tendencies of Hobbes, its father.[40] The true Christian, Brownson told Boston, must be a member of the Democratic party, the party of Christianity and progress.

By entering politics Brownson had gone beyond many of his friends, who preferred their conceptions immaculate, safe from the muddy compromises of

[38] See, for instance, "Democracy of Christianity," *BoQR*, I, 444–473 (October, 1838).

[39] "Democracy and Reform," *BoQR*, II, 485 (October, 1839).

[40] "Education of the People," *BoQR*, II, 405 (October, 1839).

the world. "Brownson's 'Boston Quarterly' is pledged to a party in politics," Bronson Alcott noted regretfully in his journal; and, now certain that the *Quarterly* could never be the organ of the Infinite, "We must have a free journal for the soul which awaits its own scribes." [41] There were tougher minds among the intellectuals, however. In December Emerson gave the introductory lecture in his series on "The Present Age." His unclouded serenity was quite different from Brownson's hot indignation; but Theodore Parker, finding the lecture *"Democratic-locofoco* throughout, and very much in the spirit of Brownson's article on Democracy and Reform in the last *Quarterly*," was moved to ask Convers Francis whether Brownson wasn't the more original of the two. [42] One solemn Bostonian came out of Emerson's lecture growling that he supposed Emerson was angling for a place in the Custom House under Bancroft. [43]

Brownson was for the moment tiring of the *Quarterly*. The strain of writing almost 150,000 words a year had told on his health, and he appended a postscript to the last issue of 1839, bidding his read-

[41] Higginson, *Margaret Fuller Ossoli*, 147.

[42] Parker to Francis, December 6, 1839, James E. Cabot, *Memoir of Ralph Waldo Emerson*, II, 400; Gohdes, *Periodicals*, 183.

[43] Cabot, *op. cit.*, 401.

ers a regretful farewell. But January found the first number of 1840 on sale, with a characteristically unabashed announcement that the magazine would continue. The promise of articles from friends and the imminence of the election of 1840 probably induced him to persevere.

3

Depressions are not ordinarily healthy for presidents, and three years in the valley of want left the country susceptible to Whig blandishments. In December 1839 the Whig convention met at Harrisburg. Passing over Henry Clay, whose ideas were too well known, it nominated William Henry Harrison of Ohio, who had not made the Kentuckian's fatal mistake of taking stands on national questions. He had to his credit, moreover, a well-advertised if dubious victory over the Indians at Tippecanoe; and his conduct in the quarter-century thereafter had been politically most inoffensive. The convention, after naming for vice-president John Tyler, a Virginian of highly uncertain Whiggism, as a bid for Southern votes, played the last act of the farce by refusing to adopt a platform. The Democrats renominated Van Buren the following May and reaffirmed the familiar Democratic policies in national affairs.

During Brownson's four years in Boston, he grew slowly convinced that power gave the dominant class an intransigence which would not yield to reason and perhaps not even to religion. "I have a fellow feeling . . . with all who struggle against power and seek to secure for the people a portion of their long lost liberty," he declared to William Lyon MacKenzie, the Canadian revolutionist, then in a Rochester prison.[44] The Whig convention of 1840, revealing the party of Money in what seemed to him a singularly vicious aspect, showed how grim the struggle was becoming. The heat of the coming election suddenly ripened his social criticism and impelled him to give his conclusions to the public. In the July issue of the *Quarterly*, just as the campaigns were swinging into action, he published his essay on "The Laboring Classes."

The article began innocently enough as a review of Carlyle's *Chartism*. But Brownson, who could not believe that slavery existed only on Southern plantations, was not the man to regard the causes of Chartism as peculiar to England. Inequality, he wrote, is universal: in all countries the actual pro-

[44] Brownson to MacKenzie, April 22, 1840, W. L. MacKenzie, *The Life and Times of Martin Van Buren* (Boston, 1846), 143.

ducer of wealth is shut off from the main social benefits. In England the tyranny of the middle class has simply forced into the open a protest that is everywhere latent. He bitterly declared Carlyle's two proposals to be no better than Morrison Pills: universal education was meaningless for the starving, a mockery at which devils may laugh but angels must weep, and general emigration would only attenuate suffering and injustice. The English sickness had gone far beyond drugs or calisthenics; it would respond, Brownson said, only to bloodletting in the "most dreaded of all wars, the war of the poor against the rich, a war which, however long it may be delayed, will come, and come with all its horrors."

Indeed, in Brownson's eyes, the injustices of capitalism now exceeded those of slavery. If there had to be a laboring population distinct from proprietors and employers, he would prefer the slavery system. "As to actual freedom one has just about as much as the other"; and the slave never tastes the terrible want and uncertainty which forever torments the free laborer. In factories, sweatshops, brothels, men and women give their lifeblood that the rich may ride in carriages.

The man who employs them, and for whom they are toiling as so many slaves is one of our city nabobs, revelling in luxury; or he is a member of our legislature, enacting laws to put money in his own pocket; or he is a member of Congress, contending for a high Tariff to tax the poor for the benefit of the rich; or in these times he is shedding crocodile tears over the deplorable condition of the poor laborer, while he docks his wages twenty-five per cent.; building miniature log cabins, shouting Harrison and "hard cider." And this man too would fain pass for a Christian and a republican. He shouts for liberty, stickles for equality, and is horrified at a Southern planter who keeps slaves.[45]

"Wages," Brownson decided, "is a cunning device of the devil, for the benefit of tender consciences, who would retain all the advantages of the slave system, without the expense, trouble, and odium of being slave-holders."

What were the prospects for the wage-earner? he asked. Plainly, very bad: man today cannot aspire to competence or independence with health and industry as his only assets; he must be backed by capital or luck. "The wilderness has receded, and already the new lands are beyond the reach of the mere laborer, and the employer has him at his mercy." [46] Brownson, almost alone, was undeceived

[45] "The Laboring Classes," *BoQR*, III, 370 (July, 1840). The comparison of slavery and free labor was, of course, a commonplace among Southern apologists for the plantation system.

[46] Brownson's comment on the western lands is probably much more accurate than the persistent theory that the frontier served as a refuge for the underpaid laborers of the East. As he explained it more fully, "Few, comparatively speaking, of the proletaries, in

by the seeming ease with which apprentices rose to be mill owners. He did not let the social fluidity hide the decisive fact that "the simple market wages for ordinary labor, has never been adequate to raise him from poverty to wealth"; and from this he boldly deduced that "the system of wages must be supplanted by some other system, or else one half of the human race must forever be the virtual slaves of the other." Our duty is "to emancipate the proletaries, as the past has emancipated the slaves." By emancipation he envisaged the establishment of such conditions for the workingman that "by the time he is of a proper age to settle in life, he shall have accumulated enough to be an independent laborer on his own capital, — on his own farm or in his own shop."

Brownson next considered ways of improving the morality of business life. He first inquired mercilessly into the theory of inner reform. "So far as the salvation of his soul will not interfere with my income," he made his manufacturer say, "I hold

---

any of the old states, can ever become landowners. Land there, is already too high for that. The new lands are rapidly receding to the west, and can even now be reached only by those who have some little capital in advance. Moreover, these new lands are not inexhaustible. Fifty years to come, if emigration go on at the rate it has for fifty years past, will leave very little for the new emigrant." "The Laboring Classes" (second article), *BoQR*, III, 473–474 (October, 1840). See also *ibid.*, 372.

it worthy of being sought; and if a few thousand dollars will aid you, Mr. Priest, in reconciling him to God and making fair weather for him hereafter, they are at your service." By advocating this theory, Brownson remarked scornfully, a man can be a reformer without losing the friendship of the rankest aristocrat. He himself could not look for the regeneration of the race from priests and pedagogues:

They have had a fair trial. They cannot construct the temple of God. They cannot conceive its plan, and they know not how to build. . . . In a word, they always league with the people's masters and seek to reform without disturbing the social arrangements which render reform necessary. . . . They merely cry peace, peace, and that too when there is no peace, and can be none. . . . Miserable panders to the prejudices of the age, loud in condemning sins nobody is guilty of, but silent as the grave when it concerns the crying sin of the times. . . . As a body they never preach a truth till there is none whom it will indict.

Following Tom Paine (whom he quoted), and Saint-Simon and Fanny Wright (whom he did not), Brownson declared the destruction of the priesthood to be the first step in advancing equality. Social ills, he thought, were not to be cured without radically changing the social structure. Make all men Christians, he challenged the priests, but leave the system of trade untouched, and the present consequences will ensue. "The only way to get rid of its evils is to change the system, not its managers. . . . If you will serve the devil, you must look to the devil for your wages; we know no other way."

Brownson's proposals for change, however, lack the hard practicality of his criticism and seem almost to repeat at several removes the error of Channing. After the chief obstacle to reform had been destroyed by overthrowing the priesthood, he looked next to the resuscitation of the Christianity of Christ. This phrase may have meant to him an actual conversion to the Gospel in the manner imagined by Saint-Simon; or it may have been simply a metaphorical description of the kindled moral impulse which Brownson knew to be essential for improving old customs and sustaining new laws. In either case, the invigorated morality was to express itself in legislation. Here he threw discretion overboard and laid out a definite program. The government must strictly limit its own power; it must then repeal all laws burdening the laboring class, demolish the banking system to save the workingmen from the subtle and sinister power of credit, root out all monopoly and privilege, and abolish the inheritance of property. This last measure, borrowed somewhat rashly from the Saint-Simonists, seemed to Brownson most fruitful; but "the rich, the business community, will never voluntarily consent to it. . . . It will be effected only by the strong arm of physical force. It will come, if it ever come at all, only at the conclusion of war, the like of which the world as yet has never witnessed, and from which, however inevitable it may seem to the eye of philosophy, the heart of Humanity recoils with horror." [47]

"The Laboring Classes" is an extraordinary performance. It is clear, direct, compelling and brilliant, written with an intensity of emotion that occasionally burns into genuine eloquence. As analysis or as polemic, it deserves a high place in revolutionary literature. Brownson actually was a revolutionist only in the sense that he thought the class struggle was not to be resolved by prayer or kindliness. He wanted to awaken labor to a feeling for its rights and for its destiny, without expecting to set up guillotines in State Street and hang Daniel Webster on the Common. Yet he did not hesitate to write with passion. Though far inferior as a systematic thinker to Marx, Brownson on the whole surpassed him as a pamphleteer. He discriminated between condemnation and invective, and almost never suffered the lapses of taste which have filled Marx's pamphlets with cheap sarcasm and personal abuse.

[47] "The Laboring Classes," *BoQR*, III, 358–395 (July, 1840).

On its critical side the essay on "The Laboring Classes" is perhaps the best study of the workings of society written by an American before the Civil War. The exigencies of the day somewhat distorted the emphasis: Brownson's disgust for the conservatism of the church led him to exaggerate the villainy of the priesthood, just as a century later radicals were moved by their hatred of reactionary newspaper-owners to overrate the influence of the press. The main lines of diagnosis, however, are accepted today; and the method, which no other American of the time used so well, has grown in recent years to be indispensable to social investigation.

In the sagacity of his analysis Brownson occupies a halfway ground between the Utopian socialists and Marx. Owen, Saint-Simon and Fourier felt keenly the injustice resulting from one man's tending a machine which another man owned; but they fatally underestimated both the inner impetus of the new technology and the inevitability of its control by enterprising persons who would exploit the want of enterprise in others. They recognized quite justly that the misery of the factory workers came from unregulated competition and, in effect, wanted to revive medieval principles of economic life: a static order in which buying and selling would be carefully governed in guild fashion according to some theory of the "just price." Marx, on the other hand, saw history much more profoundly and did not believe that man could halt the tide of economic change. He accepted the factory system and the propertyless workingmen; his solution required that unregulated competition give way to collective ownership and control. Utopian socialists tried to evade economic forces; Marx sought to harness them to his own theory of social development. The Utopians traced the poverty around them to *laissez-faire* and demanded independent communities which would ignore technological advance and stifle competition. Marx likewise traced poverty to *laissez-faire*, but pictured a dynamic state energized by an ever-developing technology which would finally strangle competition in the web of its own economic complexity.

Brownson, on the other hand, traced the poverty around him to the absence of true *laissez-faire*, and demanded that free competition be restored. Here his vision, like that of most radical thinkers of the time, save Marx and Engels, fell short. The terms of his solution show his imperfect understanding of the Industrial Revolution. His aim was to restore the personal economic relationships of the century before the machine and the corporation; and this hope was possible for him because, lacking sufficient data, he attributed the rise of corporations less to the new machine than to the contrivance of power-hungry financiers. There is a suggestion that Brownson hoped to adjust the new machines to the old morality by some kind of economic co-operation; [48] but such a plan, based on wide division of control, had to assume a very slow rate of technological change.

Yet his program expresses remarkable insight. Very few economists of the day considered a return to free competition as a remedy because they thought they already possessed it. They read Ricardo and mistook his theories of competition for a factual description of society. Brownson saw that society was everywhere victimized by more or less concealed monopoly; but, underreckoning the importance of technology in creating this monopoly, he believed salvation could be found in expelling the financiers, dismantling the system of trade they had erected and settling back into genuinely atomic competition. [49] The powers of the state, he declared, must be severely limited. Every man should have his own shop or his own farm and be subject to the same legal and social handicaps as every other man.

[48] "Our Future Policy," *BoQR*, IV, 82 (January, 1841).

[49] Brownson, it is to be understood, did *not* advocate anarchism. He believed government to be a positive good as the agent of society.

Competition should not be checked by employment, which is the first step toward a propertyless proletariat and eventually toward monopoly, nor by the piling-up of control under the thin cloak of credit manipulation. The abolition of inheritance would enable each generation to enter the field of competition on equal terms. Only under these conditions of substantial equality could political equality cease to be a sham and American democracy take on a practical significance. And without actual equality Brownson's ideal of the Christian democracy, the vast church-state, the Kingdom of God on earth, would never be realized.

No other American of the day and few Europeans inquired so deeply into the weaknesses and contradictions of industrial society. In Great Britain William Thompson and Thomas Hodgskin occupied the halfway stage between Utopian and Marxist socialism. Thompson, an Irish landowner, saw that the distribution of wealth was cluttered up with restraints and obstructions which were weighing down cruelly on the poorer classes and intensifying social inequality; he believed that Robert Owen was the prophet of the new day. Hodgskin, an ingenious English journalist, also criticized the rigidities of the existing economy and advocated a solution not unlike Brownson's in its hope of restoring a truly free market. Though Thompson and Hodgskin published their important works in the 1820's, Brownson probably never saw them. His own analysis was less rich and elaborate; it dealt more in history and less in economics; it had a more somber emphasis on the class struggle and its consequences. Among his direct contemporaries, several Chartists, especially James Bronterre O'Brien and George Julian Harney, approached some of his positions, but again there is no evidence that the American ever read their tracts. On the Continent, few socialists were as penetrating in their criticism until Marx, and Marx, though doubtless he knew nothing of Brownson, drew heavily on Thompson and Hodgskin. Sensitive men all over the world of mills and factories were finding dark revelations in the grimy misery of the workers. Marx simply constructed from their scattered criticism and abortive diagnosis a rounded and logical whole. He gave modern socialism its classic statement. Brownson was his nearest forerunner in America.

4

But his country was in no mood to admire the keenness of Brownson's analysis or to examine judicially his remedial proposals. His essay, crammed with social heresies and revolutionary appeals, and thrown into a savagely fought presidential contest, was received as a pronouncement from a leading Democrat. The Whigs, fighting a whirlwind battle, took quick advantage of Brownson's misstep, re-printing "The Laboring Classes" and giving it wide circulation as evidence of the socialistic leanings of the Democratic high command. The administration forces, dismayed to find Brownson disrobing in pub-lic, had to repudiate him and make clear that he was in no way speaking for the party.[50] "Tell Ban-croft that Brownson has played the deuce with us, by his visionary doctrines," wrote Thomas Ritchie, the Virginia editor, in great distress to the Secretary of the Treasury. "Wise, Riets [?], &c. &c. are con-stantly preaching against the President for retaining such a man in office." Levi Woodbury sent Ritchie's letter on to Bancroft with a plaintive note, "Every-body is loud in their denunciation of him. Why is he kept there? Why?" [51]

In Boston Brownson's essay excited consternation.

[50] See, for instance, the correspondence between Bancroft and W. Hall McAllister of Savannah, Georgia. "The Democracy of Massachusetts," Bancroft finally wrote, "is no more responsible for Brownson's notions, than the Whigs are for Mormonism. This is understood here." Bancroft to McAllister, August 15, 1840, Bancroft Papers.

[51] Thomas Ritchie to Levi Woodbury, October 9, 1840, Ban-croft Papers.

Even his reputation for recklessness did not explain "The Laboring Classes." William Ellery Channing was horrified. He told Elizabeth Peabody that Brownson greatly exaggerated the hardships of the workingmen who actually, he asserted, were better off than the lawyers and merchants because, not aspiring so high, they were less liable to sharp disappointment. "To me the matter of complaint is, not that the laboring class want physical comforts . . . , but that they live only for their physical natures." As for Brownson's remedies, "they are shocking or absurd." "How foolish to talk of abolishing the law of inheritance, and dividing the estates of the dead among the people!" "No good can come but from the spread of intellectual and moral power among all classes," Channing affirmed, and he thought so highly of the sentiment that he paused to underline it.[52] The stout old conservative, John Quincy Adams, was similarly aroused. He sniffed in his study at Quincy and curtly added "Brownson and the Marat-Democrats" to the Transcendentalists, abolitionists and phrenologists who were responsible for the "plausible rascalities" that troubled his old age.[53]

---

[52] Channing to Miss Peabody, September, 1840, Peabody, op. cit., 415–416.
[53] John Quincy Adams, *Memoirs*, X, 345.

Even the younger men were a bit taken aback. Brownson had received the *imprimatur* of the *Dial* in the very month that he exploded "The Laboring Classes"; but the Transcendentalists on the whole ignored the essay, or read it like Theodore Parker, who noted heavily in his journal that it was "calculated to call the philosophic to reflection." Parker, indeed, was the one most exercised by Brownson's indictment. "I like much of his article," he said cautiously, "though his property notions agree not with my view. Yet certainly the present property scheme entails awful evils upon society, rich no less than poor. This question, first, of inherited property, and, next, of all private property, is to be handled in the nineteenth century." [54]

Parker learned his lesson well, if slowly. He had so far displayed courage only in enduring the growing coldness of conservative colleagues in the ministry. In the summer of 1840, while Brownson was weathering the storm called forth by his bold pamphleteering on behalf of the people's party, Parker satisfied his social conscience by attending a comic-opera meeting of Millerites and Come-Outers at Groton and then sitting through the notorious Chardon Street Convention of eccentric reformers in Boston. Yet, at the same time, he read Saint-Simon,

[54] O. B. Frothingham, *Theodore Parker*, 134, 135.

Fourier and Brisbane, as well as Brownson, and was more than a little fluttered in his house in West Roxbury by the errant breezes of social reform stirring through New England. He soon published in the *Dial* "Thoughts on Labor," an article full of diluted Brownsonism, the vigor lost in a mass of bad rhetoric and irrelevant erudition. Then in "A Lesson for the Day, or the Christianity of Christ, of the Church and of Society" he incorporated bodily Brownson's attack on the narrowness, timidity and cowardice of the church and repeated Brownson's distinction between the Christianity of the church and the Christianity of Christ.[55] A decade after Brownson had coldly examined the relations of capital and labor, Parker discovered that merchants were frequently villains and that the social immorality he abhorred at Chardon Street might issue organically from society. He was turning into a valiant crusader against social evil; but at his best he never approached Brownson in intellectual power or originality. His advantage lay in the breadth of his influence, and he owed the respectful hearing that he finally won to men like Brownson and Evans whose daring had made Parker's success possible.

[55] Brownson believed that Parker was plagiarizing from him; see undated letter (probably 1842) with last page missing, almost certainly from Elizabeth Peabody to Brownson, Brownson Papers.

The Whigs were not content merely to present Brownson to the upper classes as a revolutionist. With the virtuosity that characterized their entire campaign, they tried also to present him to the workingmen as a slanderer. His article contained a vivid description of the wretchedness of life in the mill villages. A few factory girls, somehow persuaded to read this passage as an attack on themselves instead of on the factory system, reproved Brownson through their paper, the *Lowell Offering*. Dr. Elisha Bartlett, ex-mayor of Lowell and professional champion of the mill owners, then made a great to-do about vindicating the character of the workers in a pamphlet that hopelessly misrepresented Brownson. In like fashion, his remarks on slavery were declared to be a vicious libel on the free laborers. By now the trail was cluttered up with red herrings; and the issue remained hopelessly confused until the year after the election when Brownson's accusations no longer much mattered.[56]

Meanwhile the protest against Brownson spread to the magazines. The *Methodist Quarterly Review*, in a ferocious attack on "The Laboring Classes," used on Brownson the formulas conventionally applied by conservatives to radicals and charged him with advocating free love as well as political an-

[56] H. F. Brownson, *Early Life*, 267–276.

archy.[57] The *Christian Review* interrupted its notice of *Charles Elwood* to deny indignantly his claim that there was a class problem in America.[58] When the *Western Messenger*, on the other hand, defended Brownson, its subscription list suffered from the editors' rashness.[59] The Whigs called Brownson a Jacobin, the American Robespierre; and Brownson retorted that he planned to write a novel doing justice to Robespierre and to the French Revolution, "one of the most glorious events in human history." [60] Even his friends shied off from this wild man. Contributors had supplied eight of the seventeen articles published thus far in 1840; but after "The Laboring Classes" he received no help and was reduced to filling the October number with sermons he had preached two or three years before. Calhoun, liking most of the article, wrote Brownson that he would do well to re-examine his inheritance proposals; and even Bancroft, while approving Brownson's attack on the church, choked at his property doctrines.[61] Indeed, as Charles Sumner wrote to Professor Whewell, "Brownson has recently avowed

[57] "The Rich against the Poor," *Methodist Quarterly Review*, Third Series, I, 92–122 (January, 1841).

[58] "Charles Elwood," *Christian Review*, V, 419–442 (September, 1840).

[59] Gohdes, *Periodicals*, 34.

[60] *BoQR*, III, 517 (October, 1840).

[61] "The Convert," *Works*, V, 118.

some strange doctrines, for which he has been sadly badgered, both by politicians and philosophers." [62]

But Brownson, as Parker said, was a man who looked battles; he was covered with sweat and dust and blood and "dressed like Daniel with Goliath's sword in one hand, and that giant's head in the other." [63] His faith in the virtue and destiny of the people had sunk deep into his emotions, and he was not a man to be intimidated by all the devils in hell when he thought he was right. In the October number of the *Quarterly* he returned to the battle with a second article on "The Laboring Classes." He now began to fill in the outlines of his first inquiry into the economic basis of American society. The prevalence of agriculture, in which men were at once capitalists and laborers, had hindered the formation of classes, he wrote; but land was becoming increasingly scarce for the workingmen, and the retreat of the frontier under the present conditions would make harsh class divisions inevitable. His flinty intelligence saw how tragically the favorite liberal remedies fell short. "Universal suffrage

---

[62] Professor William Whewell, in 1841 Master of Trinity College, Cambridge, and author of *The History of the Inductive Sciences*. Sumner to Whewell, October 17, 1840, Edward L. Pierce, *Memoir and Letters of Charles Sumner*, II, 168.

[63] Parker to Francis, December 18, 1840, Frothingham, *Parker*, 140.

is little better than a mockery, where the voters are not socially equal. No matter what party you support, no matter what men you elect, property is always the basis of your governmental action." Free trade, universal education and religious culture seemed to him equally inadequate. Brushing aside these respectable nostrums, he launched into a fighting defense of his proposal to abolish inheritance, declaring it to be a logical deduction from the admitted premises of the American way of life, and saying in brave affirmation, "We believe property should be held subordinate to man, and not man to property; and therefore that it is always lawful to make such modifications of its constitution as the good of Humanity requires." [64]

Brownson's perspicacity was lost in the violence of the campaign. His two essays have never been disinterred from the bluster and libel and wind that found their way into print in 1840. The cries of rage and horror his articles provoked were but small incidents in the year which marked the change of American politics from a respectable profession into a circus. The Whigs, largely under the astute direction of Nicholas Biddle of the United States Bank, were fighting one of the most alert and in-

[64] "The Laboring Classes" (second article), *BoQR*, III, 420–512 (October, 1840).

genious campaigns of American history. Without the handicap of a platform, they contrived to be all things to all men; but they devoted their main effort toward posing as the party of the people and foisting off the Democrats as the party of aristocracy. The Whig candidate luckily was an Ohio farmer, the Democrat a suave New Yorker; and Whig orators confided to credulous audiences that Van Buren wore corsets and ate from golden plate. Then an Eastern paper commented with a sneer that Harrison would live content on his backwoods farm if he had a pension, a log-cabin and a barrel of hard cider. This remark the Democrats were not allowed to forget. The Whig strategy of ringing changes on log-cabins and hard cider soon fell into absurdity, but the country was by now stirred to a pitch of excitement where it noticed nothing. The people were treated to the unedifying spectacle of their senior statesmen giving themselves eagerly to this nonsense: Webster lamented publicly his unaccountable failure to have been born in a log-cabin, but pointed out that his elder brother and sisters had been wiser; and Clay solemnly proclaimed that the battle was between the log-cabins and the palaces, between hard cider and champagne. Political songs and torchlight processions came into their own; and the Whigs neglected no trick, however low, which

would keep popular excitement alive. Everywhere
there were log-cabins, parades, hard cider; the people shouted "Tippecanoe and Tyler too" and sang
"Little Van is a used-up man" in the streets; and
Orestes Brownson pondered the election in the cool
of his study, confidently awaiting the people's choice.

Well, the canvass for president came on in 1840 [he
wrote later] and we all went into it, with the precise issue
made up that I and my friends had wished; and we went into
it under as favorable circumstances as can ever be looked for
in the history of this country. . . . We had our full share
of the scholars and literary men of the country; also, of all
that was distinguished for eminent services in practical political
life; we had the whole patronage of the federal government,
and that of twenty states out of twenty-six.[65]

The election came, and passed, and in the gray
November Brownson heard the results: Harrison
234 electoral votes, Van Buren 60. He was filled
with violent disgust. What had happened to the virtue of the people? If they could be humbugged by
slogans and carried away by a song, if they looked on
the author of "The Laboring Classes" as their enemy and joined instead the drunken mob hurrah-
ing for "Tippecanoe," were they intelligent enough
to sustain a democracy? They had repudiated their

[65] "Popular Government," *Democratic Review*, XII (May,
1843), *Works*, XV, 286.

own party. This act struck to the heart of Brownson's belief in them. He could no longer ascribe the defects of society to the fact that the democratic principle had been obstructed: they came from democracy itself. The popular instincts that showed themselves so flagrantly in 1840 might well come next time in more dangerous form.

The flood of Whig votes washed away Brownson's faith in the people and left in its place two convictions that sharp and anguished disappointment fixed enduringly into his experience: that the people as a whole were incapable of seeking the good without more stimulation than their own natures provided; and that good government required stronger guarantees than popular suffrage and the popular virtue and intelligence. Fourth of July orations would continue, and America might roll on in its comfortable trust that *vox populi* was *vox dei;* but Orestes Brownson had put his soul into the people's cause; and in the people's defeat he lost a shining faith that did not return. The people had sold their birthright for a barrel of cider, and Brownson never forgave them.

CHAPTER IV

AT THE WICKET GATE, 1840–1842

The election of 1840 wrought a greater revolution in Brownson than it did in the government. The Whigs failed to capitalize on their victory when Harrison died from a cold shortly after a rainy inauguration, leaving Tyler thereafter to frustrate party strategy in critical moments by lapsing into his former Democratic convictions. But Brownson took the defeat severely to heart, even if its consequences were not as calamitous as he expected. Slowly his new emotions made over his old theories of government.

At first, he vehemently protested at his party's failure to return to its old position as the party of strict construction and state rights. Make the emancipation of the proletaries your objective, he told the Democrats, and work toward it by confining government to its tightest limits. When government has stepped beyond the Constitution, it has been to favor business at the expense of labor. "Hence it follows that every democrat *ought* to be a constitutionalist."[1]

The logic of this stand pointed in practice to a partnership with the one section which worshiped state rights — the South — and Brownson did not boggle at the idea. He carefully stated his disapproval of slavery; but the menace of business, he thought, was so great for workingmen and slaveholders alike that expediency excused their alliance. Here he showed a somewhat more realistic understanding of the dilemma of the workers than the persons who shouted for "Free Soil, Free Labor, Free Speech and Free Men." Lowell mill workers had more to fear from their employers than from Alabama planters, and abolition could mean for them only desperate competition with a race used to far lower standards of living. Let the workers of the North combine with the slaveholders of the South, he urged, and fight Whig attempts to reestablish the national bank, increase the tariff and assume the state debts — all measures unauthorized by the Constitution, and all demanded by the business interests. Then let them proceed to reform: a more equitable land bill, a stern hostility to monopolies, an exclusively metallic currency,[2] an improved

[1] "Our Future Policy," *BoQR*, IV, 89 (January, 1841).
[2] Brownson hoped to mitigate the suffering deflation would cause the debtor class by adjusting the real value of the debts accordingly. *Ibid.*, 108–109.

educational system, the end of imprisonment for debt and the like.

But what chance would such a program have of success? Very little, Brownson admitted ruefully. "As yet, history so far as we are acquainted, presents no instance of a political contest, in which man has remained the victor over property." [3] Still, he thought the fight worth making; and in his "Conversations with a Radical" he impenitently reproduced the radicalism that six months before had led to his excommunication by the respectable. In this article, continued through two issues of the *Quarterly*, a self-satisfied conservative starts out to repeat the conversations in which he destroyed the arguments of a dangerous radical; but in Brownson's bland presentation the conservative becomes the victim of the radical's artless logic. An essay on "The Times," signed by "V.," rehearsed much of the argument of "The Laboring Classes" with vigor and insight. The first shock of the election seemed only to confirm Brownson in his heresies.

But gradually the lesson of 1840 worked its way into his feelings. The failure of the people to live up to his theory about them turned his attention to the theory; and the outcry which greeted "The Laboring Classes," his elaboration of what he

[3] *Ibid.*, 94.

thought to be the premises of the American system, caused him to examine anew these premises. He began for the first time to study political principles systematically. He read Aristotle, corresponded with Calhoun and scrutinized with chilly detachment the place of the people in the state. Practical politics had left a bad taste in his mouth. With his delight in logic he discovered new zest in the stately generalities of political theory.

He was stimulated in his new inquiries by his growing friendship with John C. Calhoun. The great South Carolinian was perhaps the leading political philosopher of the day. His experience was unhappily too limited to serve as the basis for a successful theory of American society; but within his bounds he reasoned with cast-iron logic, and his thinking had a penetration and a severe integrity that set him far above the rival heroes of the time. By comparison Webster was turgid and Clay naïve; Benton lacked his intelligence and Van Buren had not the proportions of a great mind. Calhoun possessed in large measure the qualities that Brownson most admired: logic, courage, dignity, acumen. From 1830 Brownson had accepted the substance of his state-rights argument; and Calhoun's decision in 1837 to obey his convictions and follow his old enemy Van Buren rather than play puppet for the

United States Bank increased Brownson's respect. Their opinions coincided on the chief issues of Van Buren's administration. "I am moving towards a single end," Calhoun wrote Brownson in 1839, "to bring back the government, as far as constitutional measures are concerned, to where it was when it commenced"; [4] and Brownson could easily give this aim unqualified endorsement, if for different reasons. Indeed, Brownson's hard-headed investigation of American history in terms of economic interest represented but the lengthened shadow of Calhoun's realism, etched a little deeper and presented somewhat less covertly.

Calhoun's course after Van Buren's defeat clinched Brownson's esteem for him. He shared Brownson's desire for an ascetic financial policy without paper money and with a minimum of credit; and he led a brave fight against the proposal to distribute among the states the revenue from the public lands, a bill which was playing havoc with the state-rights ranks by appealing over principles to pocketbooks. When the *Boston Quarterly* trumpeted forth against the distribution bill, the voice was the voice of Brownson but the words were the words of Calhoun. They both regarded the measure as a blow at the Constitution. Its passage, they thought, would

[4] Calhoun to Brownson, December 30, 1839, H. F. Brownson, *Early Life*, 321–322.

empty the treasury and lead to a higher tariff, perhaps even to the repeal of the Sub-Treasury plan and the rechartering of the United States Bank.

The mad scramble of the members of Congress, tripping over their principles in the rush to vote for the bill, came as ironic vindication of Brownson's new mistrust of democracy. He had always preserved an equilibrium in his mind between popular rule and constitutionalism. Now that the excesses of popular rule were destroying the balance he put his weight forcibly on the side of constitutionalism. For the first time, he deliberately separated himself from the people's party, though not, as he thought, from the people's cause. Only within a rigorously constitutional system, Brownson decided, could the proper sort of democracy be achieved: else the government would always be the servant of special interests. He held to his old belief in the sovereignty of the people within the limits of justice; but in 1838 he had insisted on the sovereignty, and now he had come to insist on the limits. The shift had carried him from Van Buren to Calhoun. He appropriately ended the article which announced his change with a singularly unqualified commendation of the Southern statesman.[5]

[5] "The Distribution Bill," *BoQR*, V (January, 1842), *Works*, XV, 229–230.

The distribution bill induced Brownson to publish his political ideas in ordered form. Like Calhoun,
he based his analysis on Aristotle and declared government to originate legitimately in human nature.
Already he was deserting the fashionable intellectual
position. Emerson, with his placid faith in the virtue of man, Thoreau, with his thorny self-trust,
saw in government a nuisance rather than a necessity; but Brownson had lost the faith and now believed government to proceed inevitably from man's
imperfections. Its ends, he argued, were individual
liberty and social progress: justice between man
and man, and the direction of social activity to the
common good. What would determine the form of
government? "That form is the best for a people,
which in its practical workings best realizes the true
end of government." [6] He was even abandoning the
national faith in the infallibility of democracy.

He thus established a theoretical framework
against which the America of Tyler and Clay could
be measured. Democracy, he conceded, was the
proper government for the United States; but history showed amply how badly it had worked so far.
Why? Brownson's realism did not falter; and he
quickly put his old economic analysis to the service

[6] "Constitutional Government," *BoQR*, V (January, 1842),
Works, XV, 233.

of his new theory. The government has legislated perpetually for classes, for special interests, instead of confining itself to the common good. The current democratic theory, Brownson acutely observed, requires economic equality for its success; otherwise it is a mockery. Its advocates

tell us that the voice of the people is the voice of God; that what the people will is for the good of the whole; but however this may be in some refined transcendental sense, in practice the will of the people is the will of that interest in the community, which is able to command a majority, and the voice of the people is the voice of that interest.[7]

If the evils of government arise from indulging special interests, Brownson reasoned, the solution is to confine government to matters of common benefit. But, rather than circumscribe government by an *a priori* definition of common benefit, the people should have a mechanism which would define the general welfare pragmatically by enacting only laws which receive general support. He was looking for a contrivance that would automatically prevent government from running athwart the interests or rights of minorities. "Almost the sole art in constituting the government consists in devising an effective veto, one that shall operate naturally, peaceably, when,

[7] *Ibid.*, 238.

and only when, it is required." [8] The present methods of veto — the bicameral congress, the executive veto, the Constitution, periodic elections — are ineffective, he argued, because the negative power is used casually and in a sense accidentally, instead of in the protection of particular interests. But the division into states suggests an easy solution because the states correspond well enough to economic divisions. Let each state, in its separate capacity, possess the veto power; and the veto would then be no artificial creation but part of the constitution of American society. Government could act only when permitted by the concurring majorities; and thus could act only for the good of all.

This theory of the American government was essentially the same as the doctrine of "concurrent majorities" which appeared a decade later in Calhoun's posthumous *Disquisition on Government*. Calhoun had told Brownson in 1841 that his political theory was on the right track; [9] it is clear that Brownson owed much of the development of his ideas to conversations with Calhoun whom he met when his lecture tours carried him to Washington. [10]

[8] *Ibid.*, 245.
[9] Calhoun to Brownson, October 31, 1841, H. F. Brownson, *Early Life*, 302.
[10] "Popular Government," *Democratic Review*, XII (May, 1843), *Works*, XV, 293–294.

The Southerner had worked out his theory for the benefit of the slave aristocracy, and Brownson appropriated it for the benefit of the workingmen: but it applied equally well to all minorities, and it embodied a special program on which worker and planter alike could unite enthusiastically.

Regarded as political theory, the doctrine of "concurrent majorities" was a brilliant failure. Calhoun was among the first to labor to make the modern state efficient and logical by giving interests direct representation, instead of letting them exert the covert, disguised and often corrupting influence they possess under the geographical system. The problem he saw so sharply remains yet unsolved. He appreciated vividly the growing complexity of society which compelled government to respond less and less to individuals and more and more to interests. People lived in several spheres, Calhoun observed, each imposing its peculiar demands. As men they were equal; but as members of the community their conditions were diverse, their callings different and their interests often hostile. How could men vote intelligently when the system of representation prevented them from taking directly into account the interests nearest their hearts? The notion of majority democracy accepted by most Americans presumed all men to be equal and failed to acknowledge divergence of interests; but by a slight modification, Calhoun argued, the old governmental forms could serve efficiently the real needs of society. Give each state the veto power, and government would operate smoothly, recognizing that interests exist and providing a mechanism to harmonize them.

The main difficulty with the Calhoun-Brownson doctrine was the assumption that the states adequately expressed economic interests. Brownson realized the existence of bitter class differences within the states and spoke vaguely of ways of reconciling local interests; but he never discussed very concretely how the concurrence of majorities would work in the smaller units. Another defect came from Calhoun's anxiety to safeguard Southern rights, which made him insist that a single state be given power to halt governmental action. He tried to silence criticism by pointing to the Polish Diet which lasted for centuries under this system; but, as James Parton remarked, look what it did to Poland! Calhoun failed to see that government under the new conditions would have to be strong, that the growing social complexity was producing discords and collisions which would compel government to expand its authority, if only for purposes of arbitration. Any plan seeking to solve problems which baffled compromise by ignoring them must soon wreck itself.

Calhoun's rôle as the champion of the Southern aristocracy thus marred seriously the formulation of his theory. Yet it was founded on a brilliant insight into the power of economic interests in a capitalist society; and he showed remarkable intellectual virtuosity in making this insight the keystone for a defense of slavery. Most people were unaware of the conditions of control that he instinctively recognized. Brownson stood almost alone in New England in understanding the excellence of Calhoun's analysis. It gave him deeper meaning for the facts he had observed independently about the class basis of politics; and its more profound accord with his experience led him to transfer his allegiance from the workingmen, whose cause he had set out to justify, to the great apologist for slavery.

2

Brownson in his first years in New England had been much more disturbed by social problems than by intellectual perplexities. Philosophy he reserved for the scholar's idle times. Yet he always regarded the mission of Jesus as two-fold. One aim was to establish the holy kingdom on earth, but there was another — to atone for sin and prepare the soul for heaven — and this second consideration lured him into theology. On becoming a Unitarian he had thrown overboard all doubts about the existence of God and the divine origin of Christianity; but he still lacked a systematic solution for the lesser questions, and his irrepressible desire for logical completeness forced him into metaphysics.

The intellectual satisfaction he received at Walpole from Benjamin Constant induced him to continue his study of the French philosophers. In 1833 he began to read the works of Victor Cousin and found there immediate comfort. Cousin was then the leading French metaphysician, a suave and engaging thinker who translated Plato into graceful French and tried ingeniously but unsuccessfully to surmount the epistemological predicament posed by Kant. Brownson was captivated by the finish and serenity of his style and the luster of his generalizations. He was not Cousin's first disciple in America. Two of the Frenchman's books had already been translated; George Ripley was enthusiastic about Cousin's philosophy and planned to give him a prominent place in the *Specimens of Foreign Standard Literature;* even George Bancroft praised Cousin and championed the spiritual philosophy in his history. New England, indeed, was suddenly rushing to Cousin, as it rushed to Coleridge, Wordsworth, Jacobi and Schleiermacher — all European thinkers vibrant with the conviction that nature was growing and could not be caught in static formulas, that man was a part of nature, sharing in its growth, and that his strong, inarticulate emotions were profounder than logic. The continental revolt against eighteenth-century rationalism was lending the young men of New England warm encouragement in their own fight against a religion and philosophy that were becoming as mechanical as Newton's universe.

Brownson did not plunge immediately into Cousin's metaphysics. He was first attracted by the doctrine of eclecticism which proclaimed that the new philosophy must synthesize the half-truths of the old ones. This declaration, which plainly was much more a slogan than a method, made vivid use of the deep belief of the day that all the creeds of man — indeed, man's every word and every act — somehow expressed the spirit of God and were insofar true. In giving the Society for Christian Union and Progress its theoretical basis he leaned heavily on Cousin. But his inflexible trust in logic rapidly led him further; for the quest for rational justification is endless until the seeker is willing to surrender reason and rest his case on some kind of faith. Brownson, seduced into metaphysics by his passion for a complete logical explanation, shortly caught hold of Cousin's central ideas with a devotion that made him almost the official expounder of the *maître* in America.

Cousin had an initial charm for people revolted by tight philosophical systems which sacrificed human experience to rational elegance. He based his philosophy on psychology and founded his speculations on an analysis of the facts of consciousness; he disclaimed all traffic, in the manner of Hegel, with *a priori* conceptions of what man logically must be. By close reasoning he rose from his psychological observations to the absolute ideas of the true, the beautiful and the good; and in their light he returned to examine consciousness. These ideas, Cousin believed, were parts of the impersonal or spontaneous reason, which in his scheme shared the intellect with the personal or reflective reason. He thus christened anew the fashionable dualism of intuition and logic, which the Germans called *Vernunft* and *Verstand*, and the Transcendentalists, reason and understanding. Like Emerson, Cousin regarded spontaneity and reflection as the modes in which the same reason, at once divine and human, operated. To save himself from pantheism, Cousin hastily identified the divine reason with the *Logos*, the Word of God, and so made it distinct from God Himself. As the voice of God, the spontaneous reason spoke with authority and gave the absolute ideas validity beyond the minds that conceived them. The universality of the laws of thought, the Kantian categories, likewise certified to the absolute character of the spontaneous reason; Kant's error had been to regard these laws as personal rather than impersonal. Every act of perception, Cousin argued, demonstrated the independent existence of the categories (which he reduced to two) because each thought had to arise from a perceiver and an external cause: thus subject and object were given together, *"le moi"* and *"le non-moi"* were inherent in each other and equally open to the testimony of introspection.

Cousin persuaded himself in this way that he had passed from the subjective to the objective, from *"le moi"* to *"le non-moi,"* from psychology to ontology. Brought up in the shadow of the eighteenth century, he could not bear to abandon the traditional goal of philosophy — the pursuit of objective certitude along the path of logic; and he arrived confidently at conclusions deep in the realm that Kant, by denying man knowledge of reality, had ruled out of philosophical speculation. Brownson, no more pleased to give up the Absolute, overlooked for a time the weaknesses of Cousin's argument in his delight with the result. Humanity seemed to be bursting the small, dark box where Kant had confined it, and Cousin was leading the way to the sunlight where all was clear and certain.

Brownson quickly made his new enthusiasm public and introduced the readers of the *Christian Examiner* to the French philosophers, just as Ripley was telling them about the German. His *Examiner* articles aroused considerable attention and, according to Ripley, were largely responsible for the interest in philosophy that reached such alarming proportions by the time of the *Dial*.[11] He continued the propaganda even more diligently in the *Boston Quarterly Review*.

Cousin, of course, was exceedingly pleased to have so vigorous an advocate in America. A young Bostonian visited the philosopher in Paris in the winter of 1838. After discussing Henry and Ripley, Brooks and Bancroft, Cousin turned the conversation to Brownson whom he spoke of in his measured way "as a man of a great deal of talent, and indeed as a most remarkable person." "His interest in Brownson," Charles Sumner noted in his journal, "appears to be unfeignedly great."[12] Cousin had begun to exchange letters and articles with Brownson

[11] "Brownson's Writings," *Dial*, I, 25 (July, 1840). Ripley went on to say that Brownson's *Examiner* papers "formed a new era in the history of that able journal."

[12] Sumner's journal, March 9, 1838, Edward L. Pierce, *Memoir and Letters of Charles Sumner*, I, 265. C. S. Henry, a Massachusetts clergyman, had published *Cousin's Psychology* in 1834.

after the American's first essay on him in the *Examiner*. In the spring Sumner wrote eagerly to Justice Story, then a member of the Harvard Corporation, about "a very remarkable conversation" he had with Cousin. The philosopher was "very anxious with regard to the professorship at Cambridge," and told Sumner that the man for Harvard's chair in philosophy was Brownson "whom he thinks one of the most remarkable persons of the age, and wishes to be placed where he can pursue philosophy calmly, thinking his labors will redound to the advance of science throughout the globe." [13] Harvard, however, was scarcely the place for a man who was holding a job in the Custom House under George Bancroft. It preferred the prudence of a James Walker to the vigor of a Brownson, and President Quincy and the governing board hardly troubled themselves much over Cousin's rash proposal. Cousin in the meantime climaxed his appreciation of Brownson by his preface to the third edition of *Fragments Philosophiques* which was published in the summer of 1838. In Brownson, Cousin wrote, *"brille un talent de pensée et de style qui, régulièrement developpé, promet à l'Amérique un écrivain philosophique du premier ordre."* [14] Outside of France, however, Brownson was not well known in Europe. *Blackwood's* blithely

[13] Sumner to Story, May 21, 1838, *ibid.*, I, 295.
[14] Victor Cousin, *Fragments Philosophiques*, I, vi.

referred to him in 1840 as Orlando E. Brownson; and as late as 1843 Carlyle thought that he and Bronson Alcott were the same.[15]

Brownson stated Cousin's chief positions in a series of thoughtful and lucid articles for the *Quarterly*. Meanwhile he read Saint-Simon and Jouffroy. The first influenced chiefly Brownson's ideas of social reform. Yet Saint-Simon's religious vision of the future state nourished Brownson's idea of the Kingdom of God on earth and no doubt contributed to the increasingly theological shape of his thought. Brownson's excitement over Jouffroy, whom for a moment he thought to have solved the great ethical problems, soon passed; but the joy with which he greeted the Frenchman's attempt shows how anxiously he himself was trying to establish an absolute basis for ethics. About the same time, Brownson fell into a squabble with Abner Kneeland in the columns of the *Reformer* and the *Investigator* over the origin of ideas. The debate soon trailed into futility, while Boston no doubt watched it as the blind fighting the blind; but Brownson clarified his notion of causality and realized plainly that he must find another source for ideas besides sense-experience. He later explored

[15] Clarence L. F. Gohdes, *Periodicals of American Transcendentalism*, 93; F. B. Sanborn and William T. Harris, *A. Bronson Alcott*, II, 369.

the question in the *Boston Quarterly* and answered it in the fashion of M. Cousin.

Such forays and skirmishes gave the earnest young metaphysicians of Boston a chance to mouth their battle-cries and sharpen their syllogisms. Silently the armies were forming. The prophets of the soul, of reform, of Kant and Emerson, were facing the champions of experience, of orthodoxy, of Locke and Paley. Emerson suddenly blew the war-trumpet in 1838 in his sermon to the graduating class at the Harvard Divinity School, and tore the scab off the festering disagreements and antagonisms. He actually said little that Brownson or Ripley or S. D. Robbins had not said before; but he had the gift of crystallizing the impulses of the day and disclosing them with a profundity and richness of suggestion that made even those who had already voiced them wonder at facets they had overlooked and beauties they had not suspected. Their own thoughts returned to them in unanticipated grandeur.

But to the conservatives, it was their nightmares returning in unexpected reality. One shouted, "The Philistines be upon us," as Theodore Parker described it; another, "We be all dead men"; while the majority called out, "Atheism." [16] Andrews

---

[16] Parker to Ellis, August 7, 1838, Sanborn and Harris, *op. cit.*, I, 279.

Norton emerged heavily from his library and opened hostilities with a harsh newspaper attack on the Transcendentalists. This provoked several replies — one, in Parker's phrase, from the "iron pen" of Brownson in the *Post* — and soon the war spread into the magazines. Brownson, on thinking it over, liked Emerson's address less: it was vague and ill-organized, its philosophy undigested and its reasoning inconclusive — "transcendental egotism," he called it in the *Quarterly* — and he proceeded to lecture Emerson on the inadvisability of his philosophical rashness. "We wish to see a certain sobriety, a certain reserve in all speculations, something like timidity about rushing off into an unknown universe, and some little regret in departing from the faith of our fathers." [17] However queerly these worthy sentiments sounded on Brownson's lips, they indicated perfectly his religious position. For all his social radicalism and his distrust of the church as an institution, Brownson was theologically more orthodox than Emerson. In 1836 he had criticized *Nature* as pantheistic, and he was prepared even to risk his standing among the Unitarians by declaring that the Trinity, properly understood, expressed

[17] "Mr. Emerson's *Address*," BoQR, I, 512–513 (October, 1838).

significant spiritual truths.[18] He hoped to fit the new spirit into the traditional theology.

But he was far from accepting the traditional spirit. In January 1839 he directed the fire on Andrews Norton from an unexpected angle, taking as a pretext a book on theological criticism Norton had published over a year before. "When we heard this work was announced as actually published," began Brownson, "we trusted it would wipe out that suspicion of infidelity, which had long been attached to the author"; [19] and he went on to complain of the difficulty of calling a man a Christian who denied the intuition of the truths of Christianity and rested all on historical and logical grounds. Norton's philosophy, Brownson decided, is equally fatal to religious faith and sound morality. He thus contrived, in an expert piece of controversial writing, to exhibit the righteous Norton as the prophet of infidelity.

Norton meanwhile was preparing an address that would crush the rebellion of the soul and enshrine John Locke with the apostles in Unitarian theology. Early in 1839 it was finished, and he soon read "The Latest Form of Infidelity" to (with grim appropri-

[18] *Boston Reformer*, September 10, 1836; "Unitarianism and Trinitarianism," *BoQR*, II, 384 (July, 1839).

[19] "Norton on the Evidences of Christianity," *BoQR*, II, 87 (January, 1839).

ateness) the Association of the Alumni of the Divinity School. The alumni no doubt relished Norton's onslaught on the Transcendentalists; but the rebellion refused to be crushed. Ripley and James Freeman Clarke, Richard Hildreth and one Levi Blodgett (whom the initiate knew to be Theodore Parker) spoke out eloquently in its defense. Brownson, who was mainly concerned with politics, bided his time while the storm raged. In 1840, however, Norton reprinted in pamphlet form two articles from the *Princeton Review* on Transcendentalism, one of them attacking Cousin; and Brownson turned aside from writing "The Laboring Classes" to rush to the defense of his master.

Brownson's article in the *Quarterly* for July, summing up the issues of the Unitarian controversy, was perhaps the ablest that the controversy called forth. Far from killing religion, he declared, the new movement was actually reviving it by nourishing the only true source of spiritual exaltation — the soul. What more did the Transcendentalists affirm?

They differ widely in their opinions, and agree in little except in their common opposition to the old school. They do not swear by Locke, and they recognise no authority in matters of opinion but the human mind, whether termed the reason with some of them, or the soul with others. They have all felt that our old catechisms need revision, and that our old systems of philosophy do not do justice to all the elements of human nature, and that these systems can by no means furnish a solid basis for a belief in God, much less in Christianity. Here is the amount of their agreement. Some of them embrace the Transcendental philosophy, some of them reject it, some of them *ignore* all philosophy, plant themselves on their instincts and wait for the huge world to come round to them. Some of them read Cousin, some Goethe and Carlyle, others none at all. Some of them reason, others merely dream. . . . The movement is really of American origin, and the prominent actors in it were carried away by it before ever they formed any acquaintance with French or German metaphysics; and their attachment to the literatures of France and Germany is the effect of their connexion with the movement, not the cause. . . . The real aim of the Transcendentalist is to ascertain a solid ground for faith in the reality of the spiritual world.[20]

With this preamble Brownson entered into a calm and effective defense of the Transcendentalist doctrine of knowledge. Norton, he wrote, restricts faith to the few experts qualified to pass on historical evidences; by the Transcendentalist theory all men can be Christians as long as they have within them the religious impulse. Norton's doctrine of knowledge, he went on, actually denies the essential grounds of faith and can issue only in universal skepticism. Indeed, without assuming an intuition of

[20] "Two Articles from the *Princeton Review*," BoQR, III, 270, 271, 272 (July, 1840).

the presence of God, his argument for Christianity becomes empty and worthless: for, if you deny the power to perceive spiritual truth directly, how can you affirm the power to perceive any truth whatever? If you cannot be certain inwardly that God exists, how can you ever be certain that the miracles took place or that they testify to the existence of God? But the very number of the *Quarterly* that carried this article also contained the essay on "The Laboring Classes." Brownson triumphantly eliminated himself from the circles in which the Divinity School professors moved, and the orthodox were saved the trouble of trying to refute him.

3

The election of 1840 soon came, however, and it changed Brownson's philosophy as much as it changed his politics. Faith in the people had meant to him what faith in God meant to most men — properly so, because he regarded people as visible manifestations of the spirit of God. But after the disillusionment of the election he could no longer concede them so intimate a relation to their Maker. They could not be close to Him, they must therefore be divorced from Him; they could not be basically virtuous, they must therefore be basically corrupt. These ideas, rising irresistibly from intense experience, overthrew the foundations of his old beliefs and drove him on a furious search for new ones.

As long as he had dedicated his faith to a definite vision of democracy, his religion had been thin and pallid. In 1836 he described it as "the conception, or sentiment, of the Holy, that which makes us think of something as reverend, and prompts us to revere it." [21] It actually was a sentiment to Brownson, a vague feeling, a mild desire for comfort, not an inconsolable passion or an undying thirst. When he stayed with the Heckers in New York he failed even to ask a blessing at the table; and Bronson Alcott, after spending an evening with Brownson and James Walker, was moved to observe sadly in his diary that the two were "destitute of deep and fervid enthusiasm. . . . They make themselves merry, more than befits my taste, with the divine in our nature. . . . Both chop logic, both are men of understanding, neither apprehends the being of poet and seer; the high works of poetic genius, the marvels of holiness, are beyond their grasp, although both are good and useful men." [22] Before 1840 Brownson

[21] "New Views," *Works*, IV, 3.

[22] Isaac T. Hecker, "Doctor Brownson and the Workingman's Party Fifty Years Ago," *Catholic World*, XLV, 206 (May, 1887); Sanborn and Harris, *op. cit.*, I, 266.

was a man of logic with a solid grip on the practical problems. Religion meant to him either a collection of pious phrases or a metaphorical way of stating the social question, "a poetry of thought or an ornament of language." [23] His deepest emotions were mortgaged to the mission of establishing the Kingdom of God on earth.

When the election of 1840 showed that the people would not establish the Kingdom of God through their own efforts, Brownson, shrinking from the present disillusion, found solace in hopes of the future. He was turning from this world to the next, from the people to God; he lost interest in reform and grew concerned with salvation, forgot respectability and yearned for holiness. J. H. Allen first met him in this time of stress. "The hard, restless, implacably honest and domineering temper of Orestes Brownson had just been greatly softened," he wrote many years later, "by a sudden flow of religious feeling in channels which he had thought dried up." [24] The formulas Brownson had used to fill out his scheme of the universe were slowly becoming barren and inadequate as he began to think about the problems they purported to answer.

[23] J. H. Newman, *On the Scope and Nature of University Education*, 30.
[24] J. H. Allen, *Our Liberal Movement in Theology*, 86–87.

"There are no abstractions in absolute life," he determined. "God is no abstraction but an infinite concrete." [25]

The deepening of his religious sense came, not suddenly as in a mystic vision, but gradually, as if he were painfully adjusting his beliefs to emotions that had changed more than he guessed. In the spring of 1841 Theodore Parker alarmed the church by preaching his sermon on "The Transient and Permanent in Christianity" which, after annihilating the transient, left his hearers with the question so plaintively voiced by John Weiss, "Where is the permanent?" [26] Brownson cordially approved Parker's sermon and needed to qualify it very little before he gave it a whole-hearted defense. Parker spent the next year in paying the penalty for the sermon. His heterodoxy had outraged the fathers of the church who tried to restore the integrity of the sect by placing the offender in chill isolation. But not all Bostonians were so easily wounded. A group invited Parker to give a course of lectures in the winter of 1841. These lectures — later incorporated in *A Discourse of Matters Pertaining to Religion* — were an eloquent and erudite defense of Brownson's own

[25] "Church of the Future," *BoQR*, V (January, 1842), *Works*, IV, 62.
[26] H. S. Commager, *Theodore Parker*, 76.

religion of humanity. But something had changed
in Brownson. The lectures disturbed him, and he felt
strongly that they were dangerous; yet he knew not
why. Their doctrines were all familiar: but on the
lips of another he heard them with a new detachment, and they appeared in an unlovely aspect he
had not seen before.

Brownson was now frankly worried. He turned
back with a sense of dread to those books in which
he had proclaimed the *Church of the Future*. He
first picked up *New Views*, and in the *Quarterly* for
January 1842 restated its leading principles, more
thoughtfully and solidly perhaps, but without apparent change.[27] Yet somehow the "new views" were
animated by a much richer sense of religion than
they had been before; and in the closing paragraphs
was expounded a curious new doctrine of the redemption and sanctification of the race. But there
was more, and worse! In the same number Brownson — long the prophet of reason and master of
logic — suddenly turned with scorn on the guide
he had followed so long: "Alas! we have seen
enough of mere individual reason. It is impotent
when it has not, for its guide and support, the
reason of God, speaking not only to the heart, but

[27] "Church of the Future," *BoQR*, V (January, 1842), *Works*,
IV, 57–76.

through revelation and the traditions of the race."
Strange words! Even history, Brownson declared, is
inexplicable "save on the hypothesis of a constant
intervention in a *special* manner of our ever-watchful
Father." [28] This theory of history required a very
concrete religious faith. It was shocking to the enlightened generation which had divested religion of
such medieval survivals as "divine providences."

His sermons before the Society for Christian
Union and Progress began likewise to resound with
the new vigor of his faith. Up to 1841 he had presented Christianity in its most innocuous form in
order to make as few demands as possible on the
unbeliever. This policy suddenly seemed desecra-
tion; the more he pared down Christianity, the less
reason he had to offer the agnostic to become a
Christian. With his new fullness of belief he could
not bear the understatement he had hardly noticed
in his more tepid days.

At this point Brownson began to reread *Charles
Elwood.* Though written in 1834 and 1835, the book
had not been published till 1840; and its author,
speedily growing dissatisfied with it, had peremp-
torily forbidden a second edition in America, though
it was reprinted several times in England. He was

[28] "Reform and Conservatism," *BoQR*, V (January, 1842),
Works, IV, 95, 94.

pleased to discover on perusing it again that one of the characters identified philosophy and religion: Brownson himself in his essay on the *Princeton Review* had expressly separated the two, declaring philosophy to be the superior.[29] On one point, however, the novel had gone badly astray. Now that religion was becoming so vital an experience for Brownson, he could no longer agree with Constant that it originated normally as a spontaneous operation of human nature. It must be more than merely the projection of man's imagination, the shadow of his desire. Either man in the act of faith touches the truest and deepest reality, or he is a victim of his own profoundest feelings — and the second Brownson would not admit. He went on to criticize *Charles Elwood* for relying too closely on Cousin in formulating its arguments. Brownson was beginning to need a more powerful proof of man's passage to external reality.[30]

As his own ideas swelled with rich new faith, he indeed was finding Cousin altogether too pale in his religion and too superficial in adapting it to his

[29] In 1844, when he presented the volume for 1840 to Harvard College, he scrawled roughly on the margin beside this passage, "All wrong — the writer thinks differently now." This note is to be found in Volume III, page 288 of the *BoQR* at the Widener Library.

[30] "*Charles Elwood* Reviewed," *BoQR*, V (April, 1842), *Works*, IV, 316–361.

philosophy. He continued reading in the French eclectics, and luckily, in his hour of need, came on the works of Pierre Leroux.[31] Here he found what he had been looking for. Leroux had taken over Cousin's account of thought as the resultant of two elements, subject and object. If it was impossible for man to think without the presence of the intelligible in nature, Leroux reasoned, the intelligible therefore cannot be sought and found, but must present itself to the intellect. Subject and object then are given in the same act, and the reality of one is as certain as the reality of the other. He extended this principle to all activities. Man cannot live by himself alone; every fact of life is the resultant of the concurrent activity of subject and object, and partakes of the character of each. There are three general modes of communion: with nature through property, with fellow men through family and the State, and with God through humanity. Man can live and progress, Leroux concluded, only

[31] Leroux, who had begun as a Saint-Simonian and later struck out independently to construct his own system, excited other Americans than Brownson, and with somewhat different results. It was his philosophy that George Sand set out to popularize in several novels, particularly *Spiridion* (part of which Leroux wrote), *Consuelo*, and *La Comtesse de Rudolstadt*; and it was this last work which, according to a recent author (Esther Shephard, *Walt Whitman's Pose*, New York, 1938), had so strong an influence on Walt Whitman. For Leroux's relations to George Sand, see P.-Félix Thomas, *Pierre Leroux*, 66 ff.

by communion with what is not himself: all growth is by assimilation from without.

The election of 1840 had left Brownson with the discovery that man, even when confronted with the good, would not always choose it. How then to explain progress? Leroux's doctrine of assimilation suggested the answer. Humanity grew as a collective being, its capacities enlarging from generation to generation. Men sinned in Adam, not as individuals but as the race, and they were similarly redeemed in Christ.[32] The collective progress was accelerated, Leroux continued, by God's elevation of certain men into supernatural communion with Himself. Communion with these "providential men" — Jesus, Abraham, Moses, Zoroaster, Confucius, Plato and the like — enabled ordinary individuals to live a higher life. Brownson had long waited for the new Messiah: Leroux's doctrine gave his hope metaphysical meaning, and the Frenchman's somewhat arrogant statement of the doctrine, minimizing the rôle in progress of the undifferentiated mass, accorded with Brownson's new antidemocratic mood. The mystical conception of the race, moreover, with its stress on the solidarity of mankind, attracted Brownson, who was weak and bruised from leaning too

[32] "Leroux on Humanity," *BoQR*, V (July, 1842), *Works*, IV, 106–107.

heavily on individual reason. In Leroux, briefly, Brownson found the formulation of many obscure and undefined emotions which had struggled inarticulate in his consciousness since 1840. With characteristic impulsiveness he rushed to become the expositor of Leroux, as he formerly had been the expositor of Cousin. His new oracle was actually an avowed pantheist; but Brownson found the doctrine of communion invaluable in ordering his own thought and explained away Leroux's heterodoxy by saying that he didn't understand his own philosophy. "The study of his writings," Brownson wrote later, "formed an epoch in our mental history." [38]

His new emotions now demanded a more vital and concrete religious creed than the one which had sufficed him during the seven lean years before 1840. He no longer found blood and bones in Boston Unitarianism, even in the Transcendentalist variety, and he had to recast its ideas if it was to accommodate his sharp, driving faith. Who would be a better person to appeal to in this emergency than the man whose words had helped restore him to Christianity ten years before? Instinctively Brownson reached for his pen, sat down at his desk in the warm spring

[38] "An A Priori Autobiography," *BrQR*, New Series, IV (January, 1850), *Works*, I, 215.

of 1842 and wrote a long and thoughtful letter to the venerable Dr. Channing.

Since man cannot by nature commune directly with God, Brownson urged to Channing, there must be a mediator, at once God and man, who is essential to man's salvation. It is disastrous to reduce this mediator to human stature, he told the good Doctor; the "tendency to resolve God into the laws of nature — the laws of the moral world and those of the natural world" leads to atheism by draining belief of its intensity. We Unitarians misused Jesus; "Jesus became to us a law, an abstract principle according to which man was made." He is actually much more than this, much more "than a very exemplary sort of a man, a very zealous and able reformer, whom we should do well to respect and to remember along with Plato, Alfred, Luther, and Swedenborg." When He imparted divine life to His disciples, He communicated it virtually to all men, through the unity and indissolubility of the race. "If human nature were always what you say," Brownson went on, "I cannot conceive what need there was of a redeemer; if it be now what the [Calvinist] church generally affirms, that is, inherently and totally depraved, I am equally unable to conceive what the Redeemer has done." "Christianity seems to me to assume throughout as its point of departure, man's sinfulness, depravity, alienation from God and heaven." With Jesus there came new possibilities of salvation: he is the God-Man, the medium of communion between God and man whose mission is to redeem man from the original sin. This new conception, Brownson continued, lifted the halters from his deep religious passion. "I can preach now, not merely make discursions on ethics and metaphysics. . . . I now need to know nothing but Jesus and him crucified." "What before was mere thought has now become love; what was abstraction has become life; what was merely speculation has become downright, living earnestness." [34]

"The Mediatorial Life of Jesus," as Brownson called the letter when he published it in pamphlet form, was a deep and moving confession of a man who had finally justified to himself his intense need for religious faith. Shorn of its dubious metaphysics, it became an eloquent statement of the drama of sin and redemption. But Channing was an old man, bewildered by Brownson's talk of "subject" and "object" and by his borrowings from foreign philosophers whose works Channing did not know. Receiving these religious affirmations as simply a more vivid way of expressing his own Unitarianism, he welcomed what he took to be the return of the

[34] "The Mediatorial Life of Jesus," *Works*, IV, 140–172.

prodigal son, pointed out where Brownson's doctrine seemed to suggest the Universalist heresy, and
exhorted him to live calmly and earnestly according to his present principles. "God made you for
something more than to scatter random shot," he
concluded with a touch of nobility, "although those
shot may sometimes be grand ideas and may hit old
errors between wind and water." [35] He was to die
before Brownson suffered another of the sea changes
which so distressed the older man.

Theodore Parker's lectures of the winter before
now appeared in book form, and Brownson set about
reviewing them for the *Quarterly*. As he reflected
on the volume, he reluctantly decided that Parker
was reasoning straight from his premises — and they
had once been Brownson's — when he reduced religion to naturalism. But were these premises the
tenets of Christianity? Brownson finally required a
whole issue of the *Quarterly* to answer the question.
Parker kept the number on hand for several weeks
before he read it; but finding that it was, as he had
been told, "not vindictive," he wrote Brownson a
manly letter in thanks for the review, and added
that, while he wanted to avoid a cat-and-dog controversy of the kind New England knew so well,

[35] Channing to Brownson, June 10, 1842, H. F. Brownson,
Early Life, 443–444.

he intended that winter to review Brownson's writings "under three heads: *Philosophical, Theological* and *Ethico-Political*." [36] Unfortunately his theological indiscretions made the winter a more troubled one for Parker than he anticipated, and he never got farther in his study of Brownson than so characteristic a beginning.

As Brownson wrestled with the problems Parker's lectures presented, he saw with growing clarity that salvation involved the infusion, through communion, of a supernatural life into natural life. Thus alone could man be gathered to God and his original imperfections made whole. The answer to Parker was, in a word, grace. Having reached this point, he resolved the problem of the age into "Catholicity without the papacy."

[36] Parker to Increase S. Smith, October 10, 1842, John Weiss, *Life and Correspondence of Theodore Parker*, I, 188; Parker to Brownson, December 12, 1842, H. F. Brownson, *Early Life*, 238–239.

CHAPTER V

THE PALACE BEAUTIFUL, 1842–1844

By the fall of 1842 it was clear that Brownson was traveling on a different road from that of the pilgrims of the Oversoul. In his letter on "The Mediatorial Life of Jesus" he had asked Channing, "Who is there of us . . . however pure and blameless may be our lives, that does not bear on his heart the damning stain of sin?" [1] — but he had only to look round to find his answer. Emerson knew no sin, nor Alcott, nor Margaret Fuller, nor George Ripley. Ripley indeed was hard by in West Roxbury building a temple to Transcendentalist goodness, and even the sin-stained Brownson discovered that he liked Brook Farm.

Half a charming adventure, half a solemn experiment, Brook Farm represented the Transcendentalists' attempt to work out a way of life. Thoreau, near by in Concord, was the American Scholar in action, as Emerson said, whose life refuted all theories of how to live; but not everyone was independent of communities, like Thoreau, and George

[1] "The Mediatorial Life of Jesus," *Works*, IV, 151.

Ripley tried in Brook Farm to strike the medium between society and solitude for an entire group. The group was a happy one; but it was almost better to visit Brook Farm than to live there. Emerson, Alcott, Margaret Fuller and Orestes Brownson could enjoy the high times without tasting the depressions. They shared the talks and songs and theatricals, but they did not have to groom Hawthorne's "transcendental heifer" or sweep out the kitchen or rake the manure.

Brownson not only liked Brook Farm himself but sent his son there; and in the *Democratic Review* of November 1842 he wrote an article in its favor. He had to struggle hard, however, to find reasons to praise the experiment. He delighted in the people, and Ripley was his oldest and closest friend in Boston; but Brownson drew the line between liking and approving, and was a bit uneasy about the tone of the article. He later told Sam Larned that he hoped they would merit half of it.[2] Brook Farm was good, he finally said, because it was simple and unpretending. It did not aspire to reform the world. It intended no harm to the State, the Church, the family or private property.

These were fine words, and Ripley was grateful

[2] Anne C. Lynch to Brownson, November 27, 1842, H. F. Brownson, *Early Life*, 500.

for them; but he knew that a short time before Brownson would have given a different set of reasons. The two friends were drifting apart. Ripley, with all good will, could not understand this new Brownson, who was doing his best to forget the ideals they had cherished together for the last eight years; and to Brownson Ripley was well-meaning, but intellectually innocent and deaf to persuasion. Brownson was once more retiring into the deep loneliness which harshly repulses all efforts at intimacy. His new beliefs traced a magic circle round him which none could pass who knew not the charm. "We have truly sympathized as few men have done"; Ripley finally wrote him:

you have always quickened my love for humanity; and for no small share of what mental clearness I may have, am I indebted to the hours of genial, pleasant intercourse I have enjoyed with you. If I had never known you, I should never have been engaged in this enterprise. I consider it as the incarnation of those transcendental truths which we have held in common, and which you have done much to make me love. . . . With the vivid feeling that the great revolution in my life plan was the inevitable fruit of the ideas for which you most valued me, I will own to something of disappointment that you should give us so little sympathy or recognition, when a friendly word would have been cheering amidst such a tempest of abuse as fell upon us from the conservative sky.[3]

[3] Ripley to Brownson, December 18, 1842, *ibid.*, 311–315.

Young Orestes, Brownson's son, remained only a year at Brook Farm, where, wrote the kindly Ripley, he won everyone's regard save Charles A. Dana's. His father was not so fortunate. "The unpolished, vehement, and positive man," as bright young Georgiana Bruce called him, was not altogether popular on the Farm. The starry optimism of the dwellers frequently stirred him to debate where, argument failing, he sought to overawe by sheer physical massiveness, raising his voice, pounding on the table, and giving way to anger when his opponents failed to grasp his point. The artless buoyancy of most of the Brook Farmers did not equip them to understand the gloomy and logical tirades of a Brownson. Staggered by his theology, they found consolation in making him the butt of their Transcendental humor. Once in the later years, as one of the several stories goes, when his visits had grown fewer, he showed off before Ripley his newly acquired skill in Latin. Ripley, much distressed by Brownson's pronunciation, dreamed that night that he went to confession and discovered Brownson to be his priest. "Kneel my son," said the priest, "and for penance repeat after me the fifty-eighth Psalm in the Vulgate." Ripley awoke in agony, crying, "O Lord, my punishment is greater than I am able to bear!" [4]

[4] Georgiana B. Kirby, *Years of Experience*, 146, 147, 148.

Part of the Farm seems to have delighted in this story; but others awaited Brownson's visits more eagerly, Isaac Hecker particularly, the son of the family with whom Brownson used to stay in New York, a shy, thoughtful boy, who came to Brook Farm on Brownson's advice and remained to serve as the community baker. Brownson's virile force "fascinated the more delicate and sensitive temper of the young man," as George W. Curtis explained it.[5] Hecker had mysticism in his temperament — genuine mysticism, next to which the Transcendental mystics seemed dreamy sentimentalists. It required a detailed and specific theology, like Brownson's, to satisfy a youth whose visions transmuted into experience what most people accepted as abstractions. Others, too, felt the power of Brownson's personality. Several residents of the Farm were emboldened by his example to advance along the road to Rome; three or four, indeed, became Catholics eventually, among them Sophia Ripley, the wife of the founder.

Brownson's divergence from the Transcendentalists appeared at its most concentrated in Brook Farm. He had become too religious for them. He had too intense and concrete a belief to fraternize with people who ignored evil, sputtered about the infinite and

[5] Curtis to Elliott, February 28, 1890, Walter Elliott, *The Life of Father Hecker*, 56.

generalized their own vagueness into the universe. When he translated their lofty affirmations into a form which he could understand, they inevitably issued in pantheism, denial of sin, egotism, or some other species of infidelity. The Transcendentalists assumed that man pursues the good of his own accord; they valued man, the individual, above the race, above humanity; they found the source of knowledge in their own souls instead of in communion with external reality; in short, they resolved truth into an inward emotion and made religion purely subjective.

Brownson, in fact, was abandoning most of his old positions. After 1842 he gave up the *Quarterly*. Harrison's victory had reduced his income $1600 by turning him out from his job at the Chelsea Marine Hospital.[6] Brownson had several times intended stopping the *Quarterly*; and when at this point J. L. O'Sullivan of the *Democratic Review* suggested that the magazines combine with Brownson as contributing editor Brownson was inclined to accept. Thus ended the *Boston Quarterly Review*, though it still is living testimony to the candor, vitality and honesty of its editor. "Take it all in all," lamented W. H.

---

[6] Such was Brownson's salary, or so Samuel G. Goodrich charged during the Tippecanoe campaign in a speech reprinted in A. B. Norton, *The Great Revolution of 1840*, 350.

Channing, "it was the best journal this country has ever produced." [7]

The *Democratic Review* was hardly grave or dull enough to be esteemed highly in its day, but it was actually almost the best magazine of the time, lively and entertaining, intelligent without being grimly intellectual. Hawthorne, Bryant, Whittier, Longfellow, Lowell, Poe, James Kirke Paulding, Parke Godwin and Walt Whitman wrote for it; and O'Sullivan, a clever and charming Irishman, steered it on a liberal Democratic course which added materially to its popularity. The *Review* dealt in the immediacies of action and enjoyment, caring little for the swirling depths of theory.[8] Then, in 1842, it acquired Orestes A. Brownson as a steady contributor. In his first article he dismayed the subscribers by declaring that philosophy was not an independent study but a special phase of religion. This was not the way people talked in the *Democratic Review*, nor the things they talked about. He meanwhile got deep in a murky series on "Synthetic Philosophy." O'Sullivan stood the deluge of metaphysics as long as he could; but finally, in February 1843, he wrote Brownson in a model of Celtic insinuation that the

[7] Clarence L. F. Gohdes, *Periodicals of American Transcendentalism*, 81.

[8] See Frank Luther Mott, *A History of American Magazines, 1741–1850*, 677–681.

readers were "much disappointed of the expectation they had entertained of being interested in your articles." [9]

Brownson, always glad to please when it meant no violence to his convictions, readily turned from a systematic treatise on philosophy to one on government. O'Sullivan had not suspected that the flaming *sans-culotte* of 1840 was growing conservative; but Brownson had backwatered from the radicalism of his earlier days, and even while contributing to the *Democratic Review* was secretly working to secure the nomination of John C. Calhoun in 1844. He speedily showed his true colors, much to the horror of O'Sullivan as well as of the subscribers. They understood very little of Brownson's essays, and what they did understand they did not like. Their social thought assumed that, since people were generally decent individually, they would be generally decent socially; but Brownson believed that people acted socially from different motives and in different ways from their custom as individuals. The intelligence of the people, as he told the readers of the *Review* in the spring of 1843, is not sufficient for good government; and he continued in the essay to discuss democracy in so undemocratic a tone that

[9] O'Sullivan to Brownson, February 12, 1843, H. F. Brownson, *Early Life*, 347.

O'Sullivan had to preface it with an apologetic note.[10] Suspicions were aroused that Brownson was turning Whig. In July Brownson reviewed Carlyle's *Past and Present*, which he called Carlyle's best book, and dropped along the way *obiter dicta* attacking the treasured democratic belief in the right of revolution and declaring feudalism preferable to industrial capitalism; but this article was on the whole more heartening, for Carlyle's explosive rhetoric appealed deeply to Brownson's powerful feelings, and he assailed the industrial system with some of his old relish.[11]

During the summer Brownson began a series on political theory. It is no wonder that these essays completed the bewilderment of the readers of the *Review*. They were long, tedious and misty, shot through with Platonism and several times going up in the smoke of metaphysics. Even their author felt obliged to pause and apologize for his obscurity: "however unmeaning it may be to them [the complaining readers]," he explained, "it has meaning to me, and I know very well what I mean by it: but what phraseology, or whether any phraseology will suffice to communicate my meaning to their minds,

[10] "Democracy and Liberty," *Democratic Review*, XII (April, 1843), *Works*, XV, 258–281.
[11] "The Present State of Society," *Democratic Review*, XIII (July, 1843), *Works*, IV, 423–460.

I own, I am at some loss to determine." [12] In short, the essays had all the faults of abstract argument. The words were so remote from things that it would have been useless to ponder their truth, and the only consideration was whether they were gratifying. Brownson's political theory had now advanced so far that only a Catholic could have been much gratified. Certainly the readers were not; they were infuriated.

No wonder, then, that they took the quickest way out and began to cancel their subscriptions. And, when Brownson slipped and said something they could understand, they were even more indignant. The workingmen's quest for equal rights Brownson somewhere defined as a desire for "freedom for each individual to act out his individuality, or to perform his special function in the social body." [13] Now this was ingenious, but unconvincing: the mill worker wanted not free opportunity to continue being a mill worker — he had that — but free opportunity to become a storekeeper. When Brownson went on to protest his constant devotion to the workingman's cause, it struck his audience as the nakedest hypocrisy. O'Sullivan with some asperity added a note to

[12] "Origin and Ground of Government," *Democratic Review*, XIII (1843), *Works*, XV, 364.
[13] *Ibid.*, 386.

the first article, saying that "it is perhaps unnecessary to remark" that the editor held himself responsible for none of Brownson's views. In September he appended a further note trying to mollify the storm of disapproval that the articles were raising.[14] Brownson, indeed, was wrecking the *Review* with every new article, and O'Sullivan finally took steps to end his embarrassing contract. Throughout the affair he had been patient, puzzled and reasonable; but he was in the position of a man who had bought his shop a bear which was now driving the customers away. As for Brownson, he was well pleased to terminate the agreement and quickly set about reviving the *Boston Quarterly*. When O'Sullivan's publishers refused to release the name, Brownson called it *Brownson's Quarterly Review*, and under that title its first number appeared in January 1844.

2

The *Democratic Review* incident signalized Brownson's break with the Northern Democrats. Politically he had come to stand with Calhoun, against Webster and Clay on the one hand, Van Buren and Benton on the other. He still believed

[14] *Democratic Review*, XIII, 129 (August, 1843), 262 (September, 1843).

himself to be working for the laborers, but practically his energy and influence went to aiding the cause of the slaveholders. Calhoun had hinted to Brownson as early as 1841 that he was available for the next nomination.[15] Brownson needed little prodding, however, and by 1842 was in regular correspondence with Dixon H. Lewis of Alabama, a strong Calhoun man, over means of selling Calhoun to the nation. Brownson's part was to circulate pro-Calhoun articles through the North, some of which he was to write anonymously himself. He was particularly eager that the "crooked, serpentine" Van Buren should not be renominated, for his long distrust of Van Buren's political adroitness had been raised to animosity when he heard that Van Buren had named "The Laboring Classes" as the principal cause of his defeat in 1840.[16] (A decade after the Civil War Brownson was to call Van Buren "the last first-class man that sat, or probably that ever will sit, in the presidential chair of the United States."[17]) In 1843 Brownson was offered the editorship of a pro-Calhoun paper to be established in New

[15] Calhoun to Brownson, October 31, 1841, H. F. Brownson, *Early Life*, 305.

[16] "The Protective Policy," *BrQR*, I (October, 1844), *Works*, XV, 496; "Mr. Calhoun and the Baltimore Convention," *BrQR*, I (April, 1844), *Works*, XV, 477.

[17] "The Democratic Principle," *BrQR*, Last Series, I (April, 1873), *Works*, XVIII, 224.

York; [18] but the offer was recalled because of financial difficulties that made a regular editor impossible. During 1844 he wrote the leading political articles in six papers opposing Van Buren [19] and devoted the new *Brownson's Quarterly* largely to pushing Calhoun's candidacy. In the first issue, after making a lengthy and cruel attack on Van Buren, he solemnly called for a statesman, a man of principle, to appear in this hour of the country's need. Who could the savior be? The article following, to the immense surprise of no one, revealed him as John C. Calhoun. It was a piece of suave and expert apologetics. Brownson took care to disclaim all connection with or interest in Calhoun's campaign and, having established his disinterestedness, declared Calhoun's life to be a triumph of devotion to principle. But what of his astonishing record of inconsistencies? Calhoun, said Brownson, is "eminently a practical statesman"; "the presidential chair may receive new lustre and dignity from him; to him it can give none." [20]

By the next appearance of the *Quarterly*, however, Calhoun had been removed from consideration.

[18] Isaac Hecker to Brownson, September 14, 1843, H. F. Brownson, *Early Life*, 340–341.
[19] *Ibid.*, 362.
[20] "Demagoguism," *BrQR*, I (January, 1844), *Works*, XV, 434–451; "Life and Speeches of John C. Calhoun," *BrQR*, I (January, 1844), *Works*, XV, 451–472.

Brownson bravely fought on in his private campaign; but he had learned in 1840 not to put his heart into politics. When James K. Polk was finally nominated, Brownson is said in his first fury to have dashed the paper that brought the news to the floor and roared, "Who is James K. Polk?"; [21] but he soon discovered a few virtues in the candidate and contrived to work up a modicum of enthusiasm in his support. Brownson actually confessed that "in many of the abstract principles of government, we coincide much more nearly with the Whigs than we do with the Democrats; but the Whigs," he went on, "are thoroughly, and without any mitigation, the party of modern feudalism. . . . There is not one of their distinctive measures but will tend directly and with fatal force to consolidate the power of the industrial lords, and to reduce the operative classes to a state of virtual serfage." [22] Though he eventually grew disgusted with Polk and with the campaign, Brownson was pleased with Polk's victory and interpreted it as evidence that "the God of our fathers has not wholly abandoned us." [23]

[21] H. F. Brownson, *Early Life*, 360.
[22] "The Presidential Nominations," *BrQR*, I (July, 1844), *Works*, XV, 485.
[23] "The Protective Policy," *BrQR*, I (October, 1844), *Works*, XV, 496; "The Recent Election," *BrQR*, II (January, 1845), *Works*, XV, 519.

Brownson's preoccupation with abstractions did not blunt his powers of sharp, cutting analysis, as his indictment of the Whig policy showed. He still surveyed the operations of politics with the caustic realism of "The Laboring Classes." He still saw the undercover workings of economic interests, and still observed the defects of capitalism with a sagacity possessed by few of his contemporaries. If there had been any social reformers capable of understanding him, Brownson would have documented abundantly their feeling that reform was necessary. The casual remarks on society scattered through his essays in these years reflected his skill in piercing through to the realities behind the puppet-show of politics. The American democracy made a pretty picture, Brownson acknowledged; but, almost alone in his day, he saw how meaningless equality in the voting-booth was when not confirmed by equality in the market-place. The politicians seek "to turn you off with mere political equality," he told the workingmen, "while they reap all the advantages of the social state." "Universal suffrage does not, then, in giving to every man an equal vote in the state, give to every man equal ability to protect his own rights and interests." Here lies the pressing problem of society: "The great danger of modern times is this growing industrial feudalism, which is springing up

in all the more *advanced* nations of Christendom."
Economic legislation, he declared, has "fallen under
the control of, probably, less than two hundred
individuals." Our whole experience as a nation
proves that democracy does not protect labor against
the usurpations of capital. It shows the necessity of
restraints on the popular will, for in practice these
become restraints on the greed of the capitalists.[24]

His strengthened conviction that government supplied a legitimate need of human nature was
smothering his desire to return to atomic competition. "We are no believers in the sovereign virtue
of free competition. . . . There are times and cases
when government is needed to control it, to set
bounds to it; when the government itself should
take the initiative, and assume the direction."[25] Yet
what was the government doing? — and here he
reverted momentarily to his penetrating diagnosis of
a few years before.

Our industrial system is working gradually, but surely,
the subjection of the great mass of the operative classes, and
when our new lands shall have been exhausted, and the

[24] "Origin and Ground of Government," *Democratic Review*,
XIII (1843), *Works*, XV, 387; "Origin and Constitution of
Government," *BrQR*, I (April, 1844), *Works*, XV, 425, 426,
433.

[25] Brownson advocated free trade but spurned the conventional
arguments of the free traders. "The Protective Policy," *BrQR*,
I (October, 1844), *Works*, XV, 497.

price of land become so high that the laboring man can no longer hope to become a proprietor . . . we shall find established all over the country an industrial feudalism, of which the military feudalism of the middle ages was but a faint prelude. All is settling down into this new feudalism, and the whole legislation of the country, in relation to banks, tariffs and corporations generally, is rapidly hastening it.[26]

He willingly furnished detailed evidence of the burgeoning of the new feudalism. The chief economic tendency of the day, he declared, was the gradual reduction of wages to the point of minimum subsistence. The separation of capital and labor turned labor into a commodity and made it subject to the laws of supply and demand. With humane considerations thus banished, the employers sought to lower wages as much as possible, and the economic forces of the day sided with them. Improvements in machinery enabled them to dispense with labor; machines, moreover, increased the productive capacity far beyond "not the *wants*, but in the actual state of society, the *ability* of the community to consume," and this overproduction compelled the capitalists in their competition for markets to cheapen their producing costs, either by cutting wages directly

[26] "Come-outerism: or the Radical Tendency of the Day," *BrQR*, I (July, 1844), *Works*, IV, 542.

or by introducing better machinery and cutting them indirectly.[27] All the conditions of industrial capitalism, then, were conspiring to reduce workingmen to virtual slaves.

What could be done to check the new feudalism? George Ripley sponsored one solution. Brownson's old friend had helped turn Brook Farm into a Fourierist community and in 1844 himself presided over a Fourierist convention in New York City. Three years before Brownson had regarded Fourierism with moderate favor, but now he attacked it as false and anti-Christian.[28] Yet he saw no greater hope in capitalism; and in a striking passage he isolated the phenomenon which later generations have labeled the business cycle. It required extraordinary penetration to trace so early the roots of depressions to the system itself, and not to a special set of circum-

[27] *Address on Social Reform*, delivered before the Society of the Mystical Seven at Wesleyan University, Middletown, Conn., August 7, 1844, 5–6.

[28] "Social Evils, and Their Remedy," *BoQR*, IV, 265–291 (July, 1841); "Church Unity and Social Amelioration," *BrQR*, I (July, 1844), *Works*, IV, 512–526. "I require in my theory, four terms," Brownson explained to Parke Godwin of the New York *Evening Post*, a leading Fourierist, "the Church, the State, the Community or Phalanx and the Family. I see no way of working out the reforms . . . without the active presence of all four." Brownson to Godwin, May 9, 1843, Greeley-Godwin Papers. Brownson borrowed his copy of Fourier from Albert Brisbane, the chief American Fourierist and father of the late Arthur Brisbane, the Hearst columnist.

stances.[29] The Panic of 1837 had to repeat itself half a dozen times before the professional economists realized that depressions were organic in capitalism. "There is no longer any certainty of the born worker obtaining always work whereby he can provide for the ordinary wants of a human being," Brownson wrote; and this injustice results from

our vicious method of distributing the products of labor, [by which] we destroy the possibility of keeping up an equilibrium between production and consumption. We create a surplus — that is, a surplus, not when we consider the wants of the people, but when we consider the state of the markets — and then must slacken our hands till the surplus is worked off. During this time, while we are working off the surplus, while the mills run short time, or stop altogether, the workmen must want employment. The evil is inherent in the system.[30]

Yet, for all the discernment of his analysis, Brownson turned his back on practical attempts to improve conditions. His theory of government had changed. Those facts that had bulked so large in the old frame of reference meant little in the new one. Interests, for example, he no longer regarded as sinister intrusions into the pattern of society, but

[29] There is no evidence that Brownson had read Sismondi, the French economist, who made a somewhat similar analysis.

[30] "The Present State of Society," *Democratic Review*, XIII (July, 1843), *Works*, IV, 452–453.

as actual parts of the fabric of government. He was now appalled, moreover, by the complexity of the social problem: "If I had been asked twenty years ago to solve the problem, I should have solved it instantly, without the least hesitation; but the longer I live, the more I see of life, and the more I perceive of the complication of all questions, how one question runs into another, and no one can be answered as an isolated, independent question." [31]

But basically his indifference to reform sprang from his heightened religious feelings. He believed firmly that the economic system was evil; but he had rejected the proposed reforms as impracticable or dangerous, and he now sought their equivalent in religion. The theological notion of a functional society displaced in his mind the democratic notion of a society of equality; and this change made him doubt the need for external reform.[32] He was convinced furthermore of the ubiquity of original sin: "With ignorant, depraved men, can you have a rightly organized society?" [33] The first step in re-

[31] *Address on Social Reform*, 9.

[32] "The diversity of gifts and callings is essential to the very conception of society; and it is a fact which there is no getting over, if we would. It has its root in the order of Providence, in human nature, and in human society." "The Scholar's Mission" (an oration before the Gamma Sigma Society of Dartmouth, July 26, 1843), *Works*, XIX, 72.

[33] "No Church, No Reform," *BrQR*, I (April, 1844), *Works*, IV, 511.

form was plainly to communicate the divine grace which alone made reform possible. As the salvation of the soul grew urgent and living in his thought, man's material well-being lost its importance. What mattered the temporary miseries of this life when man had a heavenly world to gain?

3

During most of his life Brownson's faith had been too vague and flabby to dictate a positive religion. But now, as the force and vividness of his belief in God was increasing, he began to think instinctively of the world in its relations with the supreme and efficacious being, its Maker. Yet, as he looked on the world, it gave him back no assurance of God's existence. To account for evil he had to assume original sin, a belief which expressed strikingly the disillusion with man he felt after 1840. As God became more concrete in his emotions, so too did his conviction that, in Newman's words, "*since* there is a God, the human race is implicated in some terrible aboriginal calamity. It is out of joint with the purposes of its creator." [34] Original sin car-

[34] J. H. Newman, *Apologia Pro Vita Sua*, 218.

ried with it the necessity of divine grace, which Brownson already was formulating obscurely in his version of Leroux's doctrine of communion. As the notions of sin, God, and grace commanded more intense assent, he needed a more and more specific theology to support them. The true religion, said Pascal, "must give us an explanation of our opposition to God and to our own good. It must teach us the remedies for these infirmities, and the means of obtaining these remedies." [35] In proportion to the strength and urgency of the belief, the explanation must be definite and detailed; and Brownson's faith grew so powerful that he finally rushed to the Christian epic of sin and redemption, deeply grounded in the experience of the ages and magnificently realized in Catholic theology.

But Brownson was far from rushing to the Catholic Church. Channing had instructed him that "The Mediatorial Life of Jesus" fell into the Universalist error of actually appropriating the life of Christ to all mankind. The error vanished as Brownson's idea of communion with God solidified from the notion of general inspiration by the example of "providential men" to the notion of actual inspiration by infused grace. With grace thus an experience and not a metaphor, he perceived that it must have a

[35] Pascal, *Pensées* (Everyman), 115.

channel, and this plainly must be "the Christian Church." But he did not commit himself to specifying which sect was truly Christian. He appreciated the formidable historical argument which pointed to the Catholic Church, but he inherited the typical New England prejudices against the "Scarlet Lady" and before 1843 never seriously considered turning to Catholicism. Vermont had preserved a dread of Popery from the days when the French Catholics in Quebec used to harry their borders. The Reformation, moreover, seemed to be unmistakable evidence of the breakdown of the Church; the Protestant nations were making all the great intellectual and social advances of the age, while Catholic countries were notoriously unprogressive; and Brownson's small acquaintance with Catholics and Catholic controversial literature had not encouraged him to inquire further into Catholic doctrine. He always treated the Church respectfully; but he looked on it as an institution which had served its purpose, or as a creed expressing a positive belief next to which the Protestant sects stood in gloomy negation, but never as a church still capable of playing a vital part in progress or salvation.

Yet circumstances led him to soften his sullen Yankee prejudices. His friend Doctor Charles Poyen, who initiated many New Englanders into the mysteries of animal magnetism, was an ex-Catholic regretting his abandonment of the faith. From him Brownson gained a more favorable impression of Catholicism than the shanty Irish in the slums of Boston had given him. His immersion in Saint-Simonian writings further familiarized him with the idea of hierarchy and thus helped remove the distrust of the papacy.[36] In 1841 he began to display a distinctly warmer attitude toward the Church. He looked back from the troubled days of the Tyler administration to the serene and constant faith of the Middle Ages and longed for the deep sense of social interdependence which would end the melancholy problems of misery and injustice. During the winter of 1842–1843 he condemned anti-Catholic feeling in a series of lectures on the Middle Ages and called for a new catholic church to interpret a universal faith for the modern world, as Rome had done for the Middle Ages. In January 1843 John Hughes, Bishop of New York, spoke on the need of living according to the Christian ethic instead of forgetting it in the worship of amoral laws of political economy. The lecturer made one member of the audience feel he was hearing Brownson;[37] and

[36] "The Convert," *Works*, V, 92, 98.
[37] John Hecker to Brownson, January 7, 1843, H. F. Brownson, *Early Life*, 503.

Brownson himself decided that Catholicism was perhaps not in its senility if a chief officer of the Church
could champion such vital ideas. About the same
time, one or two Catholic journals started to give
his articles approving mention. In the spring he had
a brief interview with Benedict J. Fenwick, the
Catholic Bishop of Boston. He now began to receive
anonymous letters abusing or congratulating him on
turning toward Catholicism.

He was still fascinated by the goal of reuniting
Christendom on a truly catholic basis; and he commenced to wrestle with the problem again in a
group of essays on "The Mission of Jesus" which
ran in a new weekly journal, the *Christian World.*
Without seeing clearly where he would land, Brownson intended to draw attention to the Church as the
medium through which the Son of God redeems
mankind. The first and second essays, as he later
said, pleased his Unitarian friends; the third drew
warm approval from a Puritan journal; the fourth
threw the American Tractarians into ecstasies, and
the *New York Churchman* announced that a new era
had dawned in the Puritan city of Boston; the fifth,
sixth and seventh attracted the notice of Catholic
journals; and the eighth the publisher of the *Christian World* refused to insert. Brownson found him-

self led by invincible logic to assert the Catholic Church as the living body of Christ.[38]

Yet he still drew back from the fatal step of conversion. The iron prejudices of forty years were not to snap so easily. Submission to Catholicism was unlike his earlier religious wanderings. Then he had merely moved from one room to another, but now he would have to live in a strange, new temple. His hesitations were clear enough to his acquaintances. In the spring of 1843 Theodore Parker commented to a friend that he did not know where Brownson stood, "as I have not heard from him for eight days, when he defined his position in public. He seems tending toward the Catholic Church. God bless him, wherever he is! He has a hard head." [39] Parker was right. Brownson had a hard head, and he now busied it in a desperate effort to be faithful to Catholic principles without joining the Catholic Church.

He first planned to preach Catholic doctrine and administer the sacraments. By proclaiming the Cath-

[38] "The Convert," *Works*, V, 155–156. "Instead then of looking for a church to come," as Brownson wrote Parke Godwin in the spring of 1843, "I accept the Church that is." Brownson to Godwin, May 9, 1843, Greeley-Godwin Papers.

[39] Parker to Miss C. W. Healey, April 4, 1843, John Weiss, *Life and Correspondence of Theodore Parker*, I, 353.

olic faith within the gates of Protestantism, he pointed out, he would better the possibility of a peaceable return of the rebellious sects to Catholicism. But, as Isaac Hecker remarked with a logical implacability that suggested his master,

If you grant that the Roman Catholic Church is the true Church, there is, to my thought, no stopping-place short of its bosom. Or even if it is nearest to the truth, you are under obligations to join it. How any one can believe in either one of those propositions, as O. A. B. does, without becoming a Catholic in fact, I cannot conceive. This special pleading of exceptions, the necessity of the case, and improbable suppositions, springs more, I think, from the position of the individual than from the importance or truth of the arguments made use of. Therefore I think he will give up in time the ground upon which he now supports his course — not the object but his position.[40]

Hecker's remarks were most shrewd. Brownson was sparring for time until his emotions could transform his belief in the Church from an idea into a fact. Then he would surrender these awkward compromises which his present inner perplexity made necessary. Young Hecker was a great comfort to the lonely Brownson in these anguished days. Brownson found little sympathy among his older friends, who associated Catholicism with censers and ornate masses and the scarlet whore of Rome or with

[40] Hecker to his mother, May 9, 1843, Elliott, op. cit., 66.

drunken Irishmen beating their wives and selling
their votes, or who aloofly observed that it had its
rôle in history, no doubt, but its time had passed
and it now was an anachronism. Hecker understood
Brownson's torment, though they approached religion somewhat differently. Hecker was not em-
barrassed by the sharp and subtle dictates of his soul,
while Brownson blunted his intuitions by generalizing them into a harsh and ponderous logic: yet the
interplay of the mystic and the casuist was invaluable
for both, and their tense discussions before Brownson's fireplace at Chelsea or in the parlor at Brook
Farm stimulated each in his quest for truth.

Brownson's inner objections to Catholicism quickly
presented themselves in reasonable guise; but the
reasons were not convincing enough to halt his driving honesty and merciless logic. He must go on; he
could not stop; he had to chew these problems till
they were ready for digestion. One after another, he
subdued his qualms. Finally one main intellectual
obstacle remained before him, and he spent much of
1844 in surmounting it. He had long been worried
by the problem of guaranteeing the reality of knowledge. Until he answered it, he could not be sure
that Catholicism would give him any more certainty than Transcendentalism. The discouraging
doctrines of Kant, who had argued away the pos-

sibility of reaching absolute truth, still stood between Brownson and his sanctuary. Kant, indeed, grew to be the great topic of conversation in the Brownson home. Even the children talked of the categories of judgment and the *Ding-an-sich*.[41] Brownson himself, after several months' study, worked out a long and involved criticism of Kant's theory of knowledge which, in sum, did little more than dismiss the argument by discovering some logical difficulty in his own statement of it. "To ask if the human mind be capable of science [knowledge of reality] is absurd; for we have only the human mind with which to answer the question. And it needs science," he would conclude neatly, "to answer this question."[42] He admitted Kant's proof that the *a priori* categories were necessary for knowledge; but from it he immediately inferred that the categories, as *a priori*, must be objective, and man must therefore depend on that which is not himself. Kant showed that the objective cannot be deduced from the subjective; but nowhere, Brownson declared, did Kant convincingly deny human ability to reach the objective, to apprehend reality. After all, as Brownson would have said, if pressed — and this

[41] H. F. Brownson, *Early Life*, 413.
[42] "Kant's Critic of Pure Reason," *BrQR*, I (1844), *Works*, I, 162.

conviction underlay all the elaborate detail of his reasoning — how can Kant gainsay the apprehension of reality when I apprehend it constantly as a condition of believing in God? Having thus exorcised the fearful ghost of German idealism, Brownson proceeded more tranquilly to rest on the certitudes of Catholic theology.

The revived *Review* recorded his strugglings toward salvation. Parker, hearing of it in Rome, remarked drily, "I suppose he will devote it to the overturn of the principles established in the first series" [43] — which was just enough — but Brownson was at the same time forging new ones that gave his strongest emotions deeper satisfaction. In January 1844 he eloquently called for the restoration of the Church of God. This summons provoked an excited letter from an anonymous Philadelphian who spluttered in a burst of italics that "the church of God *is* and *has been,* through eighteen centuries." Brownson commented on the letter in April, admitting that "there is still the one catholic apostolic communion, unbroken" and resorting to clumsy equivocation to explain his position outside it. In May he finally abandoned his Unitarian pulpit and called again on Bishop Fenwick. Early in June he tired of the fight and avowed his desire to join the

[43] Parker to Francis, March 18, 1844, Weiss, *op. cit.,* I, 229.

Church. "There is no use in resisting," he told young Hecker.[44]

Brownson's increasingly concrete religious vision was endowing the tortures of damnation with a terror they had never possessed when he regarded hell as a figure of speech. He and his friends had no lease on life. They might be called to their last account at any moment. "Dying where we were, could we hope to see God?"[45] Brownson put the question to Fenwick, who suavely refrained from committing himself on the destination of Brownson's friends but impressed on him the urgency of his own union with the Church if he wanted to be saved. Fenwick was wise in declining to win Brownson by softening dogma. On thinking it over, Brownson admired Fenwick's uncompromising stand, which had the relentless character of his own reasoning, and decided to make certain of his own salvation. As for his friends, the devil would have to take the hindmost: the logic of God, Brownson regretfully concluded, was inexorable.

He lost little time in making his position amply clear. In a brisk passage in the July *Review* he spurned his old religious liberalism:

[44] "Nature and Office of the Church," *BrQR*, I (April, 1844), *Works*, IV, 484–495; Brownson to Hecker, June 6, 1844, Elliott, *op. cit.*, 147.

[45] "Bishop Fenwick," *BrQR*, III (October, 1846), *Works*, XIV, 474.

We have rejected from the Gospel all that was foreign to it, all that ignorance, superstition, false learning, false philosophy and priestcraft have added to it; we have demolished hell; scouted the devil; laughed at the fall; reduced the son of God, first, to a promising Hebrew youth, who was a successful mesmeriser, and, finally, to a mythic personage, created by the creeds and fancies of men; we have, moreover, successively disrobed God himself of his justice, his truth, his sovereignty, his paternity, his providence, at last of his personality, and resolved him into a blind force, or a mere fate or irresistible necessity. And in all this we have been guilty of no heresy, . . . have been, in fact, good, true, faithful, enlightened, liberal Christians, the reformers of the church and the restorers of primitive Christianity![46]

And, in a wonderfully characteristic manner, he sternly confronted his friends with the vital question:

Do, then, take some position: either accept the Son of God, or reject him; either accept the church as it is, or reject it altogether. For if it has become corrupt, it is a false church, was always a false church, and always must be a false church; and if it be not corrupt, but the true church, then to refuse to accept it is to refuse to submit to God. . . . Our logic allows us no alternative between Catholicism and Come-outerism. But we have tried Come-outerism.[47]

[46] "Hildreth's Theory of Morals," *BrQR*, I (July, 1844), *Works*, XIV, 248.

[47] "Church Unity and Social Amelioration," *BrQR*, I (July, 1844), *Works*, IV, 520; "Sparks on Episcopacy," *BrQR*, I (July, 1844), *Works*, IV, 559.

For his instructor in the elements of faith Brownson gained John B. Fitzpatrick, the bishop's coadjutor. Hecker also put himself under instruction as soon as he knew of Brownson's intentions, and actually made a strenuous but vain effort to persuade Henry Thoreau to do the same. Under the clear sunlight of a New England autumn Brownson struggled through scholastic theology, smothering his instinctive dislike of his tutor in the desire for eternal bliss. By the middle of October he was ready to receive the sacraments. On the twentieth of the month he took the final step and became a Catholic.

"Faith is not of ourselves, it is the gift of God"; he later wrote, "and conversion is the work of grace, not of argument or logic." [48] Catholicism came to him as a fact, not as a conclusion. He might describe his conversion (and he frequently did) as the result of drawing out logically the two discordant principles that made up Protestantism: private judgment led him into unbelief, and recoiling from unbelief he followed faith in God into Catholicism. But his conversion came actually from no such deliberate choice of alternatives. It answered a compelling inner necessity.

When Brownson embraced Catholicism, he aban-

[48] "Catholic Popular Literature," *Works*, XIX, 586.

doned not reason, but the pride which exalted individual reason above the accumulated experience of mankind and raised private intuitions above the study of objective reality. He chose the wisdom of the ages as the guide to life in the place of his own unsteady desires, which had thus far always misled him. He believed profoundly in God, in morality and in logic; and he was passionately eager to combine the three in one final whole. If God were more than man's fancy, He must be absolute reality. If morality were more than local custom, it must have absolute rewards and penalties. If logic were more than human illusion, it must refer to absolute truth. Brownson's reason, his sense of good and evil, his faith in reality and in its ineffable Creator were superbly justified and consoled in Catholic theology. But theology, intellectual awareness of the truth, was not sufficient. Brownson desired to *live* the Christian life — to love God, obey the moral law and find the truth. He needed grace, and grace came alone through the Church, which was the authoritative expounder of God's word on earth, the only institution with an intrinsic relation to the truth. Catholicism absorbed Brownson's three convictions into a full and rigorous system, which satisfied alike his head and his heart.

Eight years before Brownson had proclaimed the *Church of the Future*. This church, he declared in

New Views, would arise inevitably out of the per-
fectibility of man; and it would unite the partial
truths of the existing churches by reconciling Catholicism and Protestantism, the spirit and the flesh.
He now realized that he had misunderstood man,
who was essentially imperfect, and misinterpreted
Catholicism, which actually unified spirit and flesh.
Grace alone could cause the perfection of man and
the establishment of the true church. Brownson had
sought the *Church of the Future* through weary years
of distress and disappointment. Then he looked
around him, and discovered it to be the great church
of the past.

CHAPTER VI

THE DELECTABLE MOUNTAINS,
1844–1860

Brownson entered a new world in joining the Church. As a Catholic he no longer consorted with Unitarians, any more than as a radical he would have fraternized with State Street bankers. His faith ruled him not simply on Sunday, but all the days of the week. Luckily for his domestic comfort, his wife and children accompanied him within the gates of Rome. Theirs was a somber household at best; and hesitation over this question would have made family relations insupportable. After nearly twenty years of married life Sally well knew the futility of opposing her stern and overbearing husband. She soon found deep consolation in her new faith, however, and never regretted her conversion. The children, save only Orestes, Jr., were too young to make their own decisions and obediently followed their parents. Young Orestes, who had gone to sea when his father was still nominally a Unitarian, returned, husky and tanned, in the spring of 1845 to find his family in the Church. He was not at first convinced that he should imitate his seven brothers and sisters, and finally quit the house on Mt. Bellingham to live with a maternal aunt in Ohio. At this safe distance he exchanged letters with his father over his religious doubts. Brownson's missionary efforts were complicated by frequent inability to read his son's writing; but eventually Orestes attended a Jesuit academy in Cincinnati and by the end of the year had restored family harmony by submitting himself to the Church.[1]

Brownson's own sister and brother proved much less amenable. Daphne, his twin sister, had married and moved to the Middle West. When her husband turned out to be thriftless and a drunkard she began to write pathetic letters to her brother, pouring out her troubles and begging for money to support her family. "I do not live as neare the commands of God as I wish [I] did . . . ," she scrawled in a note to Brownson in 1842. "I pray to god to give me more religion to prepare for evry event of life."[2] Daphne later became a Catholic — or so she told Orestes, perhaps the better to play on his sympathies — but her last letters make it clear that she did not remain one. Their brother Oran meanwhile

[1] H. F. Brownson, *Middle Life*, 157–166.
[2] Daphne A. Ludington to Brownson, February 28, 1842, Brownson Papers.

solved his difficulties in another way. While Orestes was groping toward Catholicism and Daphne languished in religious emptiness, Oran placidly became a Latter Day Saint. He turned to Mormonism, he later had the impertinence to tell Orestes, for exactly the same reasons that Orestes had turned to Catholicism.[3] The Brownson family evidently suffered to some degree from religious frustration. Their inherited faith did not suit them, and their will-to-believe was too strong for them to ignore religion altogether. It was precisely this frustration, repeated in ten thousand families, that goes far to explain the sudden appearance of so many new faiths in the America of the 1830's and '40's.[4]

But Catholicism cured frustration for Brownson. He was now a man of forty-one, his complexion ruddy, and his hair and beard streaked with gray. The gauntness of his youth was disappearing; al-

[3] Oran was most businesslike in discussing religious differences. "You inform me you and family are Catholic," he wrote Orestes. "The reason assigned I understand to be because no other church professed proper authority. I have changed my opinions for the same reason because I consider the proper authority rests among the Mormons." April 5, 1846, Brownson Papers.

[4] It is noteworthy that the Brownsons were born in Vermont and moved later to rural New York. The country districts of both states were characterized by religious instability. They produced the founders of Mormonism, Millerism, and spiritualism, as well as such men as Charles G. Finney, the great revivalist, and were notorious for the delight they took in all emotional and evangelical sects.

ready he was gathering flesh, and after a few years as a Catholic he weighed nearly two hundred and fifty pounds. His new creed he embraced with characteristic vigor and enthusiasm. Catholics used to meet at his home in Chelsea for long evenings of conversation and debate, which Brownson dominated with his massive frame and companionable roar; and on many cold days he was to be found at John Brown's apothecary shop on Washington Street in Boston where he argued against Protestantism with all comers. He began now to study Catholic theology, peering at the Latin texts through gold-bowed spectacles and immersing himself in scholastic philosophy. He wore a scapular while he worked, kept a crucifix and a statue of the Blessed Virgin on his desk and at sundown recited the Rosary. For a time, he attempted to practice pious meditation according to the rules of Saint Ignatius Loyola, but he had too much energy to be satisfied by contemplation. He even dabbled in asceticism. When Isaac Hecker returned from Europe a monk, he brought Brownson a belt of knotted cords as an aid to penance and promised him a hairshirt.[5] Hecker apparently forgot the promise, though not even a hairshirt could have kept Brownson long in abasement. Humility was the one Catholic virtue he found impossible to acquire.

[5] H. F. Brownson, *Middle Life*, 276–277.

Yet he tried desperately to be humble. "Our life begins with our birth into the Catholic Church," he declared, resolutely blotting out of the record all the words he had written before conversion except only his essays on Kant and some political articles. He wanted to do intellectual penance for a lifetime of inconsequence and sin, and there seemed no better way than to purge himself of his mistakes of the past. Later he was to decide that he had indulged in "an excess of self-abnegation." [6] He made it abundantly clear, however, that he was renouncing all old errors. In a series in the *Review* he bombarded Transcendentalism, laboriously translating it into scholastic terms and condemning it as a faith that exalted "the inferior soul," the seat of concupiscence. Parker became "a vain, conceited pedant and scoffer"; and Andrews Norton, Brownson confessed, was right after all when he labeled Transcendentalism "the latest form of infidelity." The attempt to satisfy spiritual wants with Transcendentalism, he asserted, was as vain as "to fill one's self with the east wind, or to warm one's freezing hands on a cold winter's night by holding them up to the moon." [7] He later revised this opinion and conceded that Emerson and Parker were glimpsing a

[6] *Works*, XX, 252.
[7] "Transcendentalism," *BrQR*, II–III (1845–1846), *Works*, VI, 1–113.

truth and a beauty above Protestantism; but they were in error, he proclaimed, in seeking truth in the sky when it was to be found in the Church.[8] In another article he disowned eclecticism, admitting a temporary infatuation but announcing that after consideration "we have found it utterly unsatisfactory, and utterly unable to solve a single important problem." [9]

His submission to the Church encouraged others, less bold, to follow his example. The Brook Farm arguments induced William J. Davis and George Leach, as well as Hecker and Sophia Ripley, to become Catholics; and he struggled hard to convert George Ripley. For a moment Ripley looked with favor on the Church, but Brownson was finally forced to consign him reluctantly to damnation.[10] On the whole, Brownson was too cold, and his arguments too intellectual, to make him a very successful missionary.

The public in general regarded his conversion with equanimity. He had cried "Wolf" too often for them to be shocked at his latest aberration. Victor Cousin in Paris, forgetting his French polite-

[8] "Questions of the Soul," *BrQR*, Third Series, III (April, 1855), *Works*, XIV, 541.

[9] "Jouffroy's Ethical System," *BrQR*, II (January, 1845), *Works*, XIV, 267.

[10] H. F. Brownson, *Middle Life*, 96.

ness, refused to answer Brownson's letters; [11] but
most of Brownson's friends shared James Freeman
Clarke's feeling that it was "hardly worthwhile to
exert our ingenuity in exposing the fallacy of arguments, which, judging by experience, Mr. Brownson would himself be ready to confute in the course
of a year or two. No man has ever equalled Mr.
Brownson in the ability with which he has refuted
his own arguments." [12] Theodore Parker similarly
refrained from downright controversy and expressed
his impatience more covertly, as in his sermon on
"Religious Rest" which held up to public gaze the
horror of

some man of unbalanced mind, intellectual always, but
spiritual never; heady, but not hearty; roving from Church
to Church; now Trinitarian, then unbeliever, then Universalist, Unitarian, Catholic — everything by turns but
nothing long; seeking rest by turning perpetually over and becoming at last a man having experienced many theologies
but never religion; not a Christian, but only a verbal index
of Christianity — a commonplace book of theology. [13]

Not everyone, however, was so resigned to Brownson's vagaries. Richard Hildreth, who was already

[11] "Victor Cousin and His Philosophy," *Catholic World* (June,
1867), *Works*, II, 327–328.

[12] "Orestes A. Brownson's Argument for the Roman Church,"
Christian Examiner, XLVIII, 228 (March, 1850).

[13] John Weiss, *Life and Correspondence of Theodore Parker*,
II, 28. Parker preached the sermon on April 2, 1848.

deeply grieved by Brownson's notice of his *Theory of Morals*, spoke his mind in a vigorous and caustic pamphlet:

A walking *variorum* edition of all sorts of opinions, — a fifth-rate declaimer, carried away, as such folk are apt to be, by a ludicrous passion for playing all sorts of parts, — comes stalking on the stage, in the character, for the time being, of an ecumenical council . . . and having cursed me with book and bell, in due form, delivered me over to hell-fire and the execration of all good Christians, crossed himself, sprinkled himself with holy water, and kissed the great toe of the holy Saint George who killed the dragon, which respectable and undoubted relic he always carries, with profound reverence, in his breeches-pocket, proceeds to set forth — not his own views, for he goes altogether by authority . . . .[14]

Hildreth continued that he did not exactly accept "that common opinion which regards Mr. Brownson, in his last somerset, as a mere purchased pimp of the scarlet strumpet of Rome," but instead advanced the theory that Brownson had finally discovered a position where

his love of paradox, of being the promulgator of heresies strange to the community, . . . of attacking existing institutions and prevalent opinions, is amply gratified; while, at the same time, he is sure of the support, moral and pecuniary,

[14] This is an interesting, if somewhat incoherent, venture in Menckenese a century before its master. *A Joint Letter to Orestes A. Brownson and the Editor of the North American Review*, 10.

of the greatest and richest sect in the world. . . . What, even, if the Church should have a Yankee Pope? Does not Orestes I. sound as high and as probable as Gregory VII. or Gregory XVI? [15]

Brownson answered this last charge, which others besides Hildreth flung at him, by quietly pointing out that he was married.

Indeed, far from looking to Rome for support, Brownson decided to give up his *Review* and study law, with an eye to a political career. His association with Coadjutor Fitzpatrick had made him feel keenly his incompetence to speak for the Church. This personage, whom Hecker called "the hierarchical exponent of all that was traditional and commonplace in Catholic public life," [16] was prejudiced against Brownson from his first suspicion of the motives which might lead so proud a man to seek admission to the Church. Brownson, for his part, was annoyed by the smugness of one so obviously his intellectual inferior. As his tutor, Fitzpatrick insisted that he embrace the traditional arguments for belief. When Brownson wanted to develop the reasoning which had actually cleared the way for his conversion, Fitzpatrick, who regarded novelty as evi-

[15] *Ibid.*, 25.
[16] Isaac T. Hecker, "Dr. Brownson and Bishop Fitzpatrick," *Catholic World*, XLV, 7 (April, 1887).

dence of sinful pride, chilled toward him. In the excitement of conversion Brownson was eager to make all sacrifices for the faith. Turning his back on his own thought, he adopted the vested theories, though, as he said years later, they could never have persuaded him of anything had he not already become a believer. This mysterious break between his old ideas and those he professed once within the Church nourished the misgivings of people who had wondered about his latest change of faith. "It would be impossible," Rufus Griswold commented, "to link his former opinions with his present ones, by any connexion, either logical or psychological." [17]

But Fitzpatrick was now convinced of Brownson's docility, and, giving him Billuart, Saint Thomas and Saint Augustine to read, directed him to think in the conventional formulas. He was displeased, however, at Brownson's proposal to abandon the *Review*, for the Church could not afford to lose so able a pen, and he advised him that he could atone for past evils only by laboring to spread the true faith under the coadjutor's supervision. This meant, in practice, the coadjutor's censorship of all theological articles. Seeing in Fitzpatrick's offer a way of safeguarding his writing against doctrinal error, Brownson gratefully made plans to continue his journal.

[17] Rufus Griswold, *The Prose Writers of America*, 423.

The *Review* had lost most of its Protestant subscribers when its editor turned Catholic.[18] The publicity following in the wake of conversion resulted in an increased circulation among Catholics; but even this fell off considerably at the end of 1845 and continued to decline for the next few years. The *Review* itself acquired a markedly new tone. Fitzpatrick urged Brownson to be bold and aggressive, and Brownson, of course, needed little urging. He had once written with the moderation of an earnest seeker after the truth and the open-mindedness of a man prepared to find it anywhere; but he wrote now as if he had the truth and was thus justified in abusing all those who differed with him. His essays rang with the conviction of intense belief and the confidence of intense certainty. Those who denied Catholicism he regarded as pitiable and dangerous: they must be made to see their sin and cry for salvation if they had to be threatened with all the tortures of hell itself. Bigotry, he wrote, is far better than tolerance: "Every Catholic, from the fact that he is a Catholic, has the world and the devil for his enemies." [19]

[18] In 1840 the *Boston Quarterly* had less than a thousand subscribers; in 1850 it had 1400. "The Distribution Bill," *BoQR*, V (January, 1842), *Works*, XV, 221; Sarah Brownson to Betsy ——, March 13, 1850, Brownson Papers.

[19] "Recent Publications," *BrQR*, New Series, I (April, 1847), *Works*, XIX, 178–179.

In these first years Brownson combatted the world and the devil in a series of essays directed against Anglicanism, no-churchism and Transcendentalism. He aimed to destroy all the strongholds between atheism and Catholicity where Protestants might seek shelter. His attacks, strong and often savage, soon provoked answers which were equally savage if generally less strong. He actually surpassed most of his opponents in controversy; but the debates were singularly futile, for in such disputation logic was the embroidery, not the substance. Brownson's dialectical ability no doubt delighted the Catholics who could follow him, but Protestants knew from the beginning that his conclusions were wrong and could afford to overlook his reasoning. His logic skipped only one fact — that America in the 1840's was not, in his sense, religious.

He pitched into these fruitless controversies because of his passion to put Protestantism, for once, on the defensive. This belligerence he carried from his writing into his living. It led to an open quarrel with George Ripley in the winter of 1847, which they later half-patched up out of the shreds of their old friendship; and it made him a figure of constant surprise and peril for strangers. Once when a man in Benjamin Greene's bookstore scolded him for turning Catholic, Brownson angrily caught the fellow by his coat collar and tried to throw him over the stovepipe. On another occasion, finding himself in Andover on a Friday morning and seeing only meat on the breakfast table, he roared at the landlord, "Why don't you have something in your house that a Christian can eat?" When the landlord indignantly pointed at the meat, Brownson interrupted him roughly, "Why don't you have fish? No Christian eats meat on Friday." [20]

2

He frequently avowed, however, that the *Review*'s primary purpose was not to convert Protestants but to elevate the standards of the Catholic community, to encourage "a firm and bold profession of their faith, and an independent and fearless, though quiet, assertion of their rights as Christians, as citizens, as men." [21] This eloquent proclamation of Catholic rights quickly brought him to the sympathetic attention of the British Catholics. "This man *astonishes* me," a fine old English Jesuit at Rome remarked in 1845; "he is clear and strong beyond compare." [22] Newman's conversion, just a

[20] H. F. Brownson, *Middle Life*, 635, 97–98.
[21] "The Christian Register's Objections," *BrQR*, New Series, VI (October, 1852), *Works*, VII, 233.
[22] J. G. Shaw to Brownson, October 14, 1845, Brownson Papers.

year after Brownson's, signalized the renaissance of English Catholicism, and his followers in the Oxford movement looked with special favor on what seemed corresponding progress in the American Church. In December 1845 the *Dublin Review* devoted an article to high praise of Brownson's *Review* as a means of advertising it in Great Britain.[23] In 1847 W. G. Ward wrote Brownson from St. Edmund's, the oldest Catholic college in England, "Your name is well known to the students, and they have lately ordered your Review to come regularly to them." [24] In 1853, indeed, interest in Brownson was great enough to compel an English edition of the *Review.*[25]

Yet, for all their superficial resemblance, the Oxford group and Brownson reached the Church by quite different paths. The American religious situation was too sharp in its oppositions, too confident in its antagonisms, to produce the tenuity of argument that accompanied the Oxford movement. There was no strong church, like the Anglican, to mediate between Protestantism and Catholicism. Under the

[23] *Dublin Review*, XIX, 390–400 (December, 1845).

[24] Ward to Brownson, April 7, 1847, H. F. Brownson, *Middle Life*, 41–53.

[25] This was not, as Brownson believed and others have claimed, the first American review to be republished in England; that distinction belongs to Walsh's *American Quarterly*. F. L. Mott, *A History of American Magazines, 1741–1850*, 688.

circumstances, men were for the Church or against it, and they spent little time quibbling about a *via media*. Brownson thus regarded the Tractarians as effeminate and overdelicate. He suspected their attitude toward faith; he disliked their belief that Catholicism was perfecting their Anglicanism, not displacing it; in short, what was subtle to Ward appeared disingenuous to Brownson.

He made his distaste for the school amply clear in a series of attacks on its most distinguished member. Before becoming a Catholic, Newman had written *An Essay on the Development of Christian Doctrine*, which he allowed to be published after his conversion. Brownson, with the convert's zeal in maintaining orthodoxy, believed the book to be heretical; and, obtaining the approval of Fitzpatrick (who became Bishop of Boston following Fenwick's death in 1846), he set about demolishing Newman's essay. The Church, Brownson declared, asserted that the original creed was complete, that new definitions represented not additions, but formulations occasioned by new errors: "The church has no natural history, for she is not in the order of nature, but of grace." Newman, on the other hand, had argued that there had been "a real progress of the church in her own apprehension and understanding of the sacred deposit of faith committed to her charge." [26] Eighteen months later, in another article, Brownson refined his indictment somewhat, conceding that Newman meant by doctrine not the revealed truth itself, but the idea taken of it by the mind; nevertheless he had named the formative power in development as human, not divine. [27]

W. G. Ward now rushed to Newman's defense in some unsigned articles in the *Dublin Review*. He also wrote Brownson a long and friendly letter, explaining that Newman's theory of development, created by the bitter necessity of reconciling the present body of doctrine with the doctrines of the fourth century, alone made it possible for him to become a Catholic. [28] But Brownson, having given up his private theory when he joined the Church, could not sympathize with Newman's predicament. For a true Catholic, he told Ward, the problem could not exist. The alleged discrepancy between the dogma of the fourth and the dogma of the nineteenth centuries was caused by looking at the Church from the vantage of private judgment, not of faith. The *Dublin Review* and Brownson's *Review* now resumed the

[26] "Newman's Development of Christian Doctrine," *BrQR*, III (July, 1846), *Works*, XIV, 25, 9.

[27] "Newman's Theory of Christian Doctrine," *BrQR*, New Series, I (January, 1847), *Works*, XIV, 28–74.

[28] Ward to Brownson, April 7, 1844, H. F. Brownson, *Middle Life*, 41–53.

debate, which soon trailed off into recriminations on the etiquette of controversy.[29]

Brownson was outraged at bottom by Newman's assumption that a differently constituted mind might perceive truth in a different form. This doctrine, Brownson thought, made objective certainty impossible, stripped knowledge of its guarantees and thus struck at the validity of religion. He set up his own belief in the clear and the broad: faith in religion meant to him the actual apprehension of external reality. The Oxford argument that faith comes from a sum of converging probabilities, he thought absurd. Lacking Newman's dialectical subtlety, he could not see how Newman made so many concessions to the relativistic view without conceding the foundations of belief. Yet, in *The Grammar of Assent*, Newman was to begin a study of belief on premises acceptable to an agnostic, and then rise to God and Catholic theology. To Brownson's cruder logic such a demonstration was incomprehensible; he could not, as he remarked, make head or tail of it.

[29] Richard Simpson, the distinguished English Catholic, made an observation on the debate which, apart from the somewhat deceptive analogy, seems fair enough. "I think posterity will judge of their quarrel as it has done of that between Plato and Aristotle; that the latter, though the most acute and most formally logical, has failed to see what the former intended, and has therefore misrepresented him." Simpson to Hecker, April 4, 1853, Brownson Papers.

The attack on Newman damaged the prestige of the *Review* by making it seem the organ of a philosophical school instead of Catholicism. As one Catholic journalist wrote Brownson, "I want to beg you to let alone that unfortunate topic, which has done you more hurt, and in more ways than you know of."[30] The American bishops, uneasy over the squabble between the two prize converts, did their best also to divert Brownson from the issue. For a few years he left "Developmentism" alone. Then in 1852 he lost his temper over a book by John Brande Morris, another Oxford convert. In a slashing criticism of Morris's theology he accused the Tractarians of intellectual dishonesty, and went on to castigate Newman for viewing questions narrowly instead of comprehensively.[31] Newman immediately complained in the *Dublin Tablet* that he had been subjected to a personal attack, and — worse! — by a layman. Brownson, in a dignified letter, replied that Newman seemed more disturbed over attacks on himself than on his doctrine and observed that the *Review* was published under episcopal supervision. He called again for a clear and unequivocal

[30] James Alphonsus McMaster to Brownson, January 1, 1848, H. F. Brownson, *Middle Life*, 73.

[31] "Morris on the Incarnation," *BrQR*, New Series, VI (July, 1852), *Works*, XIV, 168, 175.

statement of Newman's belief.[32] Cardinal Wiseman
meanwhile declared Newman's work to be entirely
in keeping with Catholic theology and deprecated
Brownson's criticism. Newman wrote him late in
1852, "I have not allowed Dr. Brownson's rudeness
to annoy me, yet it is a very great satisfaction and
comfort to receive such an assurance as you have
written to me." [33] In July of the next year, in consideration of Newman's conviction on the charge
of libel in the Achilli case, Brownson decided to forget Developmentism: "We do not feel that any
overture of peace is due from us; but we do feel
we have done all our duty, and are free to drop
the subject." [34]

3

After his conversion Brownson wrote fewer political articles than had been his wont, partly because he was absorbed in personal problems, partly
because as a Catholic he would have little influence,
but chiefly because he wanted to keep the Church

[32] Brownson to the editor of the *Dublin Tablet*, October 15,
1852, H. F. Brownson, *Middle Life*, 386–390.
[33] Newman to Wiseman, November 14, 1852, Wilfrid Ward,
The Life and Times of Cardinal Wiseman, II, 41.
[34] H. F. Brownson, *Middle Life*, 396.

free from the passions and conflicts of party politics. The radicalism of 1840 had wholly vanished. With his glowing belief that God was all-good and all-powerful, Brownson found it hard to escape the conclusion that things on earth were as He intended them. Hence he ended the alliance between Christianity and reform which a decade before he had struggled so hard to bring about. Conditions were intolerable certainly, but men could not devise a remedy: "Who of you can lift himself up by his own waist-bands? The thing is as impossible in morals as in mechanics." [35] Socialism, indeed, by locating the good on earth became in that very fact anti-Christian; for Christianity looked on this life purely as penance or probation.[36] He begged the reformers to cease their evil work:

You kill reason, you murder the soul, you assassinate conscience, you sap society, render order impossible, take from law its moral force, from our homes all sanctity, from our lives all security, and leave us a prey to all the low, base, beastly, cruel, violent, wild, and destructive propensities and passions of fallen nature. O, mock us not with the words Brotherhood, Fraternal Love, Universal Peace! [37]

[35] "Modern Idolatry," *BrQR*, II (July, 1845), *Works*, XIX, 112.
[36] "Schiller's Aesthetic Theory," *BrQR*, III (April, 1846), *Works*, XIX, 121, 122.
[37] "Channing on Social Reform," *BrQR*, New Series, III (1849), *Works*, X, 137–206.

As for poverty, Brownson did not believe it could be cured, "and moreover, we do not wish it to be cured, for we do not believe that poverty is an evil." [38] "This world is but an inn; we lodge in it but for a night, and what matters the inconvenience which we may be required to put up with? If we gain heaven it is nothing; and if we fail of heaven, the memory of it will be lost in the presence of an infinitely greater calamity." [39]

Such zealous devotion to religious principles rendered his social analysis increasingly hazy. Instead of tracing social evil to the irrepressible conflict of interests, he traced it to the passions of men, for he argued that interests could not be evil unless they expressed passions which were also evil. He was losing sight of the conviction he had once so vigorously expressed — that in collective action men tended to act on motives they would ignore or repudiate as individuals — and he was thereby divesting his social theory of its greatest promise of usefulness. The claim that politics was the expression of conflicting interests corresponded somewhat to the actual workings of politics; but his reachings into the morality of men were incapable of verification.

[38] Review of Lysander Spooner's *Poverty, Its Legal Causes and Legal Cure, BrQR,* III, 408 (July, 1846).
[39] "Sick Calls," *BrQR,* New Series, VI (January, 1852), *Works,* X, 595.

He now offered as the solution, not a method of harmonizing interests, but a hope that grace would assist man in the pursuit of good.

So we need not trouble ourselves with philosophical, political, social or economical problems as such. Let us once acquire the virtues indispensable to salvation, and these problems will solve themselves, or cease to need solution.[40]

In national politics Brownson had grown so attached to the old order that he was pressed to contribute to the *American Whig Review*; but even this leading conservative journal found one of his articles too rabidly antidemocratic. "I should not *dare*, coward that I am," the editor confessed to Brownson, "to publish it as it stands." [41] On the whole, however, Brownson was much less concerned with domestic affairs than he had been in the past. The events that arrested him most sharply were the bloody revolutions that convulsed Europe in 1848. Eight years before, he had recommended that Lamennais's works be kept on every table, along with the Bible and *Pilgrim's Progress*; [42] but now he powerfully opposed the Frenchman's efforts to

[40] "Saint-Bonnet on Social Restoration," *BrQR*, New Series, V (October, 1851), *Works*, XIV, 235.

[41] J. D. Whelpley to Brownson, March 5, April 16, June 27, October 30, 1849, H. F. Brownson, *Middle Life*, 199–206.

[42] *BoQR*, III, 126 (January, 1840).

sprinkle holy water on social revolution. The rebels, Brownson declared, are foes to Christianity. They shout liberty! liberty! while the only true liberty lies in obedience to God. "When I hear a man declaiming lustily for liberty, I suspect it is for liberty to pick my pocket, or cut my throat." [43] In 1852 he protested fiercely against the official welcome accorded Kossuth, the Hungarian revolutionist, and watched his triumphal progress through America with deep bitterness. By now Brownson was arguing that the revolutions of 1848 were the work of one vast satanic conspiracy, hatched by modern liberalism and aiming to destroy law, order and religion.

He carried over his disgust at European lawlessness into savage attacks on the American filibustering expeditions of the early fifties. Feeling a subtle commitment to Cuba because its rulers were Catholic, he acted on the request of the Spanish minister to denounce filibustering in articles later translated into Spanish.[44] On the same principle — for Brownson saw no difference between lawlessness and liberalism — he re-entered local politics in 1853 to save Massachusetts from the grievous danger of hav-

[43] "Conversations of an Old Man and His Young Friends," *BrQR*, New Series, IV (1850), *Works*, X, 281.
[44] A. Calderón de la Barca to Brownson, September 4, September 19, November 10, 1851, January 31, 1852, H. F. Brownson, *Middle Life*, 299–310.

ing its constitution amended. "Nothing can be more fatal to the public virtue and social well-being," he warned in somber tones, "than the continual change and alteration of the constitution of the state." [45]

4

He was returning to public activity; his religious excitement, which plainly he could not sustain forever, was dying down. Urgency of belief depended for him upon novelty of doctrine. Inevitably he became used to Catholicism, settled into it and stopped regarding its every tenet with intense and deliberate adoration. The harsh language of his first days after conversion was giving way to the more placid style of a man who was a Catholic without being acutely self-conscious about it. With religion thus become second nature, he was impelled in 1849 to make the *Review* less theological. If Catholic principles were ever to influence the nation, he decided, the great social questions must be discussed from a Catholic viewpoint. At the same time he launched into a cold and cutting review of the Catholic press which he assailed as bad-mannered and uncatholic. He had found it filled with the inevitable cliques and jealousies, log-rolling and back-slapping. Many

[45] Brownson to J. P. Healy, October 17, 1853, *ibid.*, 456.

journals resented Brownson and did their best by petty and underhand attacks to lessen his influence. By the middle of the year, indeed, the *Review* faced a financial crisis. The failure of his Philadelphia agent and the collapse of the *Catholic Observer*, a weekly he had underwritten, forced him to send up urgent signals of distress. Luckily, friends from Montreal and Quebec came to his relief; and the American bishops, assembling at Baltimore for a plenary council, gave Brownson a letter of encouragement. The *Review* quickly got back on its feet and by 1853 had a larger circulation than in 1845.

Since Fitzpatrick's authority extended only to theology, Brownson's renewed interest in social affairs meant, as he told a friend, that he was "writing from himself rather than according to order." [46] But, with self-confidence restored, he was in a mood to find all supervision galling — and Fitzpatrick's especially so. He had lost all hope of working with him. The bishop had several times deserted him after ordering or encouraging him to enter the line of fire, and had shown little disposition to defend him against unfair attacks. Even when a priest entered the lists and published *The Atheism of Brownson's Review*, a slanderous book attributing to Brownson heretical propositions culled from his re-

[46] Brownson to J. W. Cummings, June 23, 1849, *ibid.*, 195.

views of infidel authors, Fitzpatrick did nothing but tell Brownson frigidly that as a critic he must expect criticism. Yet Brownson did not see how to escape Fitzpatrick's heavy hand without an open break. This unhappy situation dragged on, Brownson reluctantly bringing him theological essays before each new issue, until 1854 when Fitzpatrick went to Europe. A substitute censor then began to examine the articles at Brownson's home in Chelsea. When Fitzpatrick returned, Brownson simply failed to submit articles to him and the censorship lapsed altogether. He thereby added further strain to an already tense relationship.

Meanwhile his passion to exalt Catholicism had risen to such a pitch that it was turning even Catholics against him. Beginning in January 1853, he developed in five successive numbers of the *Review* the doctrine that obedience to the State was justified only when it meant obedience to God. Hence, the State must have divine sanction for its authority, and in this sense, wrote Brownson, the Church is supreme. These things were not to be said to Irish Catholics. They regarded ultramontanism as a slur on the bishops of their native country who had to take oaths inconsistent with the doctrine.[47] When Bishops O'Connor of Pittsburgh and Purcell of

[47] *Ibid.*, 487–488.

Cincinnati heard Brownson's bold assertion of spiritual authority, they rushed to show him, with some harshness, the error of his ways. What Catholic would not follow such august examples? Minor journals, rejoicing at the chance to harass Brownson, began snapping at him. Writers who had suffered under the lash of his criticism gladly took up the cry. Fitzpatrick, after having assured Brownson of his support on this issue, now washed his hands of him. But Brownson, preserving admirable temper in the face of rising bitterness, offered to stop the *Review* if continuing it would divide the Church, and proclaimed his willingness to retract his ultramontanism should it fall under official ban.

In the meantime the Native American or Know-Nothing party was forcing its way into the scene. Alarmed by the increase of immigration, native-born Protestants had begun around 1850 to form secret societies to combat foreign influence. In the heat of rivalry for jobs and for political power, the instinctive Anglo-Saxon suspicion of Irishmen, Germans and papists was being forged into sharp animosity. The Know-Nothings attacked Catholics with particular venom. Americans had hated the Church long before they started to hate immigrants; the Irish invasion only gave ancient fears a new edge. In 1834 a brutal mob of nativists burned a convent in Charlestown; and in the next decade similar mobs rioted and looted in the Irish sections of Boston and Philadelphia. A multitude of tracts and pamphlets, describing Catholicism with great sensationalism and practically no accuracy, fanned the flames of dislike. Honest delusion was a chief agent in the movement's growing popularity. Samuel F. B. Morse, for example, artist, inventor of the telegraph and eminent reviler of the Church, was genuinely terrified by the horror he believed to lie behind gray monastery walls and in the dark recesses of city churches. *Six Months in a Convent, Confessions of a French Priest* and, above all, the *Awful Disclosures* of Maria Monk were the type of furtive, foul-tongued writing which verified all charges for those already certain of the Church's rottenness.

Since Catholicism grew as immigration increased, the dread of Catholics was quickly merged with the dread of all immigrants. In 1853 a papal nuncio came to America to settle a dispute between the Bishop of Buffalo and the trustees of the Church over the ownership of church property. Know-Nothings found in his visit terrifying proof of the Catholic contempt for civil government. They were stopping at nothing to prove that the Church stopped at nothing. Brownson's claims for the supremacy of the spiritual order were now twisted to mean that American Catholics owed unqualified obedience to the Pope. The country was flooded with quotations — true and fabricated — from the *Review*. The unexpected consequence of Brownson's ultramontanism made his position among Catholics more uncomfortable than ever. Inexpediency was added to doctrinal unsoundness on the list of his crimes.

The rise of the Know-Nothing party, however, threw him onto another tack. Most Catholics bitterly condemned the movement as a threat to the Church — as indeed it was — but they interlarded their condemnation with enough abuse of American institutions to give some color to the Know-Nothing accusations that the Church was unpatriotic. Too many Catholics assumed that Irish and Catholic were synonymous and looked on the American Church as a Celtic institution. But Brownson saw plainly that the Church would not grow until it became acclimated to America, and obviously it could not become American so long as it remained Irish. "The sentiment which underlies native Americanism," he wrote, "is as strong in the bosom of American Catholics as it is in the bosom of American Protestants." [48] He went on to urge Catholics to prove

[48] "The Native Americans," *BrQR*, Third Series, II (July, 1854), *Works*, XVIII, 286.

by their conduct that there was no incompatibility between honest Catholicism and honest Americanism. Moreover, he declared, Catholicism would lose little by stricter naturalization laws, for the tide of immigration was about to turn; fewer Catholics would enter the country, and a greater number of radical Germans and Hungarians. Brownson endorsed only the nativist sentiment, however. The party he vigorously repudiated, but because it was un-American, not because it was against the Church. He thus carried on a brave fight to demolish the popular belief that a true patriot must be an anti-Catholic.

But all his efforts succeeded only in bringing the Irish down on him, shouting their native cries and turning to a fight with characteristic gusto. Reading between the lines of his essays, they properly perceived a strong disgust for themselves.[49] "Since Mr. Brownson's conversion to the Catholic faith in 1844," an anonymous pamphleteer caustically observed, "he has been treated with remarkable forbearance by

[49] As early as 1849 Brownson remarked in a letter, "Nobody can deny that in external decorum and the ordinary moral and social virtues the Irish Catholics are the most deficient class of our community," and went on to warn against the tendency to "identify Catholicity with Irish hoodlumism, drunkenness, and poverty." Brownson to J. A. McMaster, March 14, 1849, Brownson Papers.

Catholic editors"; [50] and they briskly set out to remedy this distressing condition. In July and August 1854 he was censured in at least nine Catholic journals for insulting honest immigrants and kindling anti-Irish feeling. The censure was in most cases far from polite; but Brownson refrained from becoming personal or vituperative in the *Review*, trying vainly to conduct the controversy on a plane which preserved the decencies of intellectual combat. In private, however, he was less restrained. The Irish, he wrote to a friend, are "deficient in good sense, sound judgment and manly character. They lack honesty and truthfulness, and are unreliable." [51] The indictment was comprehensive enough, but somewhat pointless. The Irish were in the saddle, and they continued earnestly and joyously to belabor him. The uproar finally became so great that Brownson was asked by the Archbishop of Baltimore to remove the Bishops' letter of 1849 from the back cover of the *Review*, where he had proudly placed it.

He was caught between two fires. As he remarked, he was trying to defend against Americans his right to be a Catholic and against Catholics his right to be

[50] *Brownson's Review Reviewed*, iv.
[51] H. F. Brownson, *Latter Life*, 7.

an American. The outcome was not happy. "I own I have lost some of my first fervor with regard to a portion of the American Catholic body," he wrote dolefully to a friend.

They have so misrepresented and denounced me, and are so ready to seize every opportunity to blacken my character, that I do not feel that lively confidence in them that I did. . . . [But] I love the church more and more every day.[52]

His troubles had one unexpected reverberation. In 1853 Newman became Rector of the proposed Catholic University of Ireland. Anxious to make Dublin the center of Catholic learning, he decided to overlook his recent feud with Brownson and invited him to deliver some lectures in 1854–1855. "You are the first person to whom I have applied," Newman told him.[53] But, of all subjects, Newman had suggested geography, and Brownson, not liking it, demurred. Sir John (later Lord) Acton now appealed to Brownson, urging him to ignore the title of the course and lecture on what he pleased:

The vast field of philosophy will be yours . . . and I thank God for the good fortune of my countrymen in being initiated in that magnificent science by you of all men liv-

[52] Brownson to F. X. Weninger, September 5, 1854, H. F. Brownson, *Middle Life*, 579–580.

[53] Newman to Brownson, December 15, 1853, *ibid.*, 471.

ing. . . . You alone can prepare us for the great controversies by founding among us a school and arming it with the principles of a sound philosophy. . . . In choosing History for my occupation through life I am actuated by a hope of following your example in another field.[54]

Newman later suggested a more agreeable subject and Brownson accepted. But then the thunder against Brownson which was breaking so loudly in America began to sound dimly across the ocean. Dublin was not much more enthusiastic about Brownson than Carthage had been about Cato. Newman found strong opposition to him — opposition in "quarters to which I cannot but listen" — and had to request an indefinite postponement of the engagement.[55] Brownson, replying that "the storm which recently broke out here, is only the expression of long pent-up feelings," saved Newman embarrassment by withdrawing altogether.[56] In a notice of Newman's *Loss and Gain* in the next *Review* he took occasion to retract most of his unkind remarks about the Oxford movement and to praise Newman: the treaty of peace was signed. But Newman did not forget Brownson's criticism so easily, and as late as 1857 told a friend, "I am opposed to laymen writing theology,

[54] Acton to Brownson, May 13, 1854, *ibid.*, 472, 474.
[55] Newman to Brownson, August 23, 1854, *ibid.*, 481–482.
[56] Brownson to Newman, September 12, 1854, *ibid.*, 483.

on the same principle that I am against amateur doctors. . . . For this reason I am disgusted with Brownson." [57]

5

The storm of Irish protest, following on his uncomfortable relations with Bishop Fitzpatrick, made Brownson increasingly lonely and discontented in Boston. There were more reasons for unhappiness. No longer could he stroll through Boston streets and linger freely with the people whose company he had once loved. He was a stranger to Emerson and Concord. Theodore Parker was attacking him from his pulpit. He had even quarreled with Ripley. The new friends that Catholicism gave him could not replace these old ones. But near by in New York was Isaac Hecker, and, with him, a group of lively and earnest men who wanted to make the American Church a church militant and saw in the battle-scarred Brownson their leader. Archbishop Hughes, moreover, as early as 1849 had urged him to move to New York; and in 1855 he remarked significantly to Hecker that he would like to have Brownson in his diocese. Boston was dark and cold. In New York there was friendship and apprecia-

[57] Newman to J. M. Capes, January 19, 1857, Abbot Gasquet, *Lord Acton and His Circle*, xxiv.

tion and opportunity. He hesitated for a few months, then made up his mind. In the fiery New England fall he took his family and his *Review* to New York.

The removal was, in a sense, much like stepping from darkness into daylight. Boston seemed tight and suspicious; New York, open and tolerant. Brownson was now at liberty to make his theology something more than paraphrases of the Fathers. He could freely advance his old political doctrines. He was near friends on whom he could rely, and he lived no longer under a bishop who appeared eager, whenever possible, to forsake him.[58] In short, he was ready to resume his old intellectual paths; and in his mood of independence he was peculiarly receptive to the appeals of Isaac Hecker and his friends. Hecker was one of many Catholics in America and Europe deeply disturbed by the widening rift between the Church and the world. If the Church were to prosper and gain converts, he argued, it must adapt itself to the spirit of the age; in America, for example, it must put forward the doctrines most likely to attract Americans. Gioberti, Brownson's current philosophical master, strongly advocated a

[58] As Brownson observed to Montalembert, "I think I shall be here more free to advocate our old constitutional doctrines, and I am nearer the friends on whom I have chiefly to rely." Brownson to Montalembert, December 25, 1855, H. F. Brownson, *Latter Life*, 31.

similar policy in his *Del Primato Morale e Civile degli Italiani* and was perhaps even more persuasive. Brownson was further moved toward liberalism by his increasingly warm friendship with the French liberal, the Comte de Montalembert.

The change in the social balance of power in Europe was probably most influential of all in overcoming Brownson's sturdy dislike of liberals and Protestants. In 1848 men marching under the flaming banners of liberty had threatened society. It was then time to insist on authority. But the revolutions were crushed, and society was restored to even keel; soon perhaps it listed too much in the other direction. The *coup d'état* of Louis Napoleon augured for Brownson the rise of despotism. The *Review*, he declared, must now champion liberty. The Catholic Church, which alone held the balance between liberty and authority, must throw its weight on the side where the need was greater. "All attempts," he wrote,

whether by ministers of religion or by ministers of state, to re-establish social peace on the basis of political absolutism, can end only in grave injury both to religion and society. The passion for change has become too strong to be resisted. . . . [Merely that something is does not prove it should be.] [59]

[59] "Separation of Church and State," *BrQR*, Third New York Series, II (January, 1861), *Works*, XII, 409.

This was dangerous doctrine. It denied the Church the rigidity and cold conservatism which too many Catholics mistook for the timelessness and immutability of the City of God. They felt that the Church could not readjust itself to the spirit of the age without fatal concessions, and feared liberalism because they confounded it (not inaccurately) with anticlericalism. Brownson's church, though founded on a rock, seemed to sway in the wind. When he tried to align it with the forces of progress, his coreligionists first warned him of the tragic fate of Lamennais and then whispered among themselves that he was preparing to somersault back into Protestantism. The charge was even circulated that he publicly ate meat on Fridays.[60] But Brownson, undaunted, continued on his course. In 1860 he openly declared that Catholic philosophy must be reconstructed to fit the intellectual needs of the day; and soon he was to emancipate philosophy once more from theology. A Universalist minister who still cherished *New Views of Christianity, Society and the Church* was reminded of his ideas of a quarter of a century before.[61] Even Brownson saw the similarity.

[60] A. Hechinger to H. F. Brownson, December 22, 1890, Brownson Papers.

[61] George Severance to Brownson, March 22, 1862, Brownson Papers.

In 1838 . . . we wrote and can repeat now [he said in 1862]: "But if the church, both here and in Europe, does not desert the cause of absolutism, and make common cause with the people, its doom is sealed." [62]

His social thought, however, reminded no one of "The Laboring Classes." Theodore Parker, indeed, deemed him in 1859 "perhaps the ablest writer in America against the Rights of man and the Welfare of his race." [63] But within the Church Brownson's liberalism excited considerable concern. Archbishop Hughes, a determined and somewhat wilful man, deeply devoted to the Church and to himself, did not rest easily with so independent a figure as Brownson loose in his diocese.[64] In 1856 Brownson gave the commencement address at St. John's College. Hughes, who strongly opposed Brownson's national-ist sentiments, used his position as last speaker to make an oblique attack on them.[65] This incident was

[62] "Lacordaire and Catholic Progress," *BrQR*, Third New York Series, III (July, 1862), *Works*, XX, 255.

[63] Parker, *Theodore Parker's Experience as a Minister*, 58.

[64] Brownson later claimed that Hughes once said to him, "I will suffer no man in my diocese that I cannot control. I will either put him down or he shall put me down." "Archbishop Hughes," *BrQR*, Last Series, II (January, 1874), *Works*, XIV, 492.

[65] Brownson, in a letter to Hughes dated September 1, 1856 (evidently a first draft), said with embittered dignity, "There was no equality in the case. It was crushing me with the weight of authority in a matter of simple opinion." H. F. Brownson, *Latter Life*, 73.

the signal for a revival of the vindictive criticism that Brownson had suffered two years before. The Archbishop quickly professed to be well-disposed toward Brownson, but he soon censured the *Review* for its militant tone and advised its editor to cease agitating the question of Americanizing the Catholic Church.

Two such vigorous and unruly individuals could not remain long at peace. In 1857 Brownson sought to protect himself by moving out of the diocese to Elizabeth, New Jersey. Two years later the *Review* ran several articles criticizing parochial schools, especially for the encouragement they gave immigrants to maintain their national customs, and urging Catholics to patronize public schools when they were manifestly superior. These articles gave considerable offense. In 1860 Hughes's organ, the *Metropolitan Record*, serialized a novel called *Mary Lee, or the Yankee in Ireland*. Prominent among its characters was a journalist named Dr. Horseman, a spectacled, dogmatic, tobacco-chewing, harsh-voiced Yankee, profoundly contemptuous of the Irish. New York Catholics rejoiced in the portrait, and Brownson accepted it gracefully, even regretting that the author — a Catholic novelist whom Brownson had chastised — saw fit to modify the caricature when the novel came out in book form. Yet, shortly after, the *Review* carried an article on the "Rights of the Temporal" arguing forcibly, if abstractly, that the opinions of a spiritual officer did not necessarily have spiritual sanction. "There were strong reasons for maintaining this," Brownson wrote to the Bishop of Natchez, "reasons which, could you know the real state of things in the Diocese of New York, you would not treat as trivial." [66] But the quarrel with Hughes was shortly overwhelmed by a much more serious calamity, the Civil War, though that event gave them after a time new questions to squabble over.

Brownson did not openly return to liberalism, however. Remaining deeply hostile to reformers, he gradually worked out a theory which explained both the apparent excellence and the actual evil of their intentions, and he dramatized it in a novel of 1854 called *The Spirit-Rapper: an Autobiography*. The hero of this fantastic fiction was a young man of strange abilities whom Brownson imagined as creating the current excitement over spiritualism, first by sending spirits to some neighbors (two sisters named Fox) and then by working through professional mediums like Andrew Jackson Davis. He next sought to use his power as an instrument for reform.

[66] Brownson to W. H. Elder, December 26, 1860, H. F. Brownson, *Latter Life*, 226.

"World reform, as I had sketched it to myself," mused the Spirit-Rapper in his days of repentance,

had for its object unbounded liberty, and was to be accomplished, on the one hand, by the overthrow of all existing governments, and the complete disruption of all political and civil society; and on the other, by the total demolition of the Christian Church, and extirpation of the Christian religion. . . . Without Weishaupt, Mesmer, Saint-Martin, Cagliostro, you can never explain the revolution of 1789, and without me and my accomplices you can just as little explain those of 1848.[67]

Eventually Brownson's hero grew convinced that such spiritualist phenomena as the rise of liberalism could be explained only by satanic intervention, and under the pressure of impending death he became a Catholic.

The Spirit-Rapper was a work of few merits, though it had the scandalous interest always attached to a *roman à clef*. The Fox Sisters, Joe Smith and Brownson's old friend Dr. Poyen appeared under their real names, while Fanny Wright, Emerson, Alcott, Garrison, Parker, Charles Newcomb, Mazzini, Fourier, Cabet and Proudhon entered in perfunctory disguises, and such symbolic figures as "Increase Mather Cotton" and "Thomas Jefferson Andrew Jackson Hobbs" spoke their pieces. It was an

[67] "The Spirit-Rapper," *Works*, IX, 101, 97.

overlong and oddly tedious tale, good-natured, but having throughout the air of a bad joke: the writing was never consistently flip enough to make it seem a comic allegory, and the humor was inappropriate if the reader was to presume that Brownson really believed his theory of diabolism. Yet in 1869 he set forth the theory again, more soberly argued, but still tracing spiritualism to Satan and now naming Mormonism and feminism as its two leading manifestations.[68] Plainly, he could not ally himself with liberalism if the movement had so questionable an origin. He was thus compelled to shout his admiration for progress only to the Catholic community, which had largely been immunized against him. Once again Brownson was crying in the wilderness. This time he could not even hope for a new Messiah.

6

By moving to New York, Brownson had escaped Fitzpatrick, but his thought was never to escape the consequences of Fitzpatrick's supervision. He had spent five years of his life in exhausting discussions of ultimate questions in terms which were not his

[68] "Spiritism and Spiritists," *Catholic World* (June, 1869), *Works*, IX, 332–351.

own and which he never could assimilate. He had given of his vital heat and energy to develop doctrines of whose value he was never genuinely convinced. Necessarily, his own thought was stunted, his intellectual growth fatally interrupted. As Hecker said, he was switched off the main line of his career.[69] When he returned to it, he was inevitably to travel much more slowly.

Fitzpatrick had removed Catholic truth from Brownson's intimate grasp by forcing him to hold it in its scholastic form. Eventually when Brownson's faith pierced through the formulas which left him so unsatisfied, it discovered an intrinsic relation with the ideas that had led him to the Church. Catholicism finally became a personal conviction. As he wrote later, "We attained to that intellectual freedom which we had from the first asserted the church allows, demands and secures. We thus recovered the broken link of our life, reunited our present life with our life prior to our conversion, and resumed, so to speak, our personal identity."[70]

He began tentatively to reassert his personal iden-

[69] Isaac T. Hecker, "Dr. Brownson and Bishop Fitzpatrick," *Catholic World*, XLV, 6 (April, 1887). Brownson himself had once written, "The oracle within will not utter his responses, when it depends on the good will of another whether they shall to the public ear or not." *BoQR*, I, 3 (January, 1838).

[70] "Lacordaire and Catholic Progress," *BrQR*, Third New York Series, III (July, 1862), *Works*, XX, 253.

tity in 1849, the same year that social questions returned to the *Review*. His ambition was to construct a Catholic philosophy whose formulations would not seem as archaic and irrelevant as those of St. Thomas and Duns Scotus. The intellectual pressure of the day centered on the problems of cognition inherited from Kant, and the first step for the Catholic philosopher was to prove that God existed out of something more conclusive than moral necessity. Brownson, in his blunt way, could not understand what faith meant if not the sharp and convulsing impact of absolute reality on man. "With Protestants," he wrote,

religion has only a psychological basis, is purely a matter of private experience . . . [But] religion has an objective validity, an objective evidence, independent of your experience or mine.[71]

How to establish this objective evidence? He decided first that exclusive concern with psychology or with ontologism — with knowledge by introspection or knowledge by contemplation of external reality — was dangerous, for one led to egoism by making man the source of knowledge, and the other to pantheism by implying that God is everything.

[71] "Capes's Four Years' Experience," *BrQR*, Third Series, I (July, 1853), *Works*, XX, 1.

Since thought cannot pass from the subjective to the objective, he concluded that both must contribute fundamentally to the operation of thinking. In the Aristotelian doctrine of communion, which Leroux had suggested to him, with its demonstration of the reciprocal dependence of subject and object, he saw the basis for a theory of knowledge. As stated by Leroux, however, the doctrine lent itself much more easily to pantheism than to Christianity. Brownson in 1849 began to read Gioberti, the Italian philosopher, and suddenly came to the formula he was seeking: *Ens creat existentias* — being creates existences. This, he proclaimed, is the primitive intuition preceding all knowledge and rendering it possible. The object of knowledge must combine perceptibility (the attribute of existence) and reality (the attribute of being); and, since contingent being cannot be inferred from necessary being, it must also include the idea of creation. Man, then, in the act of thought, perceives directly that nature exists, that it has been created and that there is a creator. Brownson thus solved the epistemological problem by heaping all the conditions of knowledge together into one inclusive formula. Now he could dismiss the Kantian criticism as verbal sleight-of-hand which deprived man of reality while affirming it in the very act. Gioberti had laid the ghost of epistemology.

Brownson was no longer to be fooled into fighting shadows.

But his savior had meanwhile become a thoroughly suspicious character. Gioberti's hatred of the Jesuits, his argument that the Pope must lose temporal power before he could recover spiritual supremacy, and the strongly pantheistic leaning of his philosophy were bringing him into disrepute. He used *ens creat existentias* as his keystone for ontologism, and ontologism was regarded with great mistrust by the conservatives. The ontologists maintained that all knowledge presupposed the intuition of God. The conservatives, on the other hand, believing that man ordinarily had no consciousness of God, even by reflection, denied that he could have such intuition without perceiving God in His very essence and securing the supreme spiritual satisfaction. They condemned as arbitrary and frivolous the ontologists' distinction between perceiving God in His essence and perceiving the divine ideas or the existence of God, and concluded that God could not be known by intuition unless He were confused with His creatures, which would be pantheism and heresy. In 1861 seven propositions concerning the intuition of God by man were censured by the Holy Office, and in the next year fifteen similar propositions fell under official ban.

Gioberti's disgrace became a club which Brownson's enemies in the Church used energetically against him. After all, had not Brownson proclaimed that in philosophic genius, intellectual strength, in wonderful mastery of language, Gioberti yielded nothing to Plato, "while in grasp of thought, in natural grandeur, in science, erudition, intuition, he surpasses him, and has been able to correct and complete his philosophy"? [72] Yet Brownson steadfastly insisted that he was not an ontologist. Ontologism was infinitely attractive to him as one epistemological position that clearly escaped the criticism of Kant, but he sought not to adopt it, only to make enough concessions to share its immunity without falling into its error. His foes, however, denied the possibility of compromise with ontologism. When he declared that man had an intuition of God, they pronounced it heresy without pausing to discover that he was not talking about inborn perception of God, but about the conditions necessary for knowledge. It struck him as psychologically absurd to believe that human reason could reach God without some previous suspicion of His existence and without some assurance that its conclusions were true. The primitive intuition — and by intuition he meant

[72] "The Giobertian Philosophy," *BrQR*, National Series, I (1864), *Works*, II, 221.

the irresistible presentation of an object to the mind, not the active grasping of it — alone explained how man could arrive at God and certainty. The mistake of his critics, he wrote, lay in confounding cognition with intuition. Cognition was the human act of knowing, and cognition of God he did not claim; but intuition came from the divine act, the act of God in affirming Himself by creating the human intellect, and Brownson could not see how knowledge was possible without it.[73] Moreover, he never asserted the intuition of *Deus*, only of *ens;* it took logic or revelation to ascertain that they were the same. But his defense was unconvincing, if it was ever closely examined, and his reputation as an ontologist still survives.[74]

Yet for all the uproar he clung to *ens creat existentias*. The denial of *creat* seemed to him the fatal trap which had thus far betrayed Christian philosophers. Aristotle premised that matter was eternal, but Christianity said that it was created: Aristotelian

[73] He sometimes used the terms "empirical intuition" and "ideal intuition" for cognition and intuition. This shifting in phraseology made it more difficult for his opponents to understand him.

[74] There is still fighting over his body, however, and people are making valiant efforts to show that he was really on the side of the angels. A recent attempt to justify Brownson and absolve him from charges of ontologism is Sidney A. Raemers's *America's Foremost Philosopher*.

logic, therefore, by omitting the creative act, had interposed an order of arbitrary conceptions between man and reality. Since the conventional logic did not correspond with the structure of being, all attempts to frame a true Christian philosophy had foundered. The schoolmen, for example, drew from Aristotle the distinction between limited and unlimited being, and talked of this as the difference between man and God, whereas the true distinction was between creature and creator.

The spirit-matter dualism was the most recent consequence of this disharmony between Christianity and the Western philosophical tradition. Brownson traced it back to Abelard, whose conceptualist philosophy turned contemplation away from eternal verities to men's own minds; but the chief villain in his account was Descartes "who converted philosophy from a science of principles into a science of method, from the science of human and divine things in the natural and intelligible order, into the science of knowing." [75] By following Descartes's false lead modern philosophers had frittered away their energy in investigating concepts instead of things. Hume and Kant created problems of cognition which never should have been raised; and Reid,

[75] "The Problem of Causality," *BrQR*, Third Series, III (October, 1855), *Works*, I, 404.

Hamilton, Cousin and Rosmini were wasting themselves in hunting answers for nonexistent questions. Philosophy was drowning in subjectivity.

The great need plainly was for the true logic
which would enable man to deal, not with phantasms
of his own creation, but with concrete reality. Vermont had given Brownson a faith in syllogistic reasoning that sprang directly from old-line Calvinism.
He felt that he had stumbled into past errors
through the abuse rather than the use of logic; and
he feared the unutterable desolation of man in an
irrational cosmos. The universe, he decided, was
constructed according to "the logic of the creator,
and a perfect system of logic would be a key to
all its mysteries." [76] But above all the puny efforts
of man stood the necessity of grace, without which
the finest intellect was as the chaff before the storm
in trying to understand the glory of God. Natural
reason did not penetrate into the supernatural order; and only in the supernatural order were the
central questions of philosophy adequately answered. At bottom, Brownson believed, faith alone
could produce the true Christian philosophy.

While his metaphysics were undergoing this final
systematization, his critical principles insensibly fell

[76] "Schmucker's Psychology," Democratic Review, XI (October,
1842), Works, I, 42.

into a kind of order. Brownson had many limitations as a critic. He was too stern a moralist to delight genuinely in art. His sensitivity to ugly ideas was much greater than his sensitivity to ugly language.

> We cannot understand literature for its own sake [he wrote], or say much of the form of a literary work without reference to its contents. . . . We can appreciate the principles of art; we can even admire a work of art, whether a poem, a symphony, a picture, a statue, a temple, or an oration; but we could never describe a work of art, or even our raptures on beholding it.[77]

Yet his position in the Catholic community made his criticism important. He became known as "the Reviewer," and Catholic authors awaited nervously the quarterly book columns of the *Review* in which he labored hard to raise the standard of Catholic writing. For all this concern, however, his approach to criticism was distinctly offhand. He considered works of art out of the corner of his eye and always in the light of more burning questions.

He had early determined that a great national literature could arise only when all America was animated by a live and stirring faith. In 1838 he had written that the path to literary glory lay in engaging "heart and soul in the great American

[77] "The Works of Daniel Webster," *BrQR*, New Series, VI (July, 1852), *Works*, XIX, 363.

work" — in spreading the vital belief in democracy.[78] Later, as a radical, he declared that a great national literature would emerge from the passions of the class struggle. After his conversion, he concluded that the Catholic faith alone could inspire true American art. Always he was insisting on art as a means, not an end, a vehicle of faith, formed and colored by the driving belief behind it, not an arrangement of lovely words. It was, in his final decision, the expression of the objective idea of beauty which exists in God and is perceived by the soul. Since only a Catholic could truly apprehend the beautiful, only a Catholic could create beauty. "Our theology determines our ethics, and our ethics determines our aesthetics." [79]

For all his confidence in Catholic faith, Brownson failed to rouse much enthusiasm over Catholic works. He could not stomach the conventional religious tales — "wretchedly dull as novels, and miserably defective as moral essays, or theological treatises." [80] The Catholic novel, he urged, should be Catholic in tone and atmosphere, not in set arguments and contrived endings. Too many breathed an unmis-

[78] "American Literature," *BoQR*, II, 25 (January, 1839).
[79] "Dana's Poems and Prose Writings," *BrQR*, New Series, IV (October, 1850), *Works*, XIX, 318.
[80] "Religious Novels," *BrQR*, New Series, I (January, 1847), *Works*, XIX, 146.

takably heretic air, apart from gestures to the faith, and amounted to little more than sentimental Protestant novels in new trappings. He saw clearly what this situation portended. American Catholics were exposed in everything but their religious services to Protestant attitudes and assumptions. Imperceptibly they were losing all signs of Catholicism save the creed and ritual, and soon they would be as Protestants in all but name. To escape this fate, Brownson warned his coreligionists, you must read and write and think and act as Catholics, not simply sprinkle yourselves with holy water on Sundays. For twenty years he followed this program in his literary criticism, laboring to eradicate all heathen tendencies and aiming particularly at the Protestant virtue of love. But the nineteenth century had securely established love on a pedestal; and all Brownson's efforts failed to dislodge it, though they made bitter enemies of Catholic authors who fell under the wheels of his powerful rhetoric.

His treatment of Protestant writers varied according to the pressure of his own faith. For a few years he denounced them all as if by reflex action and blamed original sin when he found any charm in them. As his intensity lessened, however, the problem of form and content became for him an aspect of the general problem of nature and grace.

Nature was good in its own order; hence a Protestant might write a laudable book — imperfect,
perhaps, but not necessarily sinful. In this more
mature approach his comments had a discernment
and merit they had previously lacked. He remarked
that *The Scarlet Letter* was a glorification of sin
and should never have been published; but he called
it a work of genius, if of genius perverted, and two
years later commended *The Blithedale Romance*
as being as good a novel as one could expect from
a non-Catholic. Emerson seemed to him incom-
parably the greatest American writer, though his
poetry was intolerably gloomy and desolate, "hymns
to the devil. Not God, but Satan do they praise." [81]
Emerson, Brownson felt, would attain his true stature
only if he joined the Church. Through the years
he addressed recurrent appeals to his old friend
to have done with vain philosophizing and prostrate
himself before God.

As time passed, Brownson's literary tastes fell
behind the new fashions. He still called for an
American literature, but when it came he rejected
it as coarse. "Those of our writers who are free,
racy, original, as some of them are, lack culture,

[81] "R. W. Emerson's Poems," *BrQR*, New Series, I (April,
1847), *Works*, XIX, 201–202.

polish, are rude and extravagant." [82] He was disgusted by the new realism. The *Police Gazette*, he said, reported actual crimes, but its actuality did not make it proper reading. And he tended always to weigh literature in the scales of faith. Unhappily, the American Catholics — who might have profited by his conclusions — were very early so deafened, or frightened, by his roar that they closed their ears against him. Brownson argued to the end, but in weary futility.

[82] "Literature, Love and Marriage," *BrQR*, National Series (July, 1864), *Works*, XIX, 495.

CHAPTER VII

JOURNEY'S END, 1860–1876

As the years went by, the nation's attention fastened with growing intensity on a single object — slavery. The issue between North and South sharpened more and more until to many it took the shape of a sword. Brownson had never shared the enthusiasm of the Boston intellectuals for the antislavery cause. On one Sunday evening in Boston he brusquely told a company of abolitionists that, if they were all imps from hell perambulating the country, they could not be more mischievous. As early as 1838, he pronounced against them for propagating methods which flouted law and thereby gave lawlessness the sanction of virtue.

After turning Catholic he grew tolerant even of slavery. Leroux gave him a new theory of property: if property were man's method of communion with nature, it was a reflection of his being, and its rights thus took precedence over law and could not be qualified by legislation. The Catholic notion of a functional society, moreover, coated slavery with a moral justification which a doctrine of equality could never have permitted. In 1844 he testily asked the "silly, sickly, restless sentimentalizers" who wanted to free the slaves whether they knew of a better relation in which black and white might live together.[1] By 1847 his defense had risen from expediency to principle:

Man, we are ready to maintain, may have property in man, a valid right to the services of his slave, — though no dominion over his soul; slavery is not *malum in se* and in no case justifiable; there is nothing in slavery that necessarily prevents the slaveholder from being a true and pious Christian; and where the master is a true Christian, and takes care that his people are instructed and brought up in the true Christian faith, and worship, slavery is tolerable, and for negroes, perhaps, even more than tolerable.[2]

He rejoiced at the Compromise of 1850, while Emerson and Thoreau shook their fists angrily at the sky and denounced the government. Emerson called the fugitive slave law a "filthy enactment . . . I will not obey it, by God," [3] and Theodore Parker publicly urged its violation; but such resistance proved to Brownson only the desperate and

[1] "The Presidential Nominations," *BrQR*, First Series, I (July, 1844), *Works*, XV, 491.
[2] "Slavery and the Mexican War," *BrQR*, New Series, I (July, 1847), *Works*, XVI, 27.
[3] R. W. Emerson, *Journals*, VIII, 236.

criminal character of abolitionism. In 1853 he made his position brutally clear. "Equality is an idle dream, an empty word . . . ," he told the students at a Catholic college in Maryland.

You of the South consist of freemen and slaves . . . and so do we of the North . . . . While you have the manliness to avow it, we have the art to disguise it from the careless observer, under the drapery of fine names. . . . [It is] our duty to accept the distinction of classes as a social fact, permanent and indestructible in civilized society.[4]

As the slavery problem became increasingly urgent, however, the shabbiness of motive behind lofty Southern principles grew increasingly visible, and Southern pressure on the North more and more irritating. Brownson, perceiving (at first, unconsciously) that it was more important now to restrain the Southerners than to restrain the abolitionists, began to amend his position. He had originally argued that slavery, like any other property, could be taken by the owner into the territories. By 1854, however, he decided that according to the *ius naturale* slavery was only a local, civil institution and consequently excluded from the territories except when allowed by positive law. All the presumptions of natural law, he began to believe, were in favor

[4] "Liberal Studies," an oration delivered before the Philomathean Society of Mt. St. Mary's College, *Works*, XIX, 432, 433.

of freedom. When the Dred Scott case split the nation in 1857, Brownson concurred in Taney's judgment that the Supreme Court had no jurisdiction, but objected to the incidental opinions and meditated gloomily the consequences of so unmistakably Southern a decision.

He seriously resented the emergence of slavery as a national problem. It was a question for the states, and the federal government could answer it only at the cost of destroying the Constitution. Yet he resented even more the attempt of the planters to rule the nation through the Democratic party. If national policy was to be subservient to the interests of slaveholders, it were almost better to end slavery. In an extraordinary passage after Buchanan's election he predicted the course of affairs for the next decade. The Southern policy, he said, would force the majority of the North into the Republican party.

No statesman, worthy of the name, can for one moment believe the free states would long submit to be thus deprived of their legitimate influence in the affairs of the country, and quietly acquiesce in the domination of some three hundred thousand slaveholders in a single geographical section. Having, as they well know, the absolute majority, having also, as they fully believe, the power, they would rebel against their southern masters, and form a northern sectional party, do their best to defeat and subject the slave interest, and in their turn attempt to bring the slaveholding states under the domination of the northern manufacturers, bankers, brokers, and stockjobbers.

If Buchanan supports the Southern policy, Brownson warned, he will "inevitably prepare the way for the accession of a northern sectional president in 1860." [5]

As the election approached, Brownson grew increasingly melancholy over the national dilemma. His patience with Southern tactics was becoming rapidly exhausted. He did not relish the invective of a Virginia editor who called him a Black Republican or the demand of a committee of influential New Yorkers that he stop attacking Southern policy, after he had once suggested in print that slavery was not God's chief gift to man. He had heard for too many years that unless he voted in a certain manner the South would dissolve the Union. He was tired, as he later remarked, of voting under threats. His first allegiance went to the Union. He finally found this strong devotion leading him to support Abraham Lincoln, whom he did not respect, and the Republican party, whose peculiar principles he could not endorse, in order to settle once and for all the ques-

[5] "Slavery and the Incoming Administration," *BrQR*, New York Series, II (January, 1857), *Works*, XVII, 55–56, 57.

tion of Southern domination. He still thought it possible to curb the slaveholders without abolishing slavery, and he was far from believing that the South would reply to Lincoln's election by secession; but "even if we had so believed," he wrote in 1862, we "should still have voted for Mr. Lincoln all the same." [6]

The war called forth Brownson's deep and genuine patriotism. While Sumter was still echoing in the nation's ears, he declared that the cause of the war was the Southern conviction that, unless they retained political power, their capital invested in slavery would be insecure.

No intelligent man at the South believed the success of the Republican party threatened directly the institution of slavery; but the whole South saw in it the fact that the political control of the Union had passed from southern hands.[7]

The rebellion must be crushed, Brownson continued; and he criticized the administration for its timidity and uncertainty. "It was not liberty for the black race," he wrote later, "so much as for the white race that we wished to secure." [8]

[6] "Emancipation and Colonization," *BrQR*, Third New York Series, III (April, 1862), *Works*, XVII, 255.
[7] "The Great Rebellion," *BrQR*, Third New York Series, II (July, 1861), *Works*, XVII, 126.
[8] "Emancipation and Colonization," *BrQR*, Third New York Series, III (April, 1862), *Works*, XVII, 257.

In October Brownson demanded a sterner prose-
cution of the war. He told those who objected to
Lincoln's acts as unconstitutional, "We know not,
and care not, whether those acts were constitutional
or not, so long as we know that they were necessary
to the maintenance of the Union," [9] and he attacked
the Catholic hierarchy and press for want of patriotism. But, most impressively, he proposed the immediate emancipation of the slaves. It was impossible,
he now believed, to annihilate the political power
of the slave interest without annihilating that interest itself. "We urge their liberation," Brownson explained, "only as a war measure, a measure
necessary to save the nation, justified and called for
by military necessity." [10] Horace Greeley devoted a
page and a half of the *Tribune* to reprinting this
powerful article, and Brownson himself made several visits to Washington to drive home the urgency
of emancipation to the president. He came away
from these interviews with no high opinion of Lincoln. "He is thick-headed; he is ignorant; he is
tricky, somewhat astute in a small way, and obstinate
as a mule . . . ," Brownson finally wrote in fever-
ish exasperation to Charles Sumner. "Is there no

[9] "Slavery and the War," *BrQR*, Third New York Series, II
(October, 1861), *Works*, XVII, 169.
[10] "Archbishop Hughes on Slavery," *BrQR*, Third New York
Series, III (January, 1862), *Works*, XVII, 186.

way of inducing him to resign, and allow Mr. Hamlin [the vice-president] to take his place?" [11]

Brownson, as this letter may suggest, was now a sick man. Some years before he had been afflicted with painful inflammation of the eyes after an evening of whist playing in New York. In 1857, on the advice of Isaac Hecker, he went to a doctor whom Hecker believed to be inspired by the Holy Ghost. This man's method, it developed, was to prescribe whisky and bloodletting and charge high fees. The treatment, in spite of its origin, did not help Brownson perceptibly.[12] Later in the year, when he moved to Elizabeth, he proceeded to aggravate his disorder by studying too long under kerosene oil lamps. A new doctor pronounced the ailment to be gout of the eyes. In 1860 Brownson began to have moments of blindness. Slowly the disease commenced to affect his feet and then his hands. He had to dictate articles and letters and then give up lecturing, the chief source of his income. Since the *Review* brought him little, he found himself growing dangerously poor.[18] In 1862 friends were inviting

[11] Brownson to Sumner, December 26, 1862, Sumner Papers.
[12] H. F. Brownson, *Latter Life*, 128.
[18] In 1861 he reported that he had lost more than $17,000 in the *Review* through the failures of agents and the refusal of readers to pay for their subscriptions. On the other hand, he made $1018.65 in a single lecture in 1858; there were 5376

248   ORESTES A. BROWNSON

him to New York so that they could buy clothes for
him. "As you are so unfortunate as to be of anoma-
lous dimensions," one wrote, "we think it best to ask
you to come in and suffer a tailor to ascertain
them." [14]

But Brownson forgot his own illness and poverty
in patriotic fervor for the nation's cause. As the war
proceeded, with floundering generalship and without
emancipation, he grew increasingly critical of the
administration. In a blunt, hard-hitting article in
October 1862 he bitterly assailed Seward, whom he
imagined to be the author of the administration's
policy, for not pressing the war more grimly.[15] His
eagerness to goad on the faltering government led
him in the fall to accept the Unionist nomination for
Congress in the third district of New Jersey. He
threw his weary bulk wholeheartedly into the canvass, stumping the entire district and speaking every
day but Sunday. The Democratic majority had been
2500 in 1860, and Brownson's religion probably lost
him more votes than his eloquence won. In November after an exhausting campaign the Democrats

people in the audience. *BrQR*, Third New York Series, II
(October, 1861), 547; James Lynch and others to Brownson,
April 20, 1858, Brownson Papers.

[14] J. K. Herbert to Brownson, August 13, 1862, Brownson
Papers.

[15] "The Seward Policy," *BrQR*, Third New York Series, III
(October, 1862), *Works*, XVII, 353–385.

carried the state, Brownson running 4600 votes behind William G. Steele, his opponent.[16] Yet he continued in the next year to deliver patriotic lectures and work earnestly for the Union.

In January 1864 he decided somewhat joylessly that he would support Lincoln's re-election. But his doubts as to Lincoln's ability continued strong, and they became known to the Radical wing of the Republican party which solicited Brownson's aid in an anti-Lincoln movement. Salmon P. Chase was the first choice of the leaders in this movement, and probably also Brownson's; but Chase declined, leaving Frémont, Butler and Grant as the chief possibilities. Brownson came out against Lincoln in April, declaring Chase, Butler and Frémont preferable to this man who, as Brownson said, for all his good humor and capacity for work, lacked the qualities of education, dignity, knowledge and philosophic thought that the situation demanded. His administration, he went on, had been weak, fluctuating and appallingly wasteful of men and money.

Brownson, impressed by the enthusiastic reports of his son who had served on Frémont's staff, and beguiled by the general's own insinuating letters, came to believe that Frémont had the necessary

[16] *New York Tribune*, October 14, November 6, 1862; *New York Times*, October 24.

energy and judgment. In July he declared for him in an article filled with absurd overpraise. Though Frémont assured Brownson that he would fight Lincoln to the end, he withdrew in September when his friends made a deal with the administration, leaving Brownson, tired and sick, committed against Lincoln and without a candidate of his own. During the hot summer, moreover, as Brownson painfully pressed himself to work for the man who was shortly to desert him, he learned that two sons had been killed, one on the battlefield, the other in an accident on his way to the army. He tried to bear the deaths stoically, but he was growing old and exhausted. In October, bitterly despondent, Brownson climaxed an attack on the tendency of democracy to elevate inferior men by asking sadly, "When such a man as Abraham Lincoln can become president, who may not hope one day also to be president?" [17]

For all the personal grief and disappointment the war brought Brownson, it thrust him back into national attention. The heat of patriotism melted the religious bars which kept him from the people he had once known so well. He renewed his friendship with George Bancroft. He started to correspond with Charles Sumner. Elizabeth Peabody, now old and

[17] "Liberalism and Progress," *BrQR*, National Series (October, 1864), *Works*, XX, 357.

too poor to pay her board, found in his defense of the Union the realization of their old vision of Christian Union and Progress. "The dream of your youth will thus be accomplished," she wrote him, "and all the disappointments, chagrins and sufferings . . . will be infinitely overpaid." [18] His articles were widely reprinted, and once more he was in demand as a lecturer. Behind the struggle and sacrifice was his indomitable spirit, fired by patriotism, which lifted his aching body into carriages and sent him, jaded and crack-voiced, onto lecture platforms before unconvinced audiences. It made him, groping and half-blind, trace out in spidery, staggering script his still vigorous essays on national policy. It kept him writing for the Union and believing in Union victory while the Frémont movement was falling down round his head, and the bodies of his sons were returning from the army. His heart was in the Union cause. He felt little else. With victory his spirit was ready to collapse.

In the meantime he had succeeded in completing his alienation from the Catholic community. Most Catholics were habitual Democrats who deeply suspected anything savoring of Yankee radicalism. Brownson had forfeited many subscription fees by

[18] Elizabeth P. Peabody to Brownson, October 16, 186?, Brownson Papers.

voting Republican in 1860, and his course during the war took him even farther away from
the confidence of his coreligionists. In an anonymous article in the *Metropolitan Record* Archbishop Hughes severely censured Brownson on the
ground that his advocacy of emancipation was an
advocacy of a war to free the slaves — an unashamed
distortion of Brownson's position. James Gordon
Bennett delightedly reprinted Hughes's article in
the *Herald*, chortling over the assault on abolitionism
and adding a few scornful words of his own for
"Weathercock Brownson." Then Greeley in the *Tribune* described the article as "an attempt to parry the
blows which Dr. Brownson powerfully deals at
Slavery and Rebellion by scurrilous attacks upon him
personally," [19] and Brownson soon made his own reply
with characteristic force. Catholic leaders erred badly,
he said, when they were persuaded

that slavery and Catholicity are the only two conservative
institutions in the country, and that to strengthen the slaveholding power would be to strengthen the Catholic Church.
. . . In regard to civilization and the future prosperity of
our religion on this continent, an anti-slavery Protestant is
worth more than a pro-slavery Catholic.[20]

[19] *N. Y. Herald*, October 8, 1861; *N. Y. Daily Tribune*,
October 9, 1861.
[20] "Archbishop Hughes on Slavery," *BrQR*, Third New York
Series, III (January, 1862), *Works*, XVII, 200.

In the same number he announced that the *Review* would hereafter seek to please Protestant as well as Catholic readers.[21] Later in the year, when Hughes triumphantly produced a letter from Pius IX calling for peace, Brownson asserted that it was either forged or obtained by a gross misrepresentation of American affairs. He even publicly reproved Catholics for want of loyalty. The result of all his patriotic ardor was, as he wrote, that the *Review*

lost the confidence of the Catholic community, and was interdicted by the Bishop of Richmond, denounced by the Bishop of Wheeling, and officially declared by the Bishop of Philadelphia and the Archbishop of Cincinnati to be no longer a Catholic review.[22]

Brownson antagonized the orthodox by his theological deviations as well as by his championship of the war. His essay on "Rights of the Temporal," which contained the oblique attack on Hughes, further shocked the conservatives in the Church by its conciliatory tone toward Protestants and by its proposal that the Church abandon its secular power and become only "the spiritual kingdom of God on earth."[23] Such sentiments soon led to Brownson's

[21] *BrQR*, Third New York Series, III, 133 (January, 1862).
[22] H. F. Brownson, *Latter Life*, 377.
[23] "Rights of the Temporal," *BrQR*, Third New York Series (October, 1860), *Works*, XII, 376–405.

denunciation at Rome. Cardinal Barnabò, the Prefect
of Propaganda, was favorably disposed toward him,
however, and finally dismissed the charges on receiving a detailed account by Brownson himself of his
belief. Brownson resented the fact that the bishops
had sought to manage him by anonymous magazine
articles and appeals to Rome instead of approaching
him openly, and he continued without wavering on
his liberal tack. He talked of the unfinished business
of Catholic theology, insisting that the Church take
account of the vital emotions of the day in formulating its doctrine. In his essays on the Reformation he
conceded virtually every necessity in the writing of
history that he had criticized in Newman a decade
before. Elsewhere he declared the *Essay on the Development of Doctrine* to be an admirable work
rather than a collection of sinister heresies; and he
contrived even, by softening his voice, to present the
doctrine of *extra ecclesiam nulla salus* in an ingra-
tiating logic which made it seem an obvious and
rather tolerant dogma. This new line resulted in a
barrage of criticism, which grew so heated that in
1863 he resolved to bar theological discussion from
the *Review* lest controversy drive him into heresy.
Nevertheless he could not refrain from touching religious questions: in 1864 he assailed the Jesuits as
a reactionary influence in the Church, and asserted

that an atheist who followed the law of God practically was in a sense a good Christian.

He was by now the subject of widespread and bitter comment. The *Dublin Review* in its series on "Theological Errors of the Day" devoted an article to Brownson's *Review;* [24] and Lord Acton spoke sadly of Brownson's "decay" as "pitiful and premature." [25] Gradually the pressure began to tell. With victory certain, there was no longer a national crisis to nerve him to independence. He was weary, and sick, and hungry for rest. He had fulfilled devotedly his patriotic duty, giving two sons and his own reputation to his country. His reward was the indifference of Protestants and the dislike of Catholics. There was no longer much demand for the *Review,* and after the Frémont fiasco little desire on his own part to continue it. He resolved finally to end it with the volume for 1864 and withdraw silently from the scene.

In December Pius IX handed down the encyclical *Quanta Cura* pronouncing anathema against all efforts to create a compromise between the Church and the spirit of the age. The liberalism that had played so large a part in his downfall was now under official

[24] "Theological Errors of the Day — Brownson's Review," *Dublin Review,* LIV, 58–94 (January, 1864).

[25] Acton to Simpson, June 31, 1862, Gasquet, *Lord Acton and His Circle,* 289.

ban. Brownson had no longer even the conviction that he had made his sacrifices in a just cause.

2

This series of crushing blows — his bereavements, the Frémont affair, the papal syllabus of errors — left Brownson terribly disheartened. It seemed, one son later recalled, as if he would never again have the strength to combat opponents as before. He was only sixty-one, but looked and felt a dozen years older with his eyes failing, his hair whitened, and his limbs tormented with pain. A group of still loyal Catholics presented him with an annuity of $1000 a year for life. On this the old man, his ability wasted and his aspirations come to nothing, prepared to retire into oblivion. "I am now nobody" became a favorite phrase which he repeated during these years with pathetic emphasis. He wrote it to Bancroft, he wrote it to Sumner, and all the letters he laboriously scrawled in the few years after the war bore it as a poignant undertone.[26] The giant was in defeat.

But he was only defeated, not silenced, and soon

[26] Brownson to Sumner, December 11, 1865, Sumner Papers; Brownson to Bancroft, undated [probably 1866], Brownson Papers.

he was driven on by a new ambition — to put in final order his thoughts on politics, ethics and metaphysics. His political ideas were most in need of re-examination because of the heavy impact of the Civil War on the state-rights doctrine of Calhoun that had so long been his own. After his conversion he had encrusted state rights with dogmas taken from the schoolmen and from the philosophers of the conservative reaction in Europe. The best way to safeguard rights vital to the old order (and thus to the Church) was to deny that government had any power to change them; and an age which found history so vastly consoling achieved this by arguing that such rights, existing long before governments, could not be modified by governmental action. Property became a sacred right "which civil society is instituted to protect"; and the written constitution was discovered to be only an imperfect copy of the "real" constitution, "the living soul of the nation," which directed and governed change by its own organic action.[27]

Brownson's apotheosis of property and his organic theory of constitutions attacked fundamentally the assumptions lying behind reform. The first limited

[27] "The Papal Power," *BrQR*, Third New York Series, I (July, 1860), *Works*, XII, 361; "Political Constitutions," *BrQR*, New Series, I (October, 1847), *Works*, XV, 561, 566.

the field of change; the second announced that change was taken care of by history, not by men. But for all the mysticism (largely borrowed from de Maistre) in its conception, the second doctrine had its obvious truth — that the form of government must suit the people and draw its life from the blood-stream of society. In the light of this idea Brownson set out to reinterpret American history, employing his old hardness of analysis but now reversing the moral evaluations. His new canon was that society required stability, not change; he still recognized the class struggle but decided that the good lay with the aristocracy, not with the proletariat. America had not yet recovered from the loss of the Tories, he began; the nation had steadily deteriorated from 1788 because of the vicious influences of democracy "against which the framers of the federal constitution intended to guard." [28] The country's great need was a stable and powerful interest like a landed aristocracy, and its great hope was to live by the common law, whose capacity for organic growth showed it to be the most authoritative expression in the temporal order of the divine law. Thus alone could America be saved from the perils of government by popular will. The nation owed its

[28] "Dana's Poems and Prose Writings," *BrQR*, New Series, IV (October, 1850), *Works*, XIX, 333, 334.

passion for democracy, he concluded in a comprehensive indictment,

to the influx of English and Scotch radicals, at the head of whom were Frances Wright, Robert Dale Owen, and Robert L. Jennings, — to the writings of Amos Kendall, William Leggett, and George Bancroft, — to the administrations of Andrew Jackson and Martin Van Buren, — and to the declamations, cant, and sentimentality of our abolitionists and philanthropists.[29]

On the threshold of the Civil War, then, Brownson had piled up a mass of evidence ascribing the evils of American society to the equalitarian frenzy. He found the defense against this madness in state rights. But war came, and he discovered abruptly that the integrity of the Union was far more important to him than the integrity of the states. He had to work out a new theory which without erasing entirely the rights of the individual states would permit him to assert national sovereignty. Gradually his political theory recovered from its dislocation by the war. By 1864 it was settling into a new equilibrium. He contended now

that the sovereignty with us vests neither in the states or the people of the states severally, nor in the Union created by the constitution of 1787, but in the political people of the

[29] "The Republic of the United States," *BrQR*, New Series, III (April, 1849), *Works*, XVI, 88–89.

United States, who have ordained and established both the several state governments and the general government; and that this political people is one people, yet capable of existing and acting only as organized into mutually independent political societies called states, and into states united. Hence, their union and their division into states are equally essential to our political system.[30]

Since the American states have never acted as separately sovereign states, he said in substance, they are not so; sovereignty then rests in the states united.

Brownson derived this view in large part from John C. Hurd's *The Law of Freedom and Bondage in the United States.* In 1865 he gave the position its rounded statement and imbedded the theory into his general system in *The American Republic: Its Constitution, Tendencies and Destiny.* This book showed a few changes of position. It was dedicated to George Bancroft "as a sort of public atonement" [31] for the invective Brownson had heaped on Bancroft in the near past. Brownson now rejected all types of aristocracy, accepted universal suffrage "in principle," discarded state sovereignty and championed

[30] The evolution of this theory can be traced from "The Struggle of the Nation for Life" [*BrQR*, Third New York Series, III (January, 1862), *Works*, XVII, 220], through the "Federal Constitution" [*BrQR*, National Series (January, 1864), *Works*, XVII, 565].

[31] Brownson to Bancroft, October 21, 1866, H. F. Brownson, *Latter Life*, 456.

Hurd's compromise theory of the Union. Behind these modifications, however, stood the familiar apparatus of Gioberti's formula, the solidarity of the race and "providential constitutions," given a new and finished setting. The book was closely reasoned and, in a strange way, full of keen insights into American government; but Brownson had by now ruined all chances of getting an unbiased hearing. Even his old friend George Ripley could remark of the work only that readers would "admire his skill in combination and his fertility of resource with the same wonder with which they watch the movements of an adroit chess player." [32]

The American Republic was the only one of his systematic studies that Brownson completed. The journalistic habits of a lifetime were too strong, and he found himself returning once more to championing Catholicism in the magazines. He wrote chiefly for Isaac Hecker's journal, the *Catholic World*, though his work was unsigned and its authorship known only to a few. While he had been absorbed in the war, a new foe had arisen to threaten the sanctity of faith. In 1859 Charles Darwin had set forth the theory of biological evolution. Friends and enemies quickly interpreted it as a gauntlet flung down to religion to signalize the opening of hostil-

[32] *New York Tribune*, December 28, 1865.

ities with theology. Defenders of science looked with scorn on the superstitions of the faithful; and the truly religious believed that preoccupation with material causes made religion a mockery by depriving God of His personal efficacy and converting Him into man-made natural law. The challenge of evolution brought the conflict into sharp issue by furnishing an account of the origin of species and the descent of man which apparently contradicted the Bible.

Brownson, with his lively solicitude for faith, had grown quickly aware of the menace of the new geology and ethnology. In 1863 he first inquired into the pretensions of science. He speedily repudiated the naïve argument that science was instantly false when it conflicted with religion. Such arguments, he observed, appealed only to those "who care nothing for science or civilization, for human intelligence and social well-being, and whose faith having been entertained without reason, no reason can disturb." Brownson himself regarded the conflict as between, not science and faith, but the opinions and conjectures of scientists and theologians. Science, indeed, could say nothing about absolute truth — and here he went to the heart of the controversy — because it dealt with appearances, not with reality. "In all that is contingent," Brownson declared, "reason has need of experience, observation, experiment, investigation; but, with these alone, we can never rise above the empirical, or attain to [truly] scientific results."

Brownson's sharp perception of the limitations of science — rare in a day which tended to confound Newton with God — sufficiently answered the claim that evolution destroyed religion. Science fed on phenomena, while faith penetrated to the *Ding-an-sich;* one ruled in the order of nature, the other in the order of grace — true science thus could not collide with true religion. The best way to tame science, thought Brownson, was for Catholics to enter the laboratories; for they alone were equipped to be really good scientists, since they alone had the correct understanding of the underlying reality. Instead of denouncing science indiscriminately, and resting their belief on pious ignorance, Catholics must *prove* the harmony of science and faith.[33]

A few years later he again criticized the foundations of science. "We do not deduce our physics from our metaphysics," he wrote,

but our metaphysics or philosophy gives the law to the inductive or empirical sciences, and prescribes the bounds beyond which they cannot pass without ceasing to be sciences.[34]

[33] "Science and the Sciences," *BrQR*, Third New York Series, IV (July, 1863), *Works*, IX, 254–268.

[34] "Faith and the Sciences," *Catholic World*, VI (December, 1867), *Works*, IX, 270.

No induction, then, could be scientific which contradicted *ens creat existentias,* for without this formula no induction was possible: hence, Brownson triumphantly concluded, any theory denying God or creation was false. He went on to a frontal attack on science, on the ground that its partial and uncertain character impugned its conclusions at any one moment, though most of these conclusions, he hastened to continue, were actually compatible with religion. He condemned evolution, however; it contradicted the doctrine of immutability of species; it blurred the sharp distinction between man, who had reason, moral responsibility and a soul, and brute beasts; and it assumed the savage to be the type of primitive man instead of realizing that the savage was primitive man corrupted.[35] In later essays he assailed the scientists who pretended that their hypotheses described objective reality, but confessed his impotence before those, like Spencer and Mill, who declared everything beyond sense-experience to be unknowable. His objection to scientists, as he remarked in a review of Draper's *Conflict between Religion and Science,* was to their insistence that the Church accept their provisional solutions as absolute truth:

[35] See "Faith and the Sciences," *supra;* "Professor Draper's Books," *Catholic World,* VII (May, 1868), *Works,* IX, 292–318.

The greater part of what our advanced thinkers call science, consists not only of assumptions, but of assumptions hardly made before they are modified or rejected for others equally baseless, to be in their turn modified or rejected. . . . Indeed, our scientists regard science, as our free-lovers regard marriage, as simply provisory, and would be disgusted with it if not at liberty to be constantly changing it. They regard truth as variable as their own views and moods.[36]

This skirmish was the next to the last act in his battle for religious certainty. Modern thought, as he looked at it, had been sapping the foundations of belief from the days of the Reformation. He had attacked Descartes, whose delight in introspection set philosophy on the wrong path, and Kant, who popularized the mischievous and hallucinatory problems of knowledge. In Newman he had discovered subtler threats to the credentials of faith. Now science was pretending to give a truer picture of reality than religion. Huxley and Comte were using it to deny the Biblical account of the making of the world and man, seeking to discredit the authority of religion by denouncing the results. The certitudes of faith were once more in danger.

In melancholy bewilderment Brownson continued the fight; but, as he grew older, he leaned more and

[36] "The Conflict of Science and Religion," *BrQR*, Last Series, III (April, 1875), *Works*, IX, 560.

more on the affirmations of faith. He had grappled with philosophical questions in candid perplexity and had never deluded himself into accepting solutions for problems he did not genuinely believe to be solved. Reason, he knew, ruled the natural order: but what conclusions of value could man obtain without supernatural aid? With characteristic honesty, after a lifetime devoted to philosophy, Brownson finally had the courage to admit the uselessness of speculation:

> We are more and more disposed to receive the revealed mysteries with the simplicity of faith. Philosophy may remove some obstacles to their intellectual acceptance, but as a rule we believe it creates more difficulties than it removes.[37]

3

The rising-up of science as a new pretender to the throne of truth struck Brownson as one more dismal portent of a dismal age. He was consoling himself for his own disappointment by indicting the times. In 1860 he had called for a sharp war to clear the moral atmosphere. The war had come, but it trailed inglorious clouds which were now befogging the nation. The politics of Reconstruction reflected the

[37] "Holy Communion — Transubstantiation," *BrQR*, Last Series, II (January, 1874), *Works*, VIII, 279.

decadence of the day from another angle. He opposed guaranteeing the Negro political and social
equality, because he realized the complexities of
social adjustment such a program would bring. The
Negro, he declared in 1864, was incapable of assuming the white man's burden and, weighed down with
it, would be in worse misery than he had been as
a slave.[38] Except for some constitutional quibbles,
Brownson thus diverged from Sumner and supported
the Lincoln-Johnson Reconstruction policy which
sought to restore government in the South to the
whites. In 1868 he joyfully voted for General
Grant, who seemed to answer Brownson's old desire
for a soldier-president. But, as he later remarked,
he found in him "neither the soldier nor the civil-
ian"; and he thought Grant's followers "not only
fearfully corrupt, but . . . manifestly consolidation-
ists, and therefore disloyal to the American constitution." He could not vote for Grant in 1872, and he
could not "without abandoning all self-respect" vote
for Greeley.[39] Finally, he did not vote at all. It was
to be his last election.

Brownson saw gloomily that the movement for
consolidation had triumphed in the Civil War. Busi-

[38] "Abolition and Negro Equality," *BrQR*, National Series
(April, 1864), *Works*, XVII, 537–560.
[39] "The Political Outlook," *BrQR*, Last Series, II (January,
1874), *Works*, XVIII, 546.

ness had conquered the slaveholders, and now the capitalists sought to perpetuate the wartime concentration of control by transforming the emergency powers into ordinary peace powers through the new amendments. He had no faith in a government with such masters — "the bankers, stock-jobbers, money-holders, railroad and other corporations." [40] "The great feudal lords had souls," he wrote, "railroad corporations have none." [41] He implored the country to return to commerce and agriculture; there its salvation lay; but his pleas disappeared with the wind, and his doctrine of property prevented him from supporting any practical measures against industrialism. No one in America surpassed Brownson in his hatred of capitalism, but probably few surpassed him in the hatred of the only forces likely to restrain the capitalists.

Brownson's social thought gradually lost the confidence that had so long sounded under his rhetoric. He now pointed to problems and observed that he failed to see how they could be solved; or, if he made suggestions, it was with an acrid conviction that no one would heed them. He even began to doubt that the Catholics could introduce honesty into the

[40] "The Political State of the Country," *BrQR*, Last Series, I (January, 1873), *Works*, XVIII, 530–531, 533.

[41] "The Democratic Principle," *BrQR*, Last Series, I (April, 1873), *Works*, XVIII, 234.

country and called them "the least reasoning, the noisiest, and the most unscrupulous class of American citizens." [42] He held out a faint hope for the nation if the South could become Catholic by conversion and colonization and leash the impulse toward centralization. But the hope was so faint that the clatter of his criticism quickly drowned it out. The nation, Brownson declared, was drenched in vice and immorality; tyrannous capital was greedily surveying the last vestiges of minority rights; and civil marriage, by withdrawing religious sanction from the family, was destroying moral purity and the inviolability of the home. The republic was on its last legs.

The bitterness of this new mood came partly from the humiliations Brownson himself was undergoing. He had during these melancholy years to submit his work to the verdict of others — and the others were not always kind. The old man grew almost pathetic in his meekness, writing on order for the *Catholic World* and deferring to younger men like Isaac Hecker and Augustine Francis Hewit, who succeeded Hecker as editor and later as superior of the Paulists. In 1868 Brownson quarreled with Hecker when the *World* sent back one essay and

[42] "Home Politics," *BrQR*, Last Series, III (October, 1875), *Works*, XVIII, 597.

mutilated another. Though the difference was patched up, he grew increasingly resentful of the patronizing manners of this man whom he could recall as a shy and frightened youth. His renewed conservatism also estranged him from Hecker, who believed the Catholic Church to be essentially democratic. By 1872 Brownson's patience was finally exhausted. He would no longer stand being treated as an inferior, and he stopped sending contributions to the *World*.

He had often thought longingly of reviving the *Review*. On a stormy day early in 1872, his wife caught a severe cold; and a short time later, as she lay dying from pneumonia, she implored him to bring his old journal to life, if only for a year, as proof to the world that his faith had never wavered. Brownson eagerly seized upon the appeal as a chance to regain his freedom and justify himself. In January 1873 the first number of the reborn journal appeared. The editor's vigor and logical force had lessened little since the war. "It is fully equal to its predecessors," commented the *Nation*, "and they formed a body of as good hard thinking on important topics as ever issued from the American press." [48]

He made amply clear that he was deserting his

[48] *Nation*, XVI, 74 (January 30, 1873).

position of the decade before, since the position could not stand the challenge of facts. If the age were evil, he sadly decided, its spirit must be evil also. Oppressed by the wickedness of the times and by the weight of his own errors, he turned savagely upon his sinful liberalism, scorned it as vile and dangerous and fell once more into rigorous orthodoxy. He attacked radicalism and reform with his old uncompromising vigor. He returned to his first opinion of Newman. He replaced his temperate attitude toward science by invective: Darwin became "utterly imbecile as a scientific reasoner," and along with Huxley and Spencer should be branded "enemies of God and man, of religion and society, of truth and justice, of science and civilization. . . . Satan's most efficient ministers." [44] He reasserted *extra ecclesiam nulla salus* in its old harshness. Everywhere he discovered evidences of corruption. The popularity of Dickens was "one of the worst symptoms of the age in which we live"; [45] another was feminism; but the great question of the time, to which all controversy ultimately reduced, was God or no God, and Brownson named Emerson, Darwin, Huxley, Spencer, Comte, the members of the Internationales and

[44] "Darwin's Descent of Man," *BrQR*, Last Series, I (July, 1873), *Works*, IX, 492, 495–496.

[45] "Religious Novels, and Woman versus Woman," *BrQR*, Last Series, I (January, 1873), *Works*, XIX, 508.

"the majority of the medical profession" as the chief villains in dethroning the Supreme Being.[46] He was declaring war on the world in order to make his own peace with heaven.

Peace with the world was growing less and less possible. The huge, red-faced old man, bearded and infirm, had never been of easy disposition. Now his sternness turned to grimness, and his intolerance to inhumanity. His wife had endured him with sweet resignation. "Whatever she may have suffered from marital harshness," wrote one son, "she was always affectionate and loving to husband and children. . . ." [47] After her death he chose to live with his daughter Sarah in Elizabeth. He found little satisfaction in his sons. A stiff father, who sent them letters that sounded like essays for the *Review*, he had always hoped that one at least would enter the priesthood, and grew old in bitter disappointment that none of them did. Henry alone was a consolation to him. "Cub of the 'Old Bear' in crossness and brightness," as Hecker called him, Henry had become a lawyer in Detroit where his father had lain sick with malaria half a century before.[48] None of the others had pleased their father, either in college

[46] "Essay in Refutation of Atheism," *BrQR*, Last Series, I–II (1873–1874), *Works*, II, 4.
[47] H. F. Brownson, *Early Life*, 485.
[48] Hecker to W. Lockhart, May 18, 1887, Brownson Papers.

or in the world. The old man felt especially disconsolate over Orestes, Jr., who, temperamentally unfit for the intellectual life his father pressed on him from the days of Brook Farm, had finally found himself as editor of a chess review and writer of burlesque melodramas. The elder Brownson apparently could not sort out the burlesque from the melodrama and wrote sadly to Henry, "Orestes has become a dramatic author. I am afraid his mind is disordered." [49]

Thus he sank into lonely old age, half-blind, deaf, smelling of tobacco, and dosing himself with all kinds of medicine to quiet the dull ache in his bones. He spent many hours, whisky and ice water by his side, in solitary games of backgammon, playing his right hand against his left. Death he dreaded, and he forbade the mention of a will. With the unthinking cruelty of age he sought to rule his home like a despot and force everyone to minister to him. "You brutal tyrant," his daughter finally cried in a moment of irritation; and Brownson answered with injured dignity, "I am of low birth, poor, unrefined, coarse, brutal, wholly beneath my lady daughter." Sarah came to believe that his infirm air was assumed wholly to excite pity. People agreed that he was

[49] Brownson to Henry F. Brownson, undated [187?], Brownson Papers.

looking younger and heartier than he had for years. He even talked of marrying again, though every word was a sword-cut for Sarah. In 1874 her loneliness was broken and she became engaged to William J. Tenney, the owner of the house in which she and her father were living. Brownson at first looked on the match favorably, but then began to resent the tenderness of others to her and seemed finally to consider every congratulation offered to Sarah an affront to himself.

After the marriage he lived alone in a large house with two Irish girls whom he called his secretaries but Sarah described as chambermaids. His former austerity was crumbling in this pathetic old age. In the saloons of Elizabeth people would say, "If you want a good square meal old Brownson's is the place to go for it"; and every night, according to the gossip that came back to Sarah, whisky flowed like water in her father's house. At nine promptly Brownson and his two girls would say the Rosary. Then pious Agnes would retire, and pert Dolly stay up to keep him company. Brownson finally returned to his daughter's home, but continued to see Agnes, who was a pretty girl of some education, and talked of marrying her. The six months with her, he told Sarah, were the happiest he ever passed in his life.

He now made the Tenney home a place of misery

and strain. Meals became especially a time of torture, with the deaf old man trying to dominate the conversation, and the others screaming to make him hear.[50] Early in 1875 Sarah had a child whom her father, carefully inspecting through his glasses, declared to be a true Brownson. The tension now lessened. Brownson became quieter and began to recover some of his old dignity. In the fall, he decided to end the *Review*, which he had somehow managed to keep going during these wretched years, and in November he went west to Detroit on a visit to Henry. Autumn gave way to winter in Detroit, and winter to spring, and the old man grew increasingly tired. In April of 1876 he became suddenly very ill and for a few days lingered helpless. The Holy Communion was brought him on Easter Sunday, after which he received Extreme Unction. At dawn on Easter Monday, April 17, he died.

[50] The account is based on the letters from Sarah to Henry, 1872–1876, Brownson Papers.

CHAPTER VIII

THE PILGRIM'S PROGRESS

"His predominant passion," Isaac Hecker said of Brownson, "was love of truth. This was all his glory and all his trouble; all his quarrels, friendships, aversions, perplexities, triumphs, labors."[1] A zealot for truth, he could not dally with lesser delights like popularity or worldly success. With so unswerving a purpose his life became strong-willed and austere. Locked in the fastnesses of his own convictions, never quite opening communication with others, Brownson was a proud and lonely man, dedicated to his search and filled with a passionate honesty that never let him rest short of final satisfaction.

His heart consumed in this unsparing quest, he put private happiness well below his high aspiration. Financial security rarely concerned him. He was rude, overbearing and cold as a person. He placed small value on friendship. Even his family felt the chilling single-mindedness of his devotion. Though he walked on many paths that might have brought

[1] Isaac Hecker, "Dr. Brownson and Catholicity," *Catholic World*, XLVI, 234 (November, 1887).

him fame or power — with the workingmen in New York, or with the Transcendentalists, or the Democratic party or the Catholic Church — he always left the traveled road to bruise himself in the thickets. Truth was an *ignis fatuus,* its small sharp flame burning obscurely just off the beaten way, but Brownson had no compunctions about rushing from certainty, and always he believed each new direction to be the right one.

Passionate honesty, however, is not the most prized of virtues. "I was and am in my natural disposition, frank, truthful, straightforward, and earnest"; Brownson wrote of himself, "and therefore have had, and, I doubt not, shall carry to the grave with me, the reputation of being reckless, ultra, a well-meaning man, perhaps an able man, but so fond of paradoxes and extremes, that he cannot be relied on." [2] Even men who agreed that consistency was the hobgoblin of small minds felt that Brownson carried inconsistency too far. The word haunted him. As early as 1834 Dr. Channing had confessed a mistrust of him because he had "made important changes of religion." [3] As these changes grew more glaring, such mistrust deepened, and his own sensitivity to the familiar accusation increased.

[2] "The Convert," *Works,* V, 46.
[3] Channing to Brownson, January 11, 1834, H. F. Brownson, *Early Life,* 107.

It was not hard to make out a devastating case against him. As Lowell observed in *A Fable for Critics:*

He shifts quite about, then proceeds to expound
That 'tis merely the earth, not himself, that turns round,
And wishes it clearly impressed on your mind
That the weathercock rules and not follows the wind;
Proving first, then as deftly confuting each side,
With no doctrine pleased that's not somewhere denied,
He lays the denier away on the shelf
And then — down beside him lies gravely himself.
He's the Salt River boatman, who always stands willing
To convey friend or foe without charging a shilling,
And so fond of the trip that, when leisure's to spare,
He'll row himself up, if he can't get a fare.
The worst of it is, that his logic's so strong,
That of two sides he commonly chooses the wrong;
If there *is* only one, why he'll split it in two,
And first pummel this half, then that, black and blue.
That white's white needs no proof, but it takes a deep fellow
To prove it jet-black, and that jet-black is yellow.
He offers the true faith to drink in a sieve, —
When it reaches your lips, there's naught left to believe
But a few silly- (syllo-, I mean) -gisms that squat 'em
Like tadpoles, o'erjoyed with the mud at the bottom.[4]

"What Weathercock Brownson says or does is of very little consequence to the community at large,"

[4] J. R. Lowell, "Fable for Critics," *Works*, IX, 44–45.

asserted the *New York Herald* more brutally. "Brownson has blown from all points of the compass in religion and in politics." [5] James Freeman Clarke offered a detailed indictment.

He has made the most elaborate and plausible plea for eclecticism, and the most elaborate and plausible plea against it. He has said the best things in favor of transcendentalism, and the best things against it. He has shown that no man can possibly be a Christian, except he is a transcendentalist; and he has also proved that every transcendentalist, whether he knows it or not, is necessarily an infidel. He has satisfactorily shown the truth of socialism, and its necessity in order to bring about a golden age, and he has, by the most convincing arguments, demonstrated that the whole system of socialism is from the pit, and can lead to nothing but anarchy and ruin. . . . He labors now with great ingenuity and extraordinary subtilty to show that there must be an infallible church with its infallible ministry, and that out of this church there can be no salvation. But formerly he labored with equal earnestness to show that there could be no such thing as a church at all, no outward priesthood or ministry.[6]

Yet, for all his inconsistency, no one could question his intelligence. Lowell in the *Fable for Critics* placed Brownson just after Emerson and Alcott; and Edgar Allan Poe said of him, "He is, in every

---

[5] *New York Herald*, October 8, 1861. The editorial went on to particularize its bill of complaint.

[6] "Orestes A. Brownson's Argument for the Roman Church," *Christian Examiner*, XLVIII, 228–229 (March, 1850).

respect, an extraordinary man." [7] There were few who did not concur in these opinions of the foremost critics of the day. Inevitably, for their own peace of mind, Brownson's contemporaries were forced to try to reconcile his undeniable ability with his equally undeniable instability. One line of argument was to pronounce him a blind follower of authority. Thus, he had first followed Fanny Wright, then William Ellery Channing, then Cousin and Leroux and the Catholic Church and Gioberti. Rufus Griswold believed that Brownson had taken everything he had of value from Comte. [8] This theory will not bear serious analysis. Brownson plainly was susceptible to influence; but the crucial question was why at certain times he was swayed in certain directions. The other popular explanation imagined him as thriving on novelty, and temperamentally incapable of remaining long in one belief. When he seemed to refute the theory by neglecting to turn Mohammedan after two years as a Catholic, a hasty postscript was added: he stayed in the Church because his intellectual somersaults before 1844 had utterly exhausted him. This theory is as patently absurd as the first.

[7] "A Chapter on Autography," *Graham's Magazine*, November 1841–January 1842, Poe, *Works*, IX, 202.
[8] R. W. Griswold, *The Prose Writers of America*, 423.

Brownson himself argued energetically, if at times somewhat speciously, to justify his shifts of belief. He maintained that apparent contradictions resulted from his habit of exploring the same questions from different viewpoints or in different terms; or he explained that his tendency to concentrate heavily on one point led to a distortion of emphasis that he never intended; or he insisted that he had not changed his ideas because his avowed theory of action remained the same. But who was to be persuaded by these suspiciously clever apologetics when he himself professed one faith on Monday and another on Tuesday?

His best defense was the true one, a simple description of his development.[9] His vision of truth changed with the permutations of his experience. Early in his career he had pointed out the danger of creeds: "There are few who do not worship their creed with more devotion than they do their God and labor a thousand times harder to support it than they do to support truth."[10] Brownson himself possessed a rare sensitivity to the hard and obstinate facts which lie in wait for theory. One event after another left its imprint on his thought, and each

[9] *Cf.* "Yes, I deny that I have *changed*, though I own that I seem to myself to have *advanced*." Introductory note to *BrQR*, I (January, 1844), H. F. Brownson, *Early Life*, 352.

[10] "My Creed," *Gospel Advocate*, June, 1829, *ibid.*, 25.

new formulation absorbed the facts that had dis-
qualified the previous one. Even when he seemed to
reassert an abandoned conviction, he did so with a
deeper understanding and a richer justification. In
1834 he advocated moral reform, and in 1848 he
again advocated it: but the difference in meaning
which underlay solutions superficially the same was
precisely the difference between the theology of
Channing and the theology of Thomas Aquinas. He
altered his beliefs, certainly, but his was the inconsistency of a firm and driving intelligence hunting
the truth, not that of caprice or stupidity.

The pursuit of truth was also pursuit of security.
With the truth he might save himself and benefit
the world. Without it he was condemned to stumble
blindly through a cold and sunless universe. He developed a dozen schemes which promised hope and
salvation, but each crumbled under him, in part from
the destructive force of his own intellect. He had not
been trained by education to accept skepticism and
live in uncertainty.[11] Doubt bred torment. With
heartbreaking intensity he longed to reach the ultimate certitudes.

The pilgrim inevitably paused before the gates of

[11] Cf. "My craving to believe was always strong, and it never
was my misfortune to be of a sceptical turn of mind." "The
Convert," Works, V, 39. Brownson's critical attitude came from
honesty, not from skepticism.

Rome. To his inexorable honesty and his thirst for certainty, Brownson added a passionate and concrete belief in God and a deep need for a rich and logical theology. Such a man could not long continue within nineteenth-century Protestantism. If his vision of God had been less definite, he might have turned Transcendentalist. If his sense of logic had been less exacting, he might have stayed a Universalist. If he had been less fervently honest, he might have remained a Unitarian, a Presbyterian or a socialist. If he had been content with anything short of absolute certainty, he might have continued forever a Protestant. But he tried Protestantism and found it wanting. Rome provided the only refuge. Entering the gates, he finally discovered a place to rest. Even when buffeted by storms of recrimination from Catholics, laymen and hierarchy alike, he never questioned the Church. To the end he remained troubled over smaller doubts; but he found in the Catholic universe the security he had sought so long, and he rested joyously in the Catholic solutions of the central problems of life.

2

In America, at a time when it was fashionable to have been born in log cabins, Brownson's rise out of

Vermont poverty was still extraordinary. He was educated in the sterner virtues — morality, thrift, conscience, self-respect — but not in letters or philosophy. Apart from the negligible period in a New York academy, he was self-taught. He first moved among cultivated men on going to New England. There he was initiated into metaphysics and political theory; there he learned French and German and, after becoming a Catholic, Latin and Italian. This eagerness and capacity for information lasted until late in life, and, in the moments snatched from lecturing and writing, he acquired a wide and thoughtful knowledge. "In certain favorite branches of study," wrote Father Hewit in a somewhat critical obituary (could Brownson expect more?), "as, for instance, in history, the history of philosophy, political ethics, and English philology — his knowledge was not only extensive but extremely accurate." [12] Unlike Theodore Parker, Brownson was not overborne by the weight of erudition. He tasted knowledge almost always with discrimination, not perhaps as an epicure — for he had been too long starved — but certainly not as a glutton. What a systematic education might have done to Brownson, or he to it, is a fascinating if unprofitable ques-

[12] *Catholic World*, XXIII, 370 (June, 1876).

tion that used to engage men as different as Acton, Poe and Hecker.

He was greater as an author than as a man. For thirty years in his magazines he commented on virtually all important questions both of the day and of eternity. As a journalist he had constantly to write on the most abstruse topics before grasping them thoroughly himself. Inevitably he was tripped by haste into inaccuracy and error. Inevitably also he had overgreat literary facility and a leaning toward garrulousness. Yet it is hard to find in any magazine of the century a more consistent record of intelligent observation.

His style, vigorous, forthright and clear, lacked subtlety and variety, gaining in cogency by its rude and unadorned strength. His best writing was tough, sinewy, concrete, hard-hitting;[13] his worst was at least clear and forceful. His grammar may often have been uncertain, but his meaning rarely. If he

[13] George Ripley told Hecker that there were passages in Brownson which could not be surpassed in the whole range of English literature. Walter Elliott, *Life of Hecker*, 182. According to Daniel Sargent, *Four Independents*, 238: "as a master of forceful English prose he had scarcely an equal, save, centuries before him, Dean Swift." The Rev. Dr. Thomas F. Coakley was even less restrained, conceding to Brownson "the energy of a Tertullian, the fire of a Cyprian, the polemic ability of an Athanasius, and the eloquence of a Chrysostom." *Catholic Builders of the Nation* (Boston, 1923), IV, 230.

frequently said the same thing too many times, this resulted in part from haste of composition. He was a master of vivid and searching irony, which hardly ever became flippancy or sarcasm. He could put obscure and complex ideas into admirably lucid form. Above all, he had a talent for metaphor; he could illuminate abstract notions with phrases which were at once accurate and pungent. Early in life he wrote that the priests would reject the religion of humanity "because it will require them to pay as much attention to the flock as they have hitherto paid to the fleece." This sentence had his peculiar and characteristic felicity; it suggests the honesty, force and liveliness of Brownson's writing. His was without question one of the best journalistic styles that America has known.

The most arresting characteristics of this "transparent and forcible prose," as Lowell called it, were its logic and its power. From the logic Brownson's writing gained an air of finality, and from the power an air of intransigence: the result was his reputation as an extremist. In reality, he tended on most issues to mediate between extremes. He championed the eclectic method, which was a perfect instrument for compromise; he tried to combine first the traditional New England theology with the new spirit of Transcendentalism, and later Catholicism with

Protestantism; he occupied middle ground in the slavery controversy; his political theory sought first to effect a balance between democracy and constitutionalism and finally between an effective national government and the rights of states; his theory of knowledge mediated between nominalism and realism, and later he compromised the epistemological problem by uniting the previous solutions into one grand formula; he admired Catholicism particularly because of its ineffable harmony between nature and grace. In short, he usually decided that each side of a question had its truth, and his inclination was to build a complete answer by heaping the truths together. Yet he always stated his position with such force and decision that his readers assumed it to be extreme.

Brownson made no pretense of being an economist, but of all his writings his economic thought is today the most striking. He reasoned on economic problems, not systematically, but in a series of flashes which momentarily revealed in blazes of white light ideas later to rule the world. Unhappily few were looking, and few benefited. His notes on the rôle of the frontier in softening class divisions in America and on the organic nature of the business cycle were brilliant insights, thrown off casually in discussions of other questions. He worked out the ideas of the class struggle and of the dominance of economic factors in history more deliberately and used them to make remarkably penetrating observations on the politics of his day. Standing on the border of the new industrial economy with his preconceptions taken from a society where relationships were predominantly personal, he saw clearly how the impersonal system of factories and banks was sloughing off the old morality. Impersonality meant soullessness; and, if soullessness were to triumph on earth, Brownson feared for God in His heaven. As a constructor of Utopias, he suffered from the belief that the old morality and the new capitalism could somehow be combined; but as a critic of industrialism he observed the interplay between ethics and industry with a keenness equalled by few of his time.

In philosophy Brownson aspired to much more than in economics, but attained to much less. He was enthusiastic rather than gifted as a metaphysician, earnest rather than skillful. Doubtless he had no equal in America; but next to Kant or Hegel, or to Newman and Mill, he appears crude and shallow. His two strong habits of mind were frequently in conflict. One was his reliance on common sense, his strong solicitude for facts; the other, his guileless trust in logic. His intellectual honesty compelled him to rest his philosophy, not only on facts, but on all the facts, and at the same time prevented him from manipulating them in a way which would render them harmless. His observations of the facts of consciousness were, for example, extremely candid and accurate. He vigorously attacked the psychologists who explained the intellect in formulas which were logically consistent but went far beyond recognizable experience. "Psychologists have never, or at least rarely, been willing to accept the primitive fact of consciousness as the primitive fact," he wrote. "What is complex or manifold, they have supposed must needs be composite; therefore, secondary; therefore, susceptible of being decomposed and resolved into its primitive elements." [14] Indeed, it was unfortunate that Brownson never completed his treatise on *Synthetic Philosophy*, less for philosophy than for psychology. He was derivative and uninteresting in his metaphysics; but his comments on the workings of man's mind showed a remarkable scrupulousness in the reading of consciousness and a fine unwillingness to make distinctions which were not confirmed by observation.

But, with all this respect for fact, Brownson retained a passion for logic. "The thing he detests most is bad logic," reported Hecker. "It makes him peev-

[14] "Schmucker's Psychology," *Democratic Review*, XI (October, 1842), *Works*, I, 52.

ish and often riles his temper." [15] Emerson would say, "We value an observation upon a brass knob, a genuine observation on a button, more than whole encyclopædias"; [16] but Brownson, after glancing at the knob and button, would pass on quickly to the encyclopedias. Emerson insisted that thought sprang from an intimate, first-hand acquaintance with things. Brownson regarded logic as the test of thought, preferring a set of criteria imposed from above to the interior conviction of truth or falsity. Emerson was intuitive, Brownson legalistic; one hoped to conquer by calling forth an inner recognition of the truth, the other by the sheer power of demonstration.

Yet Brownson was too honest not to acknowledge at times that he was placing a false value on logic. His belief that he could unravel the universe with the true logic was unassailable; but, lacking the true logic, his reliance on the imperfect logic of man was totally unwarranted. It encouraged his temperamental yearning for simple problems and easy solutions. "Either your principle is sound, or it is not," was too often the method of his argument. "If it is sound, you have no right to stop short of its legitimate consequences . . . if it is unsound,

[15] Hecker's journal, June 22, 1845, Elliott, *op. cit.*, 181.
[16] Emerson, *Journals*, IV, 400.

you have no right to act on it at all." [17] Brownson, in fact, was insensibly deceived into thinking that syllogisms were realities and that life followed logic. Logic goes by extremes, but life by compromises, for logic leaves out considerations that life cannot ignore. He nevertheless apotheosized logic and fell victim to its disastrous simplicity. For all its power his reasoning commanded respect rather than assent. He defeated his opponents but did not convince them. In fact, he grew to doubt at times that any argument could touch the soul. "It is not the office of logic to produce faith," he once wrote,

but simply to remove the intellectual obstacles to it; not to motive assent, but to demonstrate that there is no solid reason for withholding it, and that it ought to be yielded. [18]

His own life, indeed, made a laughing-stock of logic. The impact on him of vital experience again and again changed his belief by evoking new intuitions, though they emerged from his head fully dressed in syllogistic armor. He could vindicate all his conclusions superbly; but the conclusions were with equal plainness the servants of his experience and the masters of his logic. No man in America of

[17] "Come-outerism; or the Radical Tendency of the Day," *BrQR*, I (July, 1844), *Works*, IV, 554.
[18] "The Christian Register's Objections," *BrQR*, New Series, VI (October, 1852), *Works*, VII, 232.

the day handled the instrument of reason with more proficiency, or believed in it with more conviction; yet few men had careers less characterized by the stability supposed to come from reason. But his faith in logic rarely faltered.

The lonely pursuit of truth, with its worship of unflinching honesty and rigorous logic, was the secret of his failure. While the quest for goodness might have united him to his fellows and given him power to move them, the quest for truth only led to bleak isolation. He adopted the highest standards of integrity and thought for so perilous a journey. His fellows could not live by these standards, and he lost touch with them. Knowing they were fallible, he yet disliked them for it and refused to forgive their faults. Knowing they were ruled by emotion, he yet acted as if they were rational and despaired when they shrank from his elaborate argument. He swayed them by massiveness of personality, not by warmth of soul. "Though he is a friend to me," wrote Isaac Hecker, "and the most critical periods of my experience have been known to him, and he has frequently given me advice and sympathy, yet he never moves my heart . . . ." [19] Set apart by his love for truth, too proud to abandon his desolate quest, he could shout only to the wind and the waves.

[19] Hecker's journal, June 22, 1845, Elliott, *op. cit.*, 180–181.

But he fought many brave fights on the way and kept his face turned always ahead. "My *Marks* and *Scars* I carry with me, to be a Witness for me, that I have fought his Battles who now will be my Rewarder," cried Mr. Valiant-for-Truth as he prepared to pass over the river. So he passed over, and all the trumpets sounded for him on the other side.

3

Against the background of his time Orestes Brownson stands an important and expressive figure. He symbolized the intellectual restlessness and vitality of the period before specialization made it impossible for one man to work with equal facility in a dozen fields. The years before the Civil War were marked by stir and bustle, aspiration and anticipation. New paths were laid down, new ideas struck off. The people grew socially and intellectually self-conscious. They rushed to remedy the defects of their society and to repair the shortcomings of their culture. From a Vermont farm Brownson rose by his own intelligence and energy to a position of national importance. In the diversity of his interests he typified the generation. The rejection of Calvinism, the concern with workingmen's reform, the *Church of the Future*, Transcendentalism, the

Democratic party of Jackson and Van Buren, Brook Farm, Catholicism, Calhoun and state rights, spiritualism, feminism, emancipation — there was hardly a question, large or small, that agitated the country from 1830 to 1870, on which Brownson did not make comments. To many of them he made contributions.

While most reformers of the day busied themselves with evils that were remote, like slavery, or largely speculative, like intemperance and sex inequality, Brownson had the courage to face the life around him and the sharpness to see what the problem of the future was to be. When it was the height of radicalism to inveigh against the slaveholder, he was inveighing against the capitalist. His political theory mirrored the transformation of the nation. His writings on religion reflected from shifting angles the vital problems of the church. His philosophy was a significant attempt to wrestle with the relation of faith and reality. His observations on society had a profundity no other American of the time approached.

Yet Brownson is today almost forgotten. His name survives on a gravestone at Notre Dame. A slab given by the Knights of Columbus marks his birthplace at Stockbridge. In 1910 loyal Catholics set up in Riverside Park a bronze head by Samuel J. Kitson, labeled

"BROWNSON, Publicist, Philosopher, Patriot"; it stood there until 1937 when a gang of playful boys knocked it off its pedestal. This incident returned Brownson to public attention for the first time since his death sixty years before. "Riverside Statue Stumps Historians," was the headline in the ordinarily omniscient *New York Times*.

> The instability of fame was demonstrated yesterday when an investigation of the knocking down of a statue in Riverside Park at 104th Street opened difficulties in identifying the subject of the memorial. . . . The police of the West 100th Street station, in opening an investigation of the statue, listed its subject as a "well-known patriot." But a casual canvass of local historians, literary minds, and young men fresh from study at college showed that Brownson was unknown to modern minds [and so on].[20]

Why has Brownson slipped so completely into oblivion? The *Nation* remarked in 1873: "Had he

[20] *New York Times*, July 1, 1937. On July 5, the *Times* remarked editorially, ". . . the head found rolling down the slopes of Riverside Drive [was] fortunately a head in bronze which had been knocked off its pedestal by a crowd of raffish boys. The boys bore no grudge against the bearded gentleman whose bust was parked above the Hudson. They had not the slightest idea who he was, and neither, it turned out, did the older residents of the neighborhood. The inscription on the pedestal meant nothing to anybody. Not until the reporters dug up the information was the New Yorker thus honored and dishonored identified as ORESTES A. BROWNSON, a transcendentalist philosopher, controversialist and poet [sic] whose works fill nineteen [sic] volumes in the Public Library and who was famous enough as late as 1910 to rate a public monument."

written for some great newspaper, and on topics in which he and a wide audience had a common interest, it is probable that no writer of the century would have gained a surer popularity." [21] But Brownson wrote on subjects that were unpopular in his own day and have not till recently become fashionable for historical treatment. The scholars who decided what should be remembered of the days before the Civil War were little concerned with the fortunes of labor or the protests against industrialism or with the Catholic Church. Literary historians were more generous because of Brownson's friendship with people whose lives have received the minutest scrutiny. Yet even there his rôle has dwindled to unimportance. A generation after his conversion, when the Transcendentalists wrote their memoirs or sat to the indefatigable O. B. Frothingham, they had pretty much forgotten everything about Brownson save his vehemence, his instability and his Catholicism. "The lesson of his life was told for us above thirty years ago," observed J. H. Allen in 1882; "and the strong, stormful, rude, yet tender-hearted man passed away, leaving hardly a ripple in our memory to remind us of what his influence had been." [22]

[21] *Nation*, XVI, 74 (January 30, 1873).
[22] J. H. Allen, *Our Liberal Movement in Theology*, 88.

Orestes Brownson thus fell victim to the accidents of history and vanished from America's remembrance of her past. His extraordinary intelligence and profound honesty deserved a richer reward. In the last decade Catholic scholars have started on his rediscovery. Several Catholic studies of Brownson have appeared, and his name occurs frequently in Catholic journals.[23] But he belongs to all Americans, not simply to Catholics. Perhaps an age more sympathetic with men who would not compromise and would not retreat will accord him his rightful place. He is a part of the national heritage.

[23] The revival of Catholic interest in Brownson is shown by the publication of such essays as Virgil G. Michel's *The Critical Principles of Orestes A. Brownson*, Sidney A. Raemers's *America's Foremost Philosopher*, Mary Rose Gertrude Whalen's *Some Aspects of the Influence of Orestes A. Brownson* and the fourth essay in Daniel Sargent's *Four Independents*. Catholics never wholly forgot him; see the *Chicago Tribune* of June 19, 1926: "Leading Catholics of Chicago Recall the Books that Have Influenced Them." "Joseph Rend thinks that the Rev. Thomas Turnbull's 'History of the Jesuits' is one of the most wonderful books ever written. He also reads with great pleasure Brownson's 'Moral Philosophy.' . . . Thomas J. Condon also gave 'The Life of Christ' as one of his favorites. He likes all of Hilaire Belloc's books, and all of Gilbert Chesterton's, as well as Brownson's and Mons. Robert Hugh Benson's. . . . Father Francis P. Duffy of New York, the beloved former chaplain of the Rainbow division, who is here for the [Eucharistic] congress, says that the book which has done the most to develop the logical faculties of his mind is Orestes A. Brownson's 'Review.' " I am indebted for this citation to Mr. Edward T. James.

BIBLIOGRAPHY

The main body of the papers of Orestes A. Brownson is preserved in the archives of Notre Dame University. Though consisting largely of letters to Brownson, it also contains letters by him, first and final drafts of his articles and miscellaneous material. Additional Brownson letters are to be found in the George Bancroft manuscripts at the Massachusetts Historical Society, in the Charles Sumner papers at the Harvard College Library and in the Godwin-Greeley collection at the New York Public Library.

Brownson's *Works,* collected and arranged by his son Henry F. Brownson, were published in Detroit from 1882 to 1887 in twenty volumes. Virtually all the essays Brownson wrote as a Catholic are reprinted here, along with a selection of articles written before 1844. The order is topical, but the essays are, in general, identified by magazine and date. His forceful, if not altogether reliable, autobiography, *The Convert,* is contained in volume five. Many of his orations were published in pamphlet form during his lifetime. *An Address on the Fifty-Fifth Anniversary of American Independence Delivered at Ovid, Ithaca Co., New York, July 4, 1831* (Ithaca, 1831), *Address on Intemperance* (Keene, N. H., 1833), *An Address Delivered at Dedham on the Fifty-Eighth Anniversary of American Independence* (Dedham, 1834), *Babylon Is Falling* (Boston, 1837) and the *Address on Social Reform* (Boston, 1844) proved most useful in this study. There are files of the *Boston Quarterly Review* (Boston, 1838–1842) and of *Brownson's Quarterly Review* (Boston, 1844–1855; New York, 1856–1864, 1873–1875) in the Harvard College Library.

The comprehensive biography by his son was published in Detroit in three volumes under the titles of *Orestes A. Brownson's Early Life* (1898), *Orestes A. Brownson's Middle Life* (1899) and *Orestes A. Brownson's Latter Life* (1900). Badly organized and somewhat ponderous, this work makes only a perfunctory attempt to tell a connected story of Brownson's life; yet the author, in spite of his devotion to his father and his own piety, does not try to palliate or explain away the elder Brownson's career before he entered the Church. The important letters in the Notre Dame collection are reprinted. Those interested in Brownson's genealogical background should turn to Henry Bronson, *The History of Waterbury, Connecticut* (Waterbury, 1858). Virgil G. Michel, *The Critical Principles of Orestes A. Brownson* (Washington, 1918), is marred somewhat by its assumption that Brownson's æsthetic ideas over thirty years form a consistent body of doctrine, though it contains much of interest. Sidney A. Raemers, *America's Foremost Philosopher* (Washington, 1931), presents a thoughtful analysis of the epistemological predicament by one caught in it, but many of the factual statements about Brownson are erroneous. Mary Rose Gertrude Whalen, *Some Aspects of the Influence of Orestes A. Brownson on His Contemporaries* (Notre Dame, 1933), has little value. The essay on Brownson in Daniel Sargent, *Four Independents* (New York, 1935), is pleasant if somewhat inaccurate.

Brownson was through his lifetime the victim of vigorous and occasionally rather scurrilous pamphleteering. Characteristic are Charles Grandison Thomas, *Hereditary Property Justified. Reply to Brownson's Article on the Laboring Classes. By One Whose Personal Experience Should Enable Him to Feel the Wants and Sympathize with the Condition of the Laborer* (Cambridge, 1841), Richard Hildreth, *A Joint Letter to Orestes A. Brownson and the Editor of the North American Review in Which the Editor of the North American Review Is Proved to Be No Christian and Little Better than an Atheist* (Boston, 1844), Abel C. Thomas, *Civilization and Roman Catholicism. A Review of O. A. Brownson's Four Lectures* (Philadelphia, 1851), and [anonymous] *Brownson's Review Reviewed: Being a Mild and Vigorous Vindication of the Rights and Privileges of Adopted Citizens against the Assaults and Aspersions of Dr. O. A. Brownson by the Catholic Press of the United States* (Boston, 1854).

Frank Luther Mott's spirited and comprehensive *History of American Magazines, 1741–1850* (New York, 1930) has been helpful through the whole course of the work. The following editions of the standard authors were used: Ralph Waldo Emerson (Centenary Edition); James Russell Lowell (Riverside Edition); Edgar Allan Poe (Chicago, 1895).

Chapter One. For the background of the New York Workingmen's party, see Helen L. Sumner's chapters in John R. Commons and associates, *History of Labour in the United States* (New York, 1918). Frances Wright D'Arusmont, *Biography, Notes and Political Letters* (New

York, 1845), and Robert Dale Owen, *Threading My Way* (New York, 1874), contain autobiographical material. The best biographies are William Randall Waterman, *Frances Wright* (New York, 1924), and Richard Leopold's admirable "Robert Dale Owen," an unpublished thesis in the Harvard College Library.

Chapters Two and Three. Harriet Martineau, *Society in America* (New York, 1837), is excellent for the social background of the day. The Panic of 1837 is well discussed in Samuel Rezneck, "The Social History of an American Depression, 1837–1843," in the *American Historical Review*, XL, 662–687 (July, 1935). William Charvat's "American Romanticism and the Depression of 1837," which appeared in *Science and Society*, II, 67–82 (Winter, 1937), has some useful facts rather naïvely treated. For the background of the Transcendental enthusiasm, O. B. Frothingham, *Transcendentalism in New England* (New York, 1876), a thoroughly mediocre work, seems unhappily to be indispensable. James Murdock, *Sketches of Modern Philosophy Especially among the Germans* (Hartford, 1842), gives an interesting contemporary account of cross-currents of thought, though its picture of Brownson and the Transcendentalists is not very exact. Clarence L. F. Gohdes, *The Periodicals of American Transcendentalism* (Durham, 1931), assembles a good deal of important information. Among biographies, the following were useful: William Henry Channing's inaccurate *Memoir of William Ellery Channing* (Boston, 1848), Elizabeth Palmer Peabody's gossipy *Reminiscences of Rev. Wm. Ellery Channing* (Boston, 1880), *A. Bron-*

son Alcott: His Life and Philosophy (Boston, 1893) by F. B. Sanborn and W. T. Harris, John Weiss's *Life and Correspondence of Theodore Parker* (New York, 1864), Parker's own *Experience as a Minister* (Boston, 1859), O. B. Frothingham's *Theodore Parker* (Boston, 1874) and Henry Steele Commager's excellent *Theodore Parker* (Boston, 1936). Of peripheral relevance were Thomas Wentworth Higginson's charming *Margaret Fuller Ossoli* (Boston, 1884), James Elliot Cabot, *Memoir of Ralph Waldo Emerson* (Boston, 1887), George W. Cooke, *Ralph Waldo Emerson: His Life, Writings and Philosophy* (Boston, 1881), F. B. Sanborn (ed.), *The Genius and Character of Emerson* (Boston, 1884), William Ellery Channing, *Thoreau, the Poet-Naturalist* (Boston, 1902), Adin Ballou, *Autobiography* (Lowell, 1896), and *George Ripley* (Boston, 1882) by the industrious Frothingham.

The edition cited of Victor Cousin's *Fragments Philosophiques* is Paris, 1838; of C. H. de Saint-Simon's *Nouveau Christianisme*, Paris, 1832. There are many editions of H. F. R. de Lamennais, *Paroles d'un Croyant* and *Le Livre du Peuple*. *The People's Own Book*, a translation of the latter by Nathaniel Greene, a friend of Brownson's, appeared in Boston in 1839.

H. S. Foxwell's brilliant introduction to Anton Menger, *The Right to the Whole Produce of Labour* (translated by M. E. Tanner, London, 1899), sketches pre-Marxian socialist thought in England; there is further useful material in the book itself. William Thompson's chief work was *An Inquiry into the Principles of the Distribution of Wealth Most Conducive to Human Happiness* (London, 1824), while Thomas Hodgskin's was *Labour Defended against the Claims of Capital, or the Unproductiveness of Capital Proved with Reference to the Present Combinations amongst Journeymen* (1825), (with an introduction by G. D. H. Cole, London, 1922). Max Beer, *A History of British Socialism* (London, 1919), and Esther Lowenthal, *The Ricardian Socialists* (New York, 1911), provide further information about the halfway stage to Marxism.

Arthur B. Darling, *Political Changes in Massachusetts, 1824–1848* (New Haven, 1925), gives a detailed account of the rise of Jacksonian democracy in Massachusetts. The rancor and virulence of the election of 1840 are admirably suggested in A. B. Norton, *The Great Revolution of 1840* (Mt. Vernon, Ohio, 1888), written by a Whig still engaged, forty years after, in fighting the campaign.

Chapters Four and Five. The *Memoirs and Letters of Charles Sumner* (Boston, 1877), edited by Edward L. Pierce, and the *Memoirs* of John Quincy Adams (Philadelphia, 1876), edited by Charles Francis Adams, throw interesting sidelights on the period. Joseph Henry Allen, *Our Liberal Movement in Theology* (Boston, 1882), contains some valuable reminiscences. The standard work on Brook Farm is Lindsay Swift's amiable compilation, *Brook Farm* (New York, 1900). Until a better work is written, it is desirable to go directly to such sources as Georgiana Bruce Kirby, *Years of Experience* (New York, 1886), Marianne Dwight, *Letters from Brook Farm* (Poughkeepsie, 1928), *Early Letters of George William Curtis to John S. Dwight* (New York, 1898) and the material in Zoltán Haraszti, *The Idyll of Brook Farm* (Boston, 1937).

For Leroux, see P.–Félix Thomas, *Pierre Leroux: Sa Vie, Son Œuvre, Sa Doctrine* (Paris, 1904).

Chapters Six and Seven. The Life of Father Hecker (New York, 1898) by Walter Elliott and the *Life of the Most Reverend John Hughes, D.D.* (New York, 1866) by John R. G. Hassard are the best biographies of the leading American Catholic clerics of the day. The English Catholic movement is sketched in *Lord Acton and His Circle* (New York, 1906), edited by Abbot Gasquet, and in the following books by Wilfrid Ward: *William George Ward and the Oxford Movement* (London, 1889), *William George Ward and the Catholic Revival* (London, 1893), *The Life and Times of Cardinal Wiseman* (London, 1897) and the *Life of John Henry Cardinal Newman* (London, 1912). The works of Cardinal Newman are to be found in several editions. My references are to the volumes in Everyman's Library. By far the best treatment of Know-Nothingism and the forces lying behind it is Ray Allen Billington, *The Protestant Crusade, 1800–1860* (New York, 1938).

INDEX

ABELARD, philosophy of, 233.

Abolitionism. *See* Slavery.

Acton, Sir John (later Lord), writes Brownson, 216–217; on Brownson, 255, 285.

Adams, J. Q., Brownson supports, 34; "Laboring Classes" excites, 102.

Alcott, Bronson, and Charles Lane, 43; as Transcendentalist, 46, 150; regarding *Boston Quarterly*, 48, 87; publishes *Conversations with Children*, 58; on Brownson, 59, 137; writes for *Boston Quarterly*, 75; confused with Brownson, 130; as character in *Spirit-Rapper*, 225; compared with Brownson, 279.

Allen, J. H., on Brownson, 138, 296.

Allen, Joseph, as Unitarian, 50–51.

Allen, S. C., on economic classes, 37–38, 40, 70.

American Republic, The, Brownson writes, 260–261.

Anti-Masonic party, Brownson supports, 15.

Antislavery. *See* Slavery.

Aristotle, influences Brownson, 115, 118, 229, 232–233.

BALLOU, ADIN, and Brownson, 31.

Bancroft, George, Brownson writes, 61–62, 256; on Brownson's ideas, 70, 101 *n.*, 106; on economic classes, 70; as a Democrat, 70–71, 81, 101, 259; appointed Collector of Port of Boston, 72; offers Brownson post, 72, 129; writes for *Boston Quarterly*, 74–75; and Cousin, 124, 128; renews friendship with Brownson, 250; Brownson dedicates book to, 260.

Banks, speculation affects, 65–66; defects of, 69, 83; and Sub-Treasury, 83–86; Brownson on, 94; Whigs and, 113. *See also* United States Bank.

Bartlett, Elisha, misrepresents Brownson, 105.

Bennett, J. G., on Brownson, 252.

Benton, T. H., and banking system, 83; on class struggle, 85; compared with Calhoun, 115; Brownson opposes, 160.

Bibliography, 299–305.

Blackwood's Magazine, on Brownson, 48, 129–130.

Blithedale Romance, The, Brownson criticizes, 238.

Boston Quarterly Review, Brownson establishes, 73; opinions on, 48, 74, 75, 87, 155–156; contributors to, 74–75, 106; Brownson abandons, 155.

Boston Reformer, Brownson edits, 64, 65, 68, 73.

Brisbane, Albert, writes for *Boston Quarterly,* 75; Parker reads, 103–104; as Fourierist, 167 *n.*

Brook Farm, and Brownson, 150–154, 177; as Fourierist community, 167.

Brown, Thomas, influences Brownson, 24.

Brownson, Daphne A., born, 5; writes Brownson, 186.

Brownson, Henry, pleases father, 272; Brownson visits, 275; writes father's biography, 300.

Brownson, Oran, becomes Mormon, 186–187.

Brownson, Orestes A., ancestry of, 4, 300; childhood of, 5–7; moves to Ballston Spa, 7; education of, 7, 12, 284; as Presbyterian, 8–11; teaches school, 11; moves to Detroit, 11; falls ill, 12; goes to Vermont, 12; as Universalist, 12–16, 19, 21, 23; returns to New York, 12–13; marries, 13; at Utica, 17–18; as agnostic, 24–26; writes *Charles Elwood,* 25–26, 141–142; as religious independent, 26–28; in Ithaca, 27–28; in Walpole, N. H., 29; visits Boston, 29; as Unitarian, 29–31, 50–60, 145–149; installed at Canton, 31; moves to Chelsea, 41; proclaims "Church of the Future," 50–60, 183–184; moves to Boston, 52; writes *New Views,* 54–59, 140; becomes editor of *Boston Reformer,* 64, 68; holds post at Marine Hospital, 72, 155; becomes editor of *Boston Quarterly,* 73; writes "Laboring Classes," 89–108; effect of 1840 election on, 110–112, 114, 136–137, 138, 144, 148, 155; deepening religious sense of, 137–149, 169–170; attempts to recast Unitarianism, 145–149; and Brook Farm, 150–154; ends *Boston Quarterly* and becomes contributing editor of *Democratic Review,* 155; becomes editor of *Brownson's Quarterly,* 160, 270; leans toward Catholicism, 171–179; abandons Unitarian pulpit, 179; joins Catholic Church, 179–184; early reaction of, as a Catholic, 185–190, 194–210, 283; public attitude toward conversion of, 190–194; at odds with Catholic leaders, 210–216, 251–256; attempts to reconstruct Catholic philosophy, 219–234; invited to lecture in Dublin,

216–217; moves to New York, 218–219, 226; moves to New Jersey, 223, 247; writes *Spirit-Rapper*, 224–226; and Civil War, 245–251, 255, 259; later illness of, 247–248, 250, 255, 256, 273; ends *Brownson's Quarterly*, 255; receives annuity, 256; writes *American Republic*, 260–261; revives *Brownson's Quarterly*, 270, 275; last days of, 273–275; dies, 275; statue of, 294–295; revived interest in, 297 *n.*; and slavery question, 79–80, 90–91, 105, 113, 123, 161, 240–246, 252, 267, 287; in politics, 15, 22, 34–35, 64–65, 71, 85–87, 101, 110–114, 157–158, 160–163, 206, 207–208, 244–245, 248–250, 266–267; political theory of, 114–123, 158–159, 257–261, 287, 294; as social reformer, 19–23, 28, 33–41, 53–54, 61–111, 159, 164–170, 204–208, 268–269, 287–288, 294; as philosopher, 32–34, 46–50, 54–59, 123–136, 142–145, 154–155, 156–157, 177–179, 189–190, 228–234, 261–266, 288–293, 294; as writer, 30, 32, 56–57, 95, 114, 195–196, 222, 225–226, 261, 285–286; as literary critic, 234–239; appearance of, 12, 41–42, 72, 187–188, 256, 272; personality of, 14–15, 41–46, 107, 153, 154, 155, 185, 190, 223, 272–275, 276–285, 292–293; family relations of, 27, 31, 43–44, 185–187, 270, 272–275, 276; contemporary opinions on, 30, 43, 45, 46, 59, 62–63, 72, 101–102, 105–107, 128–129, 137, 138, 152, 153, 175, 190–194, 197, 217–218, 222, 255, 276, 277–280, 289–290; general appraisal of, 280–297; bibliography of, 299–301.

Brownson, Mrs. Orestes A., marries, 13; grieves at Brownson's disbelief, 24; becomes Catholic, 185; dies, 270; character of, 272.

Brownson, Orestes A., Jr., plays chess, 44; at Brook Farm, 151, 153; becomes Catholic, 185–186; disappoints father, 273.

Brownson, Relief M., settles in Vermont, 4, 5; moves to New York, 7.

Brownson, Sarah, on Brownson, 43–44; Brownson lives with, 272, 273–274; becomes mother, 275.

Brownson, Sylvester, settles in Vermont, 4–5; dies, 5.

Brownson's Quarterly Review, appears, 160; Brownson proposes to abandon, 193, 194; Fitzpatrick influences, 194–195, 210; circulation of, 195, 209; purpose of, 197; in Great Britain, 198; faces

Brownson's Quarterly Review (*Continued*)
    financial crisis, 209, 247 *n.*; censorship of, 210; attacked, 211; Bishop's letter removed from, 215; moved to New York, 219; censured, 223, 253, 255; ended, 255; revived for a time, 270, 275.

Bruce, Georgiana, on Brownson, 153.

Bryant, W. C., unpopular, 81; writes for *Democratic Review*, 156.

Buchanan, James, elected, 243; Brownson on policy of, 244.

Business cycle, Brownson expounds, 167, 287.

CALHOUN, J. C., Brownson supports, 34, 157, 160–162; and state rights, 77, 115, 257; and banking problem, 83, 115–116; on "Laboring Classes," 106; political theory of, 115–117, 120–123.

Calvinism, affects Brownson, 8–10; Brownson rejects, 10–11, 293; Universalists oppose, 12.

Carlyle, Thomas, Brownson on, 47; on *New Views*, 56; Brownson reviews works of, 89–90, 158; confuses Brownson with Alcott, 130.

Catholic Church, Brownson leans toward, 171–179; Brownson joins, 179–184; Brownson's family and, 185–187; Brownson as member

of, 187–203, 283; other converts to, 190, 197–198; in Great Britain, 197–198; assembly of bishops of, 209; nativists oppose, 211–214; Brownson's attempts to liberalize, 220–226, 251–256.

Catholic World, Brownson writes for, 261, 269–270.

Channing, W. E., influences Brownson, 26, 29, 30–31, 52, 280; on Brownson and Thoreau, 31–32; economic views of, 38, 65, 71, 78; and Brownson exchange pulpits, 42; Brownson's opinion of, 51; favors Society for Christian Union, 62–63; writes for *Boston Quarterly*, 75; termed Loco-Foco, 81; on "Laboring Classes," 102; Brownson appeals to, 145–148, 150; on "Mediatorial Life of Jesus," 171; mistrusts Brownson, 277.

Channing, W. H., on *Boston Quarterly*, 155–156.

Chardon Street Convention, Parker at, 103.

Charles Elwood, Brownson writes, 25–26, 141; notice of, 106; Brownson reviews, 141–142.

Chartism, and Carlyle, 89–90; exponents of, 100.

Chase, S. P., and anti-Lincoln movement, 249.

Choate, Rufus, in politics, 85.

Christian Examiner, Brownson writes for, 30, 33–34, 63,

128; James Walker edits, 36; found wanting, 74; influence of, 128.

Christian Register, Brownson writes for, 30.

Christian Review, on *Charles Elwood,* 26; attacks "Laboring Classes," 106.

Christian World, Brownson writes for, 174.

Christianity as a Purely Internal Principle, published, 58.

"Church of the Future," Brownson advocates, 34, 50–60, 140; prematureness of, 73; identified with Catholicism, 184.

Civil War, Brownson, Hughes and, 224; Brownson and, 245–246, 248–251, 253, 255, 259; and state rights, 257, 259.

Clarke, J. F., as Transcendentalist, 46, 134; on Brownson, 191, 279.

Clay, Henry, and banking system, 83–84; Whig party rejects, 88; in campaign of 1840, 109; compared with Calhoun, 115; Brownson opposes, 160.

Coakley, T. F., on Brownson, 285 n.

Coleridge, S. T., philosophy of, 124–125.

Come-Outers, meeting of, 103; Brownson and, 181.

Compromise of 1850, Webster supports, 85; Brownson favors, 241.

Comte, Auguste, religious views of, 265, 271–272; influences Brownson, 280.

Constant, Benjamin, and Ripley, 31; influences Brownson, 32–33, 34, 124; Brownson disagrees with, 142.

"Conversations with a Radical," Brownson writes, 114.

Cooper, J. F., Brownson approves, 81.

Cousin, Victor, influences Brownson, 34, 49, 54–55, 124–128, 280; eclectic principle of, 55, 125; as metaphysician, 124–130; praises Brownson, 128–129; Norton attacks, 134; Brownson defends, 134; Brownson dissatisfied with, 142–143; influences Leroux, 143; ignores Brownson, 190–191; Descartes influences, 233–234.

Curtis, G. W., on Brownson and Hecker, 154.

DANA, C. A., at Brook Farm, 153.

Darwin, Charles, proclaims theory of evolution, 261; Brownson denounces, 271–272.

Davis, A. J., as medium, 224.

Davis, W. J., becomes Catholic, 190.

Democratic party, Brownson supports, 22, 71; Brownson addresses, 68; Brownson attempts to justify, 85–87; renominates Van Buren, 88–89; and "Laboring Classes,"

Democratic party (*Continued*) 101; in 1840, 109–111; Brownson advises, 112–114; Brownson deserts, 160; and slavery, 243; in 1860, 248; in 1862, 248–249.

Democratic Review, on Brook Farm, 151; Brownson and, 155–160; appraised, 156.

Depression, of 1828–1829, 20; of 1837, 66–73, 82–83, 88; and business cycle, 167–168.

Descartes, René, Brownson criticizes, 233, 265.

Dial, compared to *Boston Quarterly*, 48 *n.*; approves Brownson, 103; Parker and, 104.

Dickens, Charles, Brownson on, 271.

Discourses on the Philosophy of Religion, published, 58.

Disquisition on Government, Calhoun writes, 120.

Distribution bill, controversy over, 116–118.

Draper, J. W., and Brownson, 264.

Dred Scott decision, effect of, 243.

Dublin Review, on *Brownson's Review*, 198, 255; defends Newman, 200.

Dwight, J. S., writes for *Boston Quarterly*, 75.

ECLECTICISM, and Cousin, 55, 125; attracts Brownson, 125, 143, 279, 286; Brownson disowns, 190, 279.

Economic classes, Allen on, 37–38, 70; Brownson on, 36, 53, 63–64, 66–70, 77–78, 82–83, 164–167; Bancroft on, 70; Channing on, 102. *See also* Labor; "Laboring Classes."

Economic interpretation of American history, Brownson on, 84–85, 258. *See also* Economic classes; "Laboring Classes."

Education, of Brownson, 7; Frances Wright on, 17, 18; through state guardianship, 20, 22; Brownson on, 36, 40–41, 63–64, 65, 81, 108, 113–114; parochial, 223.

Edwards, Jonathan, and Brownson, 6.

Emerson, R. W., on self-reliance, 39; as Transcendentalist, 42, 46, 48–50, 150, 189–190; on Brownson, 43; religious views of, 57, 58, 59, 126, 131, 189–190; economic views of, 62, 78–79 *n.*; on Whigs *versus* Democrats, 85; and Brownson compared, 87, 132, 279, 290; on government, 118; addresses Harvard Divinity School, 131, 132; Brownson criticizes, 132, 189–190, 271–272; at Brook Farm, 151; unsympathetic with Brownson, 218; as character in *Spirit-Rapper*, 225; Brownson on writings of, 238; on fugitive slave law, 241.

Essay on the Development of Christian Doctrine, An, debate over, 199–201; Brownson praises, 254.

Europe, revolutions in, 206–207, 220.

Evans, G. H., and state guardianship, 20; Parker and, 104.

Everett, A. H., writes for *Boston Quarterly*, 75; supports Van Buren, 86.

Evolutionary hypothesis, set forth, 261–262; Brownson's attitude toward, 262–265.

Fable for Critics, on Brownson, 278, 279.

Fenwick, B. J., Brownson visits, 174, 179; advises Brownson, 180; dies, 199.

Finney, C. G., as revivalist, 187 *n.*

Fitzpatrick, J. B., instructs Brownson, 182, 193–194; Hecker on, 193; influences Brownson, 195, 226–227; approves attack on Newman, 199; at odds with Brownson, 209–210, 211, 218.

Fourier, F. M. C., and laboring classes, 96; Parker reads, 103–104; and Brook Farm, 167; as character in *Spirit-Rapper*, 225.

Fragments Philosophiques, on Brownson, 129.

Francis, Convers, as Transcendentalist, 46; publishes book, 58; and Theodore Parker, 87.

Free Inquirer, Brownson and, 19, 22.

Frémont, J. C., and anti-Lincoln movement, 249–250, 251.

French Revolution, Brownson's attitude toward, 106.

Frontier and the working class, Brownson on, 91–92, 107, 287.

Frothingham, O. B., and Transcendentalists, 296.

Fruitlands, Charles Lane at, 43.

Fuller, Margaret, as Transcendentalist, 48, 150; writes for *Boston Quarterly*, 75; at Brook Farm, 151.

Furness, W. H., religious views of, 58, 59 *n.*

Gannett, E. S., as Unitarian, 50–51.

Garrison, W. L., attacks churches, 58–59; as character in *Spirit-Rapper*, 225.

Genesee *Republican and Herald of Reform*, Brownson and, 20, 22.

Gioberti, Vincenzo, influences Brownson, 219–220, 229–230, 261, 280; Brownson on, 231.

Godwin, Parke, writes for *Democratic Review*, 156; as Fourierist, 167 *n.*; Brownson writes, 175 *n.*

Gospel Advocate and Impartial Investigator, Brownson and, 14, 15–16, 21.

"Gospel Creed, A," Brownson publishes, 16.

Grant, U. S., and anti-Lincoln movement, 249; Brownson on, 267.

Greeley, Horace, and Brownson, 246, 252, 267.

Greene, Benjamin, Brownson at bookstore of, 42, 196–197.

Griswold, Rufus, on Brownson, 194, 280.

HARNEY, G. J., and Brownson, 100.

Harrison, W. H., Whigs nominate, 88; and campaign of 1840, 109–110; dies, 112.

Harvard University, Walker president of, 36; Brownson recommended to, 129; Emerson addresses Divinity School of, 131.

Hawthorne, Nathaniel, and Brook Farm, 151; writes for *Democratic Review*, 156.

Healy, Sally. *See* Brownson, Mrs. Orestes A.

Hecker, Isaac, on Brownson, 46, 176, 227, 276, 285, 289–290, 292; Brownson influences, 72, 154; Brownson visits, 137, 154; at Brook Farm, 154; sympathizes with Brownson, 176–177, 188, 218; under instruction, 182; on Fitzpatrick, 193; liberalism of, 219; advises Brownson, 247; edits *Catholic World*, 261, 269; estranged from Brownson, 269–270.

Hedge, F. H., as Transcendentalist, 46; religious views of, 59 *n.*

Heine, Heinrich, influences Brownson, 54, 55.

Henry, C. S., Cousin discusses, 128.

Hewit, A. F., as editor, 269; on Brownson, 284.

Hildreth, Richard, defends Transcendentalism, 134; criticizes Brownson, 191–193.

Hodgskin, Thomas, economic views of, 99–100.

Hughes, John, lectures, 173–174; approves Brownson, 218; at odds with Brownson, 222–224, 252, 253.

Hume, David, influences Brownson, 24; Descartes influences, 233.

Hurd, J. C., influences Brownson, 260–261.

Huxley, T. H., and Brownson, 265, 271–272.

IMMIGRATION, and nativist movement, 211–214.

Industrial Revolution, and Brownson, 39, 97.

Irish, censure Brownson, 210–216, 218.

Irving, Washington, praised, 81.

JACKSON, ANDREW, on government, 39; Brownson on, 40, 259; and Specie Circular, 65; and banking system, 83, 84.

Jacobi, F. H., philosophy of, 124–125.

Jefferson, Thomas, and slavery problem, 17; S. G. Allen champions, 38.

Jennings, R. L., Brownson on, 259.

Jesuits, Gioberti and, 230; Brownson assails, 254.

Jouffroy, T. S., and Brownson, 31, 34, 130.

Kant, Immanuel, and Cousin, 124, 127; Brownson and, 177–179, 228, 229, 231, 265; Descartes influences, 233; Brownson compared with, 288.

Kendall, Amos, Brownson on, 259.

Kneeland, Abner, popularity of, 44–45, 52; Brownson quarrels with, 130.

Knights of Columbus, honor Brownson, 294.

Know-Nothing movement, 211–214.

Knox, John, and Brownson, 8.

Kossuth, Louis, Brownson against, 207.

Labor, Wright-Owen program for, 20–21; Brownson on, 22–23, 36, 64–65, 97–100; Owen, Saint-Simon and Fourier on, 96; Marx on, 97. See also Depression; Economic classes; "Laboring Classes"; Wages; Workingmen's party.

"Laboring Classes, The," published, 89; on slavery, 89– 92; on wages, 91–92; on business morals, 92–93; on priesthood, 93–94; on a government program, 94– 95; critical estimate of, 95– 100; reception of, 100–107, 114–115, 161; second article on, 107–108.

Lamennais, F. R. de, and Brownson, 67, 206–207, 221.

Lane, Charles, and Brownson, 43.

Larned, Sam, and Brownson, 151.

Leach, George, becomes Catholic, 190.

Leggett, William, Brownson on, 259.

Leroux, Pierre, influences Brownson, 143–145, 171, 229, 240, 280.

Lewis, D. H., and Brownson, 161.

Lincoln, Abraham, Brownson's opinion of, 244–245, 246– 247, 249, 250.

Locke, Jane E., writes Brownson, 74–75 n.

Locke, John, revolt against, 57, 61, 131; championed, 133.

Loco-Focos, encouraged, 72; Channing and, 81; establish banking system, 84.

Longfellow, H. W., writes for Democratic Review, 156.

Lowell, J. R., writes for Democratic Review, 156; on Brownson, 278, 279, 286.

Lowell Offering, reproves Brownson, 105.

Lyceum, Brownson lectures for, 29; Brownson organizes, 31.

McAllister, W. H., Bancroft writes, 101 n.
MacKenzie, W. L., Brownson writes, 89.
Madison, James, and slavery problem, 17.
Martineau, Harriet, on Boston prudence, 30, 45; on Brownson, 45, 54.
Marx, Karl, and Brownson compared, 95; on economic classes, 96–97, 100.
Mary Lee, or the Yankee in Ireland, Brownson caricatured in, 223.
Masons, Brownson opposes, 15.
Maysville veto, Jackson and, 84.
"Mediatorial Life of Jesus, The," Brownson writes, 147, 150; Channing on, 171.
Methodism, influences Brownson, 6–7.
Methodist Quarterly Review, attacks "Laboring Classes," 105–106.
Metropolitan Record, censures Brownson, 252.
Mill, J. S., and Brownson, 264, 288.
Millerites, meeting of, 103; in New York and Vermont, 187 n.
"Mission of Jesus, The," essays on, 174.
Montalembert, C. F. de, and Brownson, 219 n., 220.
Morgan, William, disappearance of, 15.

Mormonism, Oran Brownson adopts, 186–187; and spiritualism, 226.
Morris, J. B., Brownson attacks, 202.
Morse, S. F. B., and Catholicism, 212.
"My Creed," Brownson writes, 15–16.

Nashoba experiment, and Frances Wright, 17.
Nation, on Brownson's Review, 270; on Brownson, 295–296.
Nature, Emerson publishes, 58; compared with New Views, 59; Brownson on, 62, 132.
Negroes, and Nashoba experiment, 17; Brownson on, 267. See also Slavery.
New York Herald, on Brownson, 252, 278–279.
New York Times, on Brownson, 295.
New York Tribune, on Brownson, 252.
New Views of Christianity, Society and the Church, authors influencing, 54–55; theories set forth in, 55–58; reception of, 56, 59–60, 73; Brownson restates principles of, 140.
Newcomb, Charles, as character in Spirit-Rapper, 225.
Newman, J. H., on original sin, 170; conversion of, 197–198; Brownson differs with, 199–203, 265, 271; invites Brownson to lecture, 216–

217; Brownson praises, 217; on Brownson, 217–218; Brownson compared with, 288.

Norton, Andrews, enemies on, 59; rebellion against, 61; attacks Transcendentalists, 131–132, 133–134, 189; Brownson attacks, 133, 135–136; Brownson condones, 189.

O'Brien, J. B., as Chartist, 100.

O'Connor, James, admonishes Brownson, 210–211.

Ontology, Cousin and, 127; Brownson and, 228, 231; Gioberti and, 230.

O'Sullivan, J. L., edits *Democratic Review*, 155, 156–160.

Owen, Robert, influences Brownson, 19; economic views of, 96–97; influences William Thompson, 99.

Owen, Robert D., reform program of, 19–23; Brownson on, 259.

Oxford movement, Brownson and, 198, 201, 202, 217.

Panic of 1837, Brownson and, 66–73; results of, 82, 88; cause of, 83.

Parker, Theodore, and *Boston Quarterly*, 48, 75; and Carlyle, 56; on Emerson, 87; on "Laboring Classes," 103; reform interests of, 103–104; on Brownson, 107, 132, 175, 179, 191, 218, 222; religious views of, 131, 134, 139–140, 148–149; Brownson on, 189–190; as character in *Spirit-Rapper*, 225; on fugitive slave law, 241; and Brownson compared, 284.

Paulding, J. K., writes for *Democratic Review*, 156.

Peabody, Elizabeth, bookstore of, 46–47; Channing writes, 62–63, 71, 102; writes for *Boston Quarterly*, 75; writes Brownson, 250–251.

Philanthropist, The, Brownson edits, 27, 29.

Pilgrim's Progress, Brownson recommends, 206.

Pius IX, letter from, 253; encyclical of, 255.

Plato, and Cousin, 124; and Gioberti compared, 231.

Poe, E. A., on *Charles Elwood*, 25 *n.*; writes for *Democratic Review*, 156; on Brownson, 279–280, 285.

Police Gazette, Brownson on, 239.

Political theory, Brownson turns to, 114–123, 287; of Calhoun, 115–117, 120–123; Brownson's essays on, 158–159; Brownson re-examines, 257–261, 287. *See also* State rights.

Polk, J. K., nominated, 163; Brownson on, 163.

Poyen, Charles, influences Brownson, 172–173; as character in *Spirit-Rapper*, 225.

Presbyterianism, Brownson adopts, 8–9; Brownson forswears, 10–11.

"Present Age, The," Emerson lectures on, 87.

Princeton Review, Brownson's essay on, 142.

Purcell, J. B., admonishes Brownson, 210–211.

QUINCY, JOSIAH, Brownson recommended to, 129.

RECONSTRUCTION, Brownson and, 266–267.

Reformer. See *Boston Reformer*.

Religion, affects Brownson's childhood, 5–7; Brownson's early doubts concerning, 7–16; more doubts concerning, 23–27; reform through, 33–34, 64; in the pulpit, 44–45; Brownson's ideas for reform in, 50–60; and working class, 61, 66–67. *See also* sects by name.

Remarks on the Four Gospels, published, 58.

Republican party, and slavery issue, 243; Brownson supports, 244–245, 248–249; the Radical wing of, 249–250.

Ricardo, David, influence of, 98.

Ripley, George, admires Brownson, 30, 31, 43, 50; as Transcendentalist, 46, 134, 150; and *Boston Quarterly*, 48, 75; and Brook Farm, 52, 150–153, 167; Brownson on, 52, 61–62; religious views of, 57, 58, 59 *n.*, 190; and Cousin, 124; on Brownson's writings, 128, 261, 285 *n.*; at odds with Brownson, 152, 153, 196, 218; and Fourierism, 167.

Ripley, Sophia, Brownson influences, 154, 190.

Ritchie, Thomas, on Brownson, 101.

SAINT-SIMON, C. H., COMTE DE, religious views of, 33, 54, 93, 94, 130, 173; economic views of, 67, 94, 96–97; Parker reads, 103.

Sand, George, and Leroux, 143 *n.*

Sargent, Daniel, on Brownson, 285 *n.*

Scarlet Letter, The, Brownson criticizes, 238.

Schleiermacher, F. E. D., influences Brownson, 54; philosophy of, 124–125.

Seward, W. H., Brownson supports, 15; Brownson assails, 248.

Shackford, Charles, and Emerson, 59.

Simpson, Richard, on debate over Newman, 201 *n.*

Skidmore, Thomas, advocates agrarianism, 20.

Slavery, Frances Wright and, 17; W. L. Garrison and, 58–59; Brownson and, 79–80,

90, 113, 161, 240–246, 252, 287.

Socialism, forms of, compared, 96–98. *See also* Brook Farm; Fourier, F. M. C.; Marx, Karl; Owen, Robert; Saint-Simon, C. H.

Society for Christian Union and Progress, Brownson sponsors, 54; attitude toward, 62–63; influence of Cousin on, 125; Brownson preaches before, 141.

Society of Free Inquirers, formed, 44–45.

Spencer, Herbert, Brownson on, 264, 271–272.

Spirit-Rapper, The, Brownson writes, 224–226.

State guardianship, Wright-Owen proposal for, 20.

State rights, Brownson upholds, 76–77, 80, 113, 120, 122, 257; Calhoun and, 77, 115, 122; Brownson rejects, 259–260.

State Street, Brownson distrusts, 62, 67; and banking system, 84.

Steele, W. G., defeats Brownson, 249.

Story, Joseph, informed of Brownson's qualifications, 129.

Sub-Treasury plan, advocated, 83–86; threatened, 117.

Sumner, Charles, on Brownson, 106–107, 128–129; Brownson writes, 246–247, 250, 256; Brownson differs with, 267.

TANEY, R. B., Brownson agrees with, 243.

Thompson, William, economic views of, 99–100.

Thoreau, H. D., Brownson influences, 31–32; approves *Boston Quarterly*, 74; on government, 118; Emerson on, 150; Hecker and, 182; and slavery issue, 241.

Tractarians, Brownson on, 199, 202.

Transcendentalists, form club, 45–46; Brownson shares interests of, 46–50; on "Laboring Classes," 103; on intuition and logic, 126; attacked and defended, 131–136; and Brook Farm, 150–154; Brownson differs with, 154–155, 189–190.

Tyler, John, Whigs nominate, 88; and campaign of 1840, 110; becomes president, 112.

Unitarian, Brownson writes for, 30, 35.

Unitarianism, Brownson's regard for, 26–27; Brownson adopts, 29–31, 124; journal of, 47–48; found wanting, 50–52, 57–58; and the Trinity, 132–133; and Transcendentalism, 134, 145; Brownson's efforts to recast, 145–149; Brownson abandons, 179.

United States Bank, struggle over, 38; influence of, 83; rechartering of, 83–84, 113, 117; bill vetoed, 84; Biddle

United States Bank (*Cont'd.*) and, 84, 108; Calhoun and, 115–116.

United States Marine Hospital, Brownson appointed to, 72.

Universalism, influences Brownson, 7–8, 12; Brownson adopts, 12–13; Brownson doubts, 13–16, 19, 23; censures Brownson, 21.

VAN BUREN, MARTIN, and Brownson, 64–65, 116, 160, 161–162, 259; Bancroft supports, 70; rewards Bancroft, 72; encourages Loco-Focos, 72; financial policy of, 83–86; renominated, 88; and campaign of 1840, 109–110; compared with Calhoun, 115.

WAGES, demand for higher, 20; Brownson on, 91–92; reduced, 166–167.

Walker, James, on Brownson, 36; Harvard prefers, 129; Alcott on, 137.

"Wants of the Times, The," Brownson preaches on, 45, 53.

Ward, W. G., and Brownson, 198, 199, 200; defends Newman, 200.

Wayland, Francis, on *Charles Elwood*, 26.

Webster, Daniel, and banking system, 83–84; influence of, 85; and campaign of 1840, 109; compared with Cal-

houn, 115; Brownson opposes, 160.

Weiss, John, on Parker's sermon, 139.

Western Messenger, heeds Brownson, 47–48; contributors to, 59 *n.*; defends Brownson, 106.

Whewell, William, Sumner writes, 106–107.

Whig party, Brownson opposed to, 73, 81, 85–86, 113, 163; convention of, 88, 89; denounces Brownson, 101, 105, 106; and campaign of 1840, 108–111, 112.

Whitman, Sarah H., writes for *Boston Quarterly*, 75.

Whitman, Walt, writes for *Democratic Review*, 156.

Whittier, J. G., writes for *Democratic Review*, 156.

Winchester, Elhanan, influences Brownson, 7–8.

Woodbury, Levi, on Brownson, 101.

Wordsworth, William, philosophy of, 124–125.

Workingmen's party, and state guardianship, 20–21; Brownson and, 21–22, 34, 64; S. G. Allen candidate of, 37–38.

Wright, Frances, and slavery problem, 17; lectures, 17–18; influences Brownson, 18–23, 71, 93, 280; and Workingmen's party, 20, 34; as character in *Spirit-Rapper*, 225; Brownson on, 259.